A Peter Fabrizius Reader

Austrian Culture

Harry Zohn
General Editor
Vol. 12

PETER LANG
New York • Washington, D.C./Baltimore • San Francisco
Bern • Frankfurt am Main • Berlin • Vienna • Paris

Max Knight and Joseph Fabry

A Peter Fabrizius Reader

Selected Stories, Exilia, Verses, and Essays from Two Worlds

Foreword by
Harry Zohn

PETER LANG
New York • Washington, D.C./Baltimore • San Francisco
Bern • Frankfurt am Main • Berlin • Vienna • Paris

Library of Congress Cataloging-in-Publication Data

Fabrizius, Peter.
   A Peter Fabrizius reader: selected stories, exilia, verses, and essays from
two worlds / by Max Knight and Joseph Fabry; foreword by Harry Zohn.
      p.   cm. — (Austrian culture; vol. 12)
   I. Title. II. Series.
PT2611.A29A6   1994   818'.5409—dc20   93-34647
ISBN 0-8204-2347-5   CIP
ISSN 1054-058X

Die Deutsche Bibliothek-CIP-Einheitsaufnahme

Fabrizius, Peter:
A Peter Fabrizius Reader; selected stories, exilia, verses, and essays from two
worlds/by Max Knight and Joseph Fabry; foreword by Harry Zohn.
- New York; San Francisco; Bern; Baltimore; Frankfurt am Main; Berlin;
Wien; Paris: Lang, 1994
   (Austrian culture; Vol. 12)
   ISBN 0-8204-2347-5
NE: GT

Cover design by James Brisson.

The paper in this book meets the guidelines for permanence and durability of
the Committee on Production Guidelines for Book Longevity of the
Council on Library Resources.

© Peter Lang Publishing, Inc., New York 1994

Printed in the United States of America.

Acknowledgments

The stories and articles presented in this book originally appeared in the newspapers, magazines, journals, and proceedings identified at the conclusion of each piece.

The following selections are taken from published books:

"Morgenstern" in *Christian Morgenstern's Galgenlieder,* Berkeley: University of California Press, 1966.

"Nestroy," in *Johann Nestroy, Three Comedies,* New York, Unger, 1967.

"Fritzi" and "A Master Cobbler" in *Return to the Alps,* San Francisco: Friends of the Earth, 1970.

"Karl Kraus," in Harry Zohn, ed., *Karl Kraus, In These Great Times,* Montreal: Engendra Press, 1976.

"Ogden Nash," in *Ogden Nash, Der Kuckuck führt ein Lotterleben,* Vienna: Paul Zsolnay, 1977.

"A Birthday Present" in *The Original Blue Danube Cook-book,* Berkeley: Lancaster-Miller, 1979.

"I Become One of Them," in *Swing Shift,* San Francisco: Strawberry Hill Press, 1982.

"Gallant Knight," in *A Florentine Chansonnier from the Time of Lorenzo the Magnificent,* Chicago: University of Chicago Press, 1983.

"Touching with One Hand," in One and One Make Three, Story of a Friendship, Berkeley: Benmir Books, 1988.

"Prelude in Prison," in *The Next to Final Solution, A Belgian Detention Camp for Hitler Refugees,* New York: Peter Lang, 1991.

"Animal Jingles," in *Zany Zoo,* Berkeley: Kalmar Pub-lishing, 1993.

Contents

If not indicated otherwise, contributions were written jointly (Peter Fabrizius).
* One asterisk: Max Knight (Kühnel)
** Two asterisks: Joseph Fabry (Epstein)

Jugendsünden

Transition

Exilia

Features

Autumn Leaves

Verses

Essays

Epilogue

Foreword

"Peter Fabrizius" has been a living legend to me most of my life.

One of the two Viennese newspapers I read daily was the *Telegraf*, the late edition of which was delivered to our home toward evening, though it was on the newsstands in the early afternoon. I later found out why our copy was always late and a bit the worse for wear: our middle-aged "newsboy" (a quintessential Viennese who was shocked and dismayed when he discovered, in 1938, that he was not an "Aryan") delivered one paper to two people, one of whom only "rented" it for a few hours. (I mention this bit of trivia to indicate that a city and a country in which people could not even afford to buy a newspaper was bound to be fair game for Hitler).

In the *Telegraf* I read short stories that delighted me with their colorful settings, their verve, wit, whimsy, and unexpected twists at the end, and that often contained a stated (or implied) moral which even a very young person could appreciate. I had no idea that "Peter Fabrizius" was the joint pseudonym of two young doctors of law named Max Eugen Kühnel and Josef Epstein. Those entertaining and uplifting stories were just what depression-ridden Austria needed, and between 1931 and 1938 Joe and Max fabricated hundreds of them, using such additional (and unlikely) pseudonyms as Brandy von Brandenburg (the name of Joe's pedigreed terrier) for multiple submissions.

Two decades later, in the 1950s, when they were named Max Knight and Joseph Fabry, I had the pleasure of reading some "Peter Fabrizius" stories with my students in C.H. Bell's school editions, which first revealed to me the authors' motto, "One and one make three." Later still I learned that several other school editions had appeared in England. Fortunate the Anglo-American students who cut their Teutonic teeth on the prodigious prose of Peter Fabrizius!

However, though there were some correspondence and telephone conversations, I had to wait another decade for our first personal meeting, which took place in California on the eve of the publication of their autobiography entitled *One and One Make Three* (Benmir Books 1988).

Joseph Fabry and Max Knight chose to tell the life story of "Peter Fabrizius" with first-person chapters by each, Max and Joe, alternating with third-person accounts by their joint *alter ego*, Peter;

this makes for an uncommonly lively stereoscopic presentation with a unique shifting perspective that brings out the author's (or authors') "multility" (a term that has been coined for the mercurial Heinrich Heine). The account of the two authors' young years in Vienna is a worthy companion to the autobiographies of such other former Viennese as Joseph Wechsberg, Richard Berczeller, George Clare, Edmund Schechter, Stephen Kalmar, and Robert Starer. But this book properly gives pride of place to their life in America, which makes it a heart-warming and inspiring American success story. Those people, mostly Jews, who had to flee from Nazi Austria after the *Anschluss*, became known as 'thirty-eighters,' a term created in analogy to the 'forty-eighters' who came to America after the abortive 1848 revolutions in Germany and Austria (and in some cases became 'forty-niners' when they heard that there was gold in California). Well, what do two spirited thirty-eighters add up to? The spirit of seventy-six, of course!

W. H. Auden diagnosed our century as the "age of anxiety." I would more specifically call it the century of the (physically and psychologically) displaced person, because in our time upheaval, uprooting, exile, and worse have been the lot of millions. In this sense the lives of Joe and Max are truly exemplary. Before they were privileged to enjoy the freedom and opportunities of this country, the authors were fated to experience the uncertainties and face the perils of an emigration that separated them for the first time since their meeting in law school. Even before the *Anschluss*, the two men had succeeded in having their stories published in England. Max became the 'first swallow' to reach England and, unlike Joe, was able to help his parents reach a safe haven. After Joe's release from a Belgian detention camp, the friends were reunited in London and continued their unique mutual-support system, each developing an "ability to become a successful refugee who saw shipwreck as a challenge to build a new life." The two men repeatedly displayed true grit as well as true wit, and in their attempts to "survive chaos, uprooting, and loss of values" their *chutzpah* often stood them in good stead. Max's original name, Kühnel, combines the adjective *kühn* (bold, daring) with the softening suffix -*el* (as in Hansel and Gretel). In an effort to obtain guarantees for his parents, Max left no stone unturned in London, using "Rothschild psychology" on Baron Lionel, a distant relative, and on a Lord who was as frosty and immovable as his name, Winterton. Turning ignorance and inexperience into an advantage and playing an 'as if' game became a pattern. Years later Max obtained a job on the Manchurian and Chinese desks of the U.S. Office of War Information, and Joe parlayed minimal experience as a California gardener into work as an agricultural expert that ultimately led to a twenty-five-year editorship of agricultural publications for the University of California. Time and time again the friends charmed Dame Fortune (or Lady Luck) into smiling on them – eventually, anyway. In all vicissitudes Peter Fabrizius was their good fairy or guardian angel. This *nom de plume* became a *nom de guerre* when the authors' pens, singly and jointly, had to be tools for survival.

Joe arrived in Boston in the spring of 1940 (a few months before I did), but Max, obliged to wait until his immigration quota "matured," had to undertake a long voyage, from England via Canada and Japan, to Shanghai (where he became an English teacher and found his beginning students at Downtown University clamoring for Shakespeare!). Readers will not soon forget Max's account of his torment of Tantalus (or *crise de conscience)* when he found himself, en route to the Far East, on the Canadian side of Niagara Falls, and entry into the United States with the holiday crowds seemed to be his for the faking. But the Peter Fabrizius "duography" is, among other things, the eminently ethical story of how emigrants become immigrants, and Max preferred not to become too quiet an invader *(The Quiet Invaders: The Story of the Austrian Impact Upon America* being the title of a book by E. Wilder Spaulding in which he and Joe are listed).

As a small child I heard the United States described as "*das Land der unbegrenzten Möglichkeiten.*" Peter Fabrizius must have thought of it that way, too, for in "his" autobiography we read that "America truly was the land of unlimited opportunities." After Max had reached this country, and before and after he and Joe were sworn in as American citizens (together, of course), the friends engaged in various "ladder-building" activities and did not allow a number of temporary occupations (beam boy, janitor, shipfitter, etc.) to deflect them from their literary aspirations. They have written uplifting chapters in the generally sad saga of refugee writers in the United States. Thomas Mann, Bertolt Brecht, Erich Maria Remarque, and Lion Feuchtwanger already had a sizable American readership when they came to these shores, but the lot of most others was frustrating hack work at best and destitution and desperation at worst. Even though the "short short story" had been originated by an American (W. S. Potter, known as O. Henry), Joe and Max discovered that there no longer was much interest in their literary specialty, their kind of finely spun, lighthearted tale with a surprise ending that they had published in 14 languages in 39 countries, and that "Peter Fabrizius could not be naturalized." Still, at least half his name was preserved in Joe's new American name, and his initials lived on in Pacific Features, the feature story and news agency through which the friends presented the peaceful face of the American West to the world. Their multifarious and wide-ranging freelancing activities as factfinders, feature writers, broadcasters, and translators are detailed in their autobiography, as is their long tenure on the editorial staffs of the University of California at Berkeley. When they retired from these positions, Max took the University Press home, as it were, continuing to write, edit, translate, and run writing workshops. It must have given him great satisfaction to translate a seminal work by his former Viennese legal mentor, Hans Kelsen (*The Pure Theory of Law*) and to publish (first in private printing, then commercially) *The Original Blue Danube Cookbook*, containing the treasured recipes of his mother. Joe, having revisited Vienna in 1965 as a sort of Ripp von Winkel, started a new career as the chief American spokesman of Viktor Frankl and the interpreter of his logotherapy ("health through meaning"), writing and lecturing widely on existential psychology and presiding over an institute and even a press. When Joe published his book *The Pursuit of Meaning* in 1968, he realized that "for the first time in our lives, Max and I were writing in different fields."

Despite having been on the same wavelength and having sustained a friendship for more than a half-century, Joe and Max are no Tweedledum and Tweedledee, no tandem talkers like Koby and Loby in Dürrenmatt's *The Visit*, no "Oliver Twin" (their sometime pseudonym). When Joe and his wife ("a female Max") decided to transcend the faith of their fathers and become active members of the Unitarian Church (in contrast to Max's "religion of nature"), "Peter Fabrizius passed the test" and the friends continued on their "long and battle-tested path," ultimately a "duoquest" rather than a "uniquest" (the title of Joe's magazine). Their lifelong loyalty reminds one of Schiller's ballad *Die Bürgschaft*, which assures us that "friendship is not an empty delusion."

*

A Fabrizius Reader, an omnium-gatherum in both English and German, is a rich feast indeed. Reflecting six decades of joint and separate literary labors, it contains both published and unpublished work in sometimes surprising profusion. It is representative of virtually every aspect of the two authors' remarkable productivity, versatility, and adaptability. After all, how many writers have appeared in the *Neue Freie Presse* and the *Delphian Quarterly*, the *Neues Wiener Tagblatt* and the *San Francisco Chronicle*, the *Michigan Quarterly* and the *North China Daily News*? The articles, stories, and translations included here range from 'Raising Ostriches in California' to 'The Royal Road to the Spiritual Unconscious,' from renditions of Karl Kraus, Johann Nepomuk Nestroy, and Ogden

Nash to 'Fred Hickenloopers seltsame Sammlung' (ostensibly the story of a brazen brassiere braggart, but actually a hilarious hoax in the manner of Karl Kraus, whose satiric zoo included a *Grubenhund* and a *Laufkatze* that were not canines or felines, an idea that somehow foreshadowed Max's *Zany Zoo*). Bert Brecht and logotherapy, encounters with Sigmund Freud in Vienna and London, Frau Kühnel's culinary competence, the flying fishes of the Sierra Nevada, the problems of Englishing humorous verse, ruminations on how an emigrant turns into an immigrant and how a former emigrant becomes the ancestor of a new generation – all these meditations and mediations are grist on the gifted authors' mill, and they are sure to inform, amuse, move, and delight numerous readers, both Europeans (or ex-Europeans) and Americans.

Today each author is an octogenarian patriarch presiding over a colorful California clan. The spirit of Fabrizius, standing for a 'web' of order, meaning and *joie de vivre*, has never petered out. It is alive wherever religion is understood in its original sense of *religare* (that which binds people together), wherever there are wit and whimsy, resilience and resourcefulness, artistry and articulateness, contentment and contemplativeness, craftsmanship and cosmopolitanism, and sophistication rather than sophistry. Yes, Peter Fabrizius lives!*

Brandeis University   Harry Zohn
Boston 02254, USA
May 1993

*Sadly, Max Knight died August 31, 1993.

Jugendsünden

Erste Gedichte

Der Zucker

Der Zucker dachte im Kaffee:
"Soferne ich es überseh',
muss ich mich wohl dazu entschliessen,
das bitt're Dasein zu versüssen;
wenngleich . . . " Hier ward er unterbrochen.
Schon war in ihn hineingekrochen
das braune Nass, und deshalb fing er
zu wanken an – und dann zerging er.

(*Neue Freie Presse,* Vienna, December 19, 1929).

Storch (Ja, hätt' er . . .)

Ein Storch liebt eine Störchin sehr.
Ach, man umschlang sich voll Begehr
und fiel sich derart um den Hals,
dass (aus Verwicklung jedenfalls)
zum Knoten ward ihr Hals geschlungen –
So haben sie sich umgebrungen.

Ja - hätt' er einer Gans hofiert,
da wär ihm dieses nicht passiert.

(*Neue Freie Presse,* July 14, 1932)

4

Schneck

Leise
um sich
selbst im Kreise
kriecht der Schneck aus
dem Gehäuse. Immer grösser
wird der Bogen, weiter windend
rund gezogen. Heller schimmert die Spirale,
als vom Tor mit weitem Strahle blitzt des Tages
Licht; es strecken sich die Fühler aus - o Schrecken!
Schwere Regentropfen nässen
Schneck, der seinen Schirm vergessen. Doch er lässt das Wetter
Wetter sein; es ist doch netter, sich in trocknen,
wenn auch engen Wandelgängen froh zu drängen.
Immer kürzer wird der Bogen, tiefer tauchend
drum gezogen; Schneckens Reise
schliesst im Kreise.
Im Gehäuse
lacht er
leise.

(*Neue Freie Presse*, Vienna, November 19, 1931)

Der Knopf

Als Thomas, der Meisterdetektiv, mit seinem Freund Georgie die Trambahn betrat, fiel ihm ein Knopf auf, der auf dem Platz lag, auf den er sich eben setzen wollte. Mit einer geschickten Bewegung seiner geübten Finger nahm er ihn in die Hand und betrachtete ihn aufmerksam durch seine Lupe, schweigend in den Anblick vertieft. Georgie wusste, dass er seinen Freund jetzt nicht stören dürfe und bezahlte die Fahrkarten für beide. Da huschte ein Lächeln über die vom vielen Huschen schon etwas abgenützten Lippen des Detektivs. Er legte die Lupe weg und sagte:

"Der Mann, der diesen Knopf verlor, ist ein höherer Offizier der Marine. Er wohnt im vierten Distrikt, Ellstrasse 14, etwa 58 Jahre und unverheiratet. Auf Äusserlichkeiten gibt er wenig. Heute um acht kannst du ihn am Grossen Platz 38 antreffen."

Wohl kannte Georgie die geradezu unglaublichen Fähigkeiten seines berühmten Freundes. Dennoch war er verblüfft und ersuchte Thomas um die Erklärung, wie er zu diesen Angaben gekommen sei. Thomas liess wieder ein Lächeln huschen und wie er damit fertig war, lehnte er sich zurück: "Dieser Knopf zeigt den Anker unserer Marine. Folglich gehört ihr der Träger an, denn Marine Uniformen sind gesetzlich geschützt. Da der Knopf goldene Farbe zeigt, muss der Besitzer ein höherer Offizier sein, denn die niederen Chargen tragen silberfarbene, die Kadetten graue Knöpfe. Seit ungefähr drei Jahren trägt die Marine neue Uniformen. Da nun dieser Knopf, wie ich aus der Zeichnung des Ankers ersehe, noch der alten Monturgattung angehört, schliesse ich, dass der Offizier bereits in Pension ist, da er ja sonst gezwungen wäre, die jetzt eingeführten Uniformen zu tragen. Mit 55 Jahren kann man frühestens in Pension gehen, also ist der Mann mindestens 58 Jahre alt. Er ist unverheiratet, denn diesen Knopf hat ein Mann, vermutlich er selbst, angenäht, was man aus den leichten Scharten an der Rückseite des Knopfes ersehen kann, die von einer Nadel herrühren. Diese stach der Nähende statt in die Öse des Knopfes daneben, eine typisch männliche Ungeschicklichkeit beim Knopfannähen. Nun seine Adresse! Der Mann muss in derselben Station ausgestiegen sein, in der wir einstiegen. Sonst wäre der Knopf in diesem dichtbesetzten Wagen längst von dem Sitz entfernt worden. Knapp neben jener

6

Haltestelle nun, in der Ellstrasse 14, liegt die Offiziersgarnison. Daher kenne ich seinen Wohnort. Es ist jetzt halb 7 Uhr. Du wirst die Ankündigung des Europetheaters (Grosser Platz 38) gelesen haben, dass es heute um 8 Uhr eine Sondervorstellung für alte Militärs gibt. Da die Zeit zum Umkleiden und zum Weg mit eineinhalb Stunden anzusetzen ist, vermutete ich, dass du ihn heute dort treffen könntest. Dass er kein Gewicht auf Äusserlichkeiten legt, schloss ich aus der matten Farbe des Knopfes. "

Georgie war so begeistert, Thomas so in Gedanken versunken, dass sie ein Stück zu weit fuhren.

Der Mann, der tatsächlich den Knopf verloren hatte, war eine Frau. Vielmehr eine, die es werden wollte, die 19-jährige, reizende kleine Tilly, die von der Garderobiere des Europetheaters beauftragt worden war, zu der heute stattfindenden Vorstellung einen Marinemantel aus der Kostümverleihanstalt zu holen. Dies hatte Tilly schon vor drei Tagen besorgt, hatte den Weg aber gar nicht per Trambahn, sondern zu Fuss zurückgelegt und dabei den Knopf verloren. Ein kleines Kind fand das in der Sonne glänzende, glatt polierte Ding und erkor es zu seinem Lieblingsspielzeug, wodurch es seinen Glanz verlor. Einige Tage später liess das Kind den Knopf in der Strassenbahn liegen, an der Stelle, wo er nachher von Thomas gefunden wurde. Die schartenartigen Kratzer an der Rückseite, die den Offizier in den Augen des grossen Detektivs zum Junggesellen gemacht hatten, stammten von einem missglückten Versuch des Kleinen, den Knopf aufzuspiessen. Tilly, die Verlustträgerin des Knopfes, wohnte nicht im vierten Distrikt, sondern im zwölften, und hätte dem, der ihr auf Grund knopflich-knifflicher Erwägungen 58 Jahre angedichtet hatte, sicherlich die Augen ausgekratzt.

Und abends um 8? Da sass sie nicht unter den weissbärtigen Veteranen des Europetheaters, sondern mit einem jungen Mann am Schillerplatz. Zufällig kamen auch Thomas und Georgie dorthin. Und im Vorbeigehen sagte der Detektiv zu seinem Freund: "Aus den kussähnlichen Geräuschen schliesse ich. . ."

Diesmal hatte er recht.

(*Neue Freie Presse*, Vienna, March 27, 1930)

Das Geschäftsprinzip

"Womit kann ich dienen?" erkundigte sich der junge Verkäufer des Warenhauses 'Alles für jeden' und starrte die hübsche Dame jenseits des Pultes in einer Weise an, die nicht durch den Grundsatz der Firma gedeckt war, 'Komm den Kunden zart entgegen"

"Ich brauche ein Geschenk für einen achtjährigen Jungen", sagte die Dame sinnend, "nicht zu teuer, aber nicht aussehen, als hätte ich es in einem Ramschgeschäft gekauft. Es soll pädagogisch wirken und dem Jungen doch Freude bereiten. Es soll..."

"Ich bin vollkommen im Bilde. Was Gnädigste benötigen, ist eine Kinderflöte, Marke 'Rattenfänger'. Es weckt in dem Kinde musikalische Talente, und macht Freude. Niemand würde der Flöte ansehen, dass sie in die Preiskategorie unserer Gelegen-heitskäufe von fünf Schilling fällt."

Er wickelte die Flöte ein und wies die Dame an die Kassa.

Einige Sekunden später stand sie jedoch wieder vor ihm.

"Ich habe mir die Sache überlegt," begann sie zaghaft. "Der Junge wird den ganzen Tag Lärm mit der Flöte machen, und seine Eltern sind sehr nervös. Sie müssen das Instrument zurück-nehmen. Bezahlt habe ich es ohnehin noch nicht."

"Zurücknehmen kann ich leider nichts," erwiderte der Verkäufer höflich, "das ist gegen unser Geschäftsprinzip. Aber ich kann es Ihnen gegen etwas Gleichwertiges umtauschen."

Nach dem Grundsatz der Firma 'Geschwindigkeit ist keine Hexerei' häufte er vor der hübschen Dame einen Berg von Kinderspielsachen.

"Wenn ich mir einen Vorschlag erlauben darf, Gnädigste, dann nehmen Sie einen Fussball. Sport stählt den Körper des Kindes und bereitet für den Lebenskampf vor. Auch kann man Fussball nicht in der Wohnung spielen, und so werden die Nerven der Eltern geschont."

"Ein Fussball ist so unpersönlich," wandte die Dame ein.

"Wie können Gnädigste nur so etwas behaupten!" Der Verkäufer brachte aus dem Innern des Leders die Gummiblase zum Vorschein, "man spricht doch von seiner 'Seele'! Er packte den Ball ein und betrachtete seine Kundin mit Erleichterung, wie sie zur Kassa ging. Knapp davor machte sie kehrt.

"Es geht doch nicht," sagte sie, "der Junge wird den ganzen Tag

8

auf den Wiesen spielen, wird nichts lernen und erhitzt nach Hause kommen. Sie müssen den Ball zurücknehmen!"

"Zurücknehmen nicht", erwiderte der Jüngling, und sein Lächeln wirkte etwas krampfhaft, "das ist gegen unser Geschäftsprinzip. Vielleicht gegen etwas Gleichwertiges umtauschen ?"

Sie tauschten.   Karl May war zu phantasieverderbend, ein Schmetterlingnetz zu grausam, ein Stoppelrevolver zu gefährlich und ein Zauberkasten zu demoralisierend.

Schliesslich einigten sie sich auf das Kinderbuch 'Summ, Bienchen, summ.'

Die Dame verstaute das Buch unterm Arm und entfernte sich. Knapp vor der Tür holte sie der Verkäufer ein.

"Gnädigste haben vergessen, das Buch zu bezahlen," flötete er, doch die von der Firma geforderte Höflichkeit fiel ihm etwas schwer.

"Das Buch ?" machte die Dame erstaunt, "ich soll Ihnen das Buch bezahlen ?"

Dem Verkaufer perlte der Schweiss von der Stirne. "Sie haben es doch schliesslich und endlich gekauft!"

"Das wohl. Dafür habe ich Ihnen den Ball zurückgegeben."

"Das ist der selbe Preis. Zahlen Sie also bitte den Fussball."

"Für den Fussball habe ich Ihnen die Flöte zurückgegeben."

"Du meine Güte, zahlen Sie eben die Flöte! "

"Die Flöte habe ich ja nicht gekauft!"

Der Verkaufer starrte sie mit offenem Munde an. In seinem Kopf begann sich alles zu drehen. Sogar der Grundsatz der Firma 'Höflichkeit geht vor Recht' geriet in den Hintergrund.

"Sie sind eine unausstehliche Person!" stiess er hervor und fühlte sich wesentlich erleichtert.

Die Dame fuhr auf, wie von einer Natter gestochen. "Waas?" schrie sie. "Was haben Sie gesagt? Ich bin eine unausstehliche Person? Das werden Sie sofort zurücknehmen!"

"Zurücknehmen nicht", röchelte der Verkäufer, "das ist gegen unser Geschäftsprinzip. Aber ich kann es Ihnen gegen etwas Gleichwertiges umtauschen."

(*Neues Wiener Journal*, March 3, 1936)

Der Bazillus der Vergesslichkeit

Professor Fürnkranz war ein Mann der exakten Wissenschaft. Jene lächerlich wirkende Lebensfremdheit und Vergesslichkeit vieler seiner Kollegen empfand er als schmerzlich, ja sogar als standeswidrig. Sein Forschersinn war nicht gewillt, sich mit ihr als etwas Unumstösslichem abzufinden. Vergesslichkeit war seiner Meinung nach das Symptom einer noch unbekannten Erkrankung der Gehirnsubstanz. Wie jede andere Krankheit musste auch sie ihren Erreger haben, der sich unter gewissen Lebensbedingungen entwickelt, unter anderen wieder zugrunde geht.

Professor Fürnkranz stellte sich die Aufgabe. den Bazillus der Vergesslichkeit zu entdecken. Gleich bei Beginn stiess er auf Schwierigkeiten. Denn die Vergesslichkeit ist eine spezifisch menschliche Eigenschaft, die man bei Tieren nicht beobachten kann. Daher fielen die für die exakte Wissenschaft so wichtigen Tierversuche weg. Die menschlichen Kranken, die an Vergesslichkeit litten, waren aber zumeist berühmte Professoren, zu denen er nicht einfach gehen konnte, um mit ihnen Versuche anzustellen. Ausserdem riskiert ein Mediziner immer eine spöttische Abfuhr, wenn er mit einer neuartigen Entdeckung vor die Wissenschaft tritt, ehe er sie durch exakte Versuche hieb- und stichfest erwiesen hat.

In diesem Zeitpunkt bescherte ihm ein gütiges Schicksal den Laboratoriumsdiener Watzek. Dieser konnte es, was Vergesslich-keit anlangt, mit jedem Professor aufnehmen. Länger als einen Monat konnte er nie in Stellung bleiben, da Aufträge durch sein Gehirn in sein Unterbewusstsein fielen, wie durch ein Sieb.

Watzek war glücklich: bei Professor Fürnkranz hatte er einen Dauerposten gefunden. Seine Vergesslichkeit wurde nicht gerügt, sondern genau aufgezeichnet. Dankbar für die ihm unbegreiflich milde Behandlung liess er mit sich alle, auch die unbequemsten Versuche anstellen, die der Professor für notwendig hielt.

Zuerst musste er sich vierzehn Tage nur von Obst und rohem Gemüse nähren. Dann versuchte es der Professor mit salz- und gewürzloser Kost, später gab er Watzek nur halbrohes Fleisch zu essen. Ganze Tage musste er in frischer Luft verbringen, dann durfte er wieder eine ganze Woche das Haus nicht verlassen. Versuchsweise lebte er alkoholfrei, einige Zeit musste er täglich zwei

10

Liter Wein trinken und dreissig Zigaretten rauchen. Da er Nichtraucher war, wurde ihm totenübel, aber seine Vergesslichkeit besserte sich nicht.

Dann ging Professor Fürnkranz zu einer Kneippkur über. Watzek musste bis zu einer Stunde in immer kälterem Wasser sitzen. Er bekam zwar einen gehörigen Schnupfen, aber der erste Erfolg stellte sich ein: die Vergesslichkeit Watzeks besserte sich mit einem Schlage, fast alle Aufträge wurden ausgeführt. Professor Fürnkranz triumphierte. Er wartete nur die Verkühlung Watzeks ab (er wollte sein Versuchsobjekt nicht gefährden), dann setzte er die Kaltwasserkur fort.

Aber die Wissenschaft lässt sich nicht so leicht besiegen. Watzek war wieder vergesslich wie zuvor. Er verwechselte im Laboratorium Gas- und Wasserleitung und schloss den Bunsen-brenner an den Wasserhahn. Als Professor Fürnkranz später die Gasflamme aufdrehte, schoss ein Springbrunnen zur Decke.

Der Professor stand vor einem Rätsel. Als er Watzeks Bad bis auf acht Grad herabgesetzt hatte, ohne dass der Vergesslich-keitskoeffizient sank, musste er zugeben, von einem Irrlicht auf den falschen Weg gelockt worden zu sein.

Er versuchte es nun mit Dampf- und Schwefelbädern, Schlammpackungen und Höhensonne. Erst als Watzek in seiner Zerstreutheit nach einer Schlammpackung statt in die Duschräume auf den kalten Korridor trat und sich neuerdings verkühlte, besserte sich seine Vergesslichkeit.

Nun wurde Professor Fürnkranz vom Strahle der Erkenntnis getroffen: die Verkühlung war es, die die Vergesslichkeit verdrängte! Man hat in der Medizin schon oft Fälle beobachtet, wo eine Krankheit durch den Bazillus einer anderen geheit wurde. Der Vergesslichkeitsbazillus wird also durch den Schnupfenbazillus verdrängt.

Professor Fürnkranz begann nun ein wissenschaftliches System auszuarbeiten. Als Grundlage nahm er ein Fü (1 Fürnkranz, das ist jene Vergesslichkeitsmenge, die ein Durchschnittsmensch in seinem dreissigsten Lebensjahr produziert). Seine weiteren Forschungen mit Watzek bestätigten die Richtigkeit seiner Theorie: in dem Mass, in dem Watzeks Erkältungen zunahmen, schwand seine Vergesslichkeit. Ein Abflauen des Schnupfens brachte eine Steigerung der Vergesslichkeit. Professor Fürnkranz registrierte seine Forschungsergebnisse durch rote und grüne Kurven.

Nachdem der Professor seinem Diener versuchsweise den zwölften Schnupfen injiziert und wieder kuriert hatte, hielt er den Zeitpunkt für gekommen, mit seiner Entdeckung in die Öffentlichkeit zu treten. "Watzek," sprach er feierlich, "Sie sollen der erste sein, der die Ergebnisse meiner Forschung erfährt. Sie haben mir wackere Dienste geleistet und sind vor keiner Unannehmlichkeit zurückgescheut. Sie sind zerstreut. Die Versuche haben ergeben, dass Sie von 20 Aufträgen, die man Ihnen gibt, im Durchnitt bloss drei durchführen. Sind Sie aber verkühlt, führen Sie, durchschnittlich genommen, von 20 Auftragen 17 durch. Wie ist dieses Phänomen zu erklären ?"

Diese Frage war durchaus rhetorisch gemeint, aber Watzek wusste das nicht. "Das Phänomen", sagte er, "erklärt sich folgendermassen: Wenn ich vom Herrn Professor einen Auftrag bekomme, mache ich mir einen Knoten ins Taschentuch. Weil ich aber das Taschentuch im Sack hab', vergess ich auf den Knoten und auf den Auftrag. Bei Schnupfen brauche ich das Taschentuch immer wieder, dann sehe ich den Knoten und erinnere mich."

Professor Fürnkranz hat seine Versuche aufgegeben.

(*Die Stunde*, Vienna, August 27, 1936)

Frag mich nichts!

"Vatti," rief mein Sprössling Fredi, "habe ich nicht eine weisse Zunge ?" Er zeigte zögernd eine rosige Spitze.

"Fühlst du dich nicht wohl?" fragte ich besorgt.

"N–ja, das schon," gestand er, "fühl' mal meinen Puls, vielleicht hab' ich Fieber."

Der Puls schlug normal. Meine Diagnose war gestellt. "Du willst die Schule schwänzen! Was ist morgen los?"

"Der Lehrer hat eine so blöde Frage gestellt."

"Der Lehrer stellt niemals blöde Fragen. Wie lautet sie?"

"Wir sollen einen Aufsatz schreiben. Über das Thema: Warum läuft die Telegraphenleitung immer neben dem Eisenbahngeleise?"

"Und wegen einer so einfachen Frage willst du schwänzen? Pfui, schäm' dich! Das hätte ich nie von dir gedacht!"

"Also, Vati, sag' mir: warum läuft die Telegraphenleitung neben dem Eisenbahngeleise?"

"Warum? Hm. Darauf kannst du wohl selber kommen."

"Ich weiss es aber nicht. Schorschi weiss es auch nicht. Ich hab' ihn gerade angerufen."

"Umso mehr Grund, dass Du selbst draufkommst. Nein, mein Kind, ich sage es dir nicht. Denk' bis abends nach und wenn du es dann immer noch nicht weisst, will ich dir helfen."

Ich nahm meinen Hut und hatte einen leidlich guten Abgang. Im Kaffeehaus traf ich Otto an, der finster in seinen Mocca starrte.

"Du, Otto!" rief ich ihn an. "Kannst du mir sagen warum die Telegraphenstangen immer neben dem Eisenbahngeleise laufen?"

"Was geht das dich an?" knurrte er.

"Das ist keine Art, wissenschaftliche Fragen zu erledigen," rügte ich. "Wenn ich zum Beispiel frage, warum man dich nicht mehr mit Mimi sieht, könntest du mir antworten, es geht mich nichts an. Frage ich aber, warum die Erde um die Sonne kreist und nicht umgekehrt, dann ist eine solche Antwort unangebracht. Und ebenso ist es mit der Frage: Warum läuft die Telegraphenleitung immer neben den Eisenbahnschienen?"

"Andere Sorgen hast du wirklich nicht?" stöhnte Otto auf. "Wie ich aus deiner taktlosen Anspielung erkenne, weisst du ganz gut, dass Mimi mir den Laufpass gegeben hat und mich mit irgend einem

Schurken betrügt. Wahrscheinlich mit dir, das traue ich dir schon zu! Und da hast du die Stirne, mich zu fragen, warum die Wasserleitung neben dem Telephon läuft!"

Ich habe einen feinen Instinkt dafür, wann meine Anwesenheit erwünscht ist und wann nicht. In solchen Augen-blicken mache ich mich davon, bevor man noch deutlicher wird.

Zwei Tische weiter sass Max. "Hallo!" begrüsste ich ihn. "Mit Otto ist heute ein ernsthaftes Thema nicht zu erörtern. Kannst du mir vielleicht sagen, warum die Telegraphenleitung neben den Eisenbahnschienen läuft?"

Max riss verwundert seine Augen auf. "Warum soll sie nicht neben den Eisenbahnschienen laufen?" war alles, was er hervorbrachte.

Diese Frage hatte ich mir selbst schon gestellt. Ich konnte daher blitzschnell entgegnen: "Nun sieh mal, wenn du ein Eisenbahngeleise beobachtest, wirst du bemerken, dass es niemals seinen geraden Weg geht. Es biegt einmal nach rechts, dann nach links, schlängelt sich in grossen Bogen durchs Tal, windet sich einen Berg hinauf und auf der anderen Seite wieder hinunter, kriecht durch Tunnels, und macht alle möglichen Biegungen. Ein Telegraphendraht hat das nicht notwendig. Warum geht er nicht durch Feld und Wald schnurstracks in kürzester Luftlinie von einem Ort zum andern, sondern begleitet schön brav das Geleise auf all seinen Umwegen?"

Max zog seine Stirne kraus. "Ich muss gestehen," sagte er schliesslich, "ich habe noch niemals darüber nachgedacht. Aber die Sache scheint nicht so einfach, wie sie auf den ersten Blick aussieht. Wir wollen das Problem einmal logisch durchdenken: was bedeutet es also, wenn eine Telegraphenleitung neben den Eisenbahnschienen herläuft?"

"Nun," fragte ich gespannt, "was bedeutet das?"

"Das würde bedeuten," dozierte Max nachdenklich, "dass man Morsezeichen durch den Draht schicken und sich verständigen kann."

"Sehr gut. Und was würde es bedeuten, wenn neben einer Eisenbahnschiene kein Telegraphendraht liefe?"

"Das würde bedeuten, dass man sich auf dieser Strecke drahtlos verständigt."

"Wir wollen die Kernfrage nicht unnötig komplizieren", sagte ich streng ."Lass gefälligst die drahtlose Telegraphie, das Radio, die Telepathie und die Gedankenübertragung ganz aus dem Spiel. Sag' mir lieber, warum die Telegraphenstangen neben dem Eisenbahngeleise laufen."

"Mich wirst du nicht anschreien, mein Lieber", rief Max

14

gereizt. "Denk allein über deine blöden Fragen nach. Ich telegraphiere ohnehin nie!"

Ich sah ihm neiderfüllt nach, wie er sich davonmachte. Meiner väterlichen Autorität konnte ich nicht so einfach davonlaufen.

Als ich das Kaffeehaus verliess, traf ich Fritz. Ich riskierte einen letzten Versuch.

"Fritz!" beschwor ich ihn. "Kannst du mir sagen, warum die Telegraphenstangen neben den Eisenbahnschienen laufen?"

"Das ist doch klar!" antwortete er.

"Nun," fragte ich hoffnungsfroh.

"Wenn die Telegraphenstangen *zwischen* den Eisenbahn-schienen liefen, wären sie ein recht unangenehmes Verkehrs-hindernis."

Als ich nach Hause kam, sass Fredi betrübt vor seinem Tisch.

"Fredi!" sagte ich, bevor er noch etwas fragen konnte. "Zeig' mal deine Zunge ."

Er streckte sie chamäleonartig heraus.

"Und nun den Puls!"

Fredi gehorchte mit unheimlicher Schnelligkeit.

"Nun, mein Kind," sagte ich, "krank bist du gerade nicht, aber Vorsicht ist die Mutter der Weisheit. Du bleibst morgen im Bett, verstanden?"

Fredi verstand und stellte keine einzige Frage. Er wusste aus seiner eigenen Schulerfahrung, dass Fragen nur unangenehm sind und einen in Verlegenheit bringen.

(*Mocca*, Vienna, November 1936)

Der Fremdenführer

...s waren eigentümliche Umstände, unter denen ich meinen
...ligen Schulkollegen Oskar nach fünfzehnjähriger
...ollenheit wiederfand. Der Küstendampfer, der mich mit
...n Touristen von Stadt zu Stadt brachte, schwankte ein wenig
...war eben im Begriff, über einen im Weg stehenden Deckstuhl
...pern, als mich ein elegant gekleideter junger Mann auffing
...och rechtzeitig rettete. Dieser junge Mann war eben jener
...den ich seit fünfzehn Jahren nicht mehr gesehen hatte, und ich
..., dass er Fremdenführer war und die Ausländer in den
...städten spazierenführte.
...Kennst du dich denn so gut aus?" fragte ich naiv und erinnerte
...chwach, dass Oskar seinerzeit in Geschichte durchgefallen
...ber Oskar hatte ein System und mit liebenswürdiger
...enheit war er auch bereit, es zu erklären. "Weisst du, die Sache
...r einfach. Man muss sich ein Schema zusammenstellen und
...sprechenden Daten jeweils einsetzen. Ich sage in jeder Stadt
...e, nur die Jahreszahlen, Kaisernamen usw. werden geändert,
...ganz leicht."
...r zog aus der Brusttasche einen stark abgenutzten Zettel.
...t werden die Leute zur grössten Kirche geführt. Für Kirchen ist
...de Erklärung zu geben." Er las von dem Zettel: "Dieses
...ne Kunstwerk der Gotik (Romanik, Renaissance, des Barock)
...sprünglich ein kleines Kapellchen. An seinen Ursprung knüpft
...ne Sage . . . (folgt beliebige Sage: Lebensrettung, Quellfund,
...im Dickicht etc.). Seine erste Errichtung fällt ins . . .
...ndert, doch ist von dem damaligen Kirchlein nichts mehr
...n, da es von den Hunnen (Avaren, Magyaren, Türken etc.)
...t wurde. An der gleichen Stelle wurde dann von Franz
...ich, Ludwig, Karl) dem Frommen (Gütigen, Glorreichen)
...ndert Jahre später der heutige Bau errichtet und mit reichen
...verken bedacht. Ich mache Sie auf die holzgeschnitzten
...ühle aufmerksam. Beachten Sie den Gesichtsausdruck des
...Engels von links! Welch tiefe Verinnerlichung! Die Säulen
...s überseeischem Marmor, haben ein Gewicht von zwanzig

Vienna Made in USA

Mister Knowbetter, Eigentümer der "Newpeeper Tagespost",
tat den Mund auf und sprach: "Gilly soll sofort zu mir kommen!"

Wenn in irgend einer anderen Redaktion der Welt der Chef
einen seiner Angestellten zu sich rufen lässt, so wird dieser die Türe
des Allerheiligsten mit einem leisen Schwächegefühl im Magen
öffnen. Nicht so Mister Gilly. Er trat ein wie ein Geldbrief-träger:
im vollen Bewusstsein, stets willkommen zu sein. Er hatte auch
Grund dazu. Seiner Idee, die Sonntagsbeilage "Im Fluge durch die
Welt!" verdankte das Blatt eine Auflage von 15,000, wo ganz
Newpeep bloss 10.000 Einwohner besass. Aus Gillys Feder stammten
auch die sensationellen Reiseberichte aus aller Welt. Er war zwar
noch niemals aus Newpeep herausgekommen und phantasierte sich
seine Artikel aus Reiseschilderungen anderer zusammen, aber er
wusste, was seine Leser lesen wollten und diese waren ebenfalls
niemals aus Newpeep herausgekommen.

"Hallo, Gilly!" begrüsste ihn der Chef. "Haben Sie schon jemals
etwas von einer Stadt gehört, die Wien heisst?"

"Gewiss!" Es gab nichts, was er nicht gewusst oder worüber er
nicht wenigstens genaue Auskunft gegeben hätte. "Wien, das liegt da
oben zwischen dem Nordpol und dem Schwarzen Meer!"

"Wundervoll, wie Sie alles im Kopf behalten!" bewunderte ihn
sein Chef. "Ich lese hier einen Artikel in einer Bostoner Zeitschrift.
Diese Wiener sollen ein so gemütliches Volk sein - schreiben Sie eine
Reiseschilderung über sie. Natürlich sensationell, wie immer!"

Gilly nahm den Artikel aus Boston, auch hatte er schon zwei in
Hollywood gedrehte Wiener Filme gesehen. Das genügte für ein
Genie wie ihn. Er setzte sich an seine Maschine und schrieb:

Hollodaro!
Ein Besuch in Wien, der lustigsten Stadt der Welt

Nach einer tagelangen Reise durch die Reisfelder Ungarns und
die Bananenwälder der Türkei, begrüsst uns die wild-romantische
Gletscherwelt Wiens, der Hauptstadt von Australia. Bunte
Häuschen, wie von Künstlerhand an die Felswände der lieblichen
Gebirgstäler hingeworfen, durchbraust von der blauen Donau, so
entbietet Wien dem Fremden einen freundlichen Willkomm.

Der erste Eindruck der Stadt ist überwältigend: überall Buntheit, Heiterkeit, aus allen Häusern tönt Musik. Dabei gehen alle Passanten ganz langsam, Eile kennt der Wiener nicht. Nur ab und zu geht ein Bursch auf ein Mädchen zu, nimmt es um die Taille und tanzt ein paar Schritte Walzer. Automobile gibt es in Wien nicht, wohl wegen seiner gebirgigen Lage. Das charakter-istische Fahrzeug, das auch ich benutzte, ist der sogenannte 'Fiaker', ein vierrädriges, schwarzes Holzgestell, das von sechs federgeschmückten Schimmeln gezogen wird. Die Strassen sind eng und winkelig. Die Männer tragen entweder Uniform oder wenigstens eine Kappe mit einer Nummer. Diese Leute nennt man "Dienstmänner" und sie ersetzen dem Wiener die Post, Spediteur und das Auskunftsbüro. Die Mädchen tragen weisse, blaugetupfte Kleider, weisse Schürzen und Häubchen; man nennt sie Wäschermädchen, weil sie den ganzen Tag an der schönen blauen Donau Wäsche waschen. Mehrmals am Tage ziehen Militärkapellen durch die Stadt. Wenn die Wiener die mit-reissende Musik hören, verklären sich alle Gesichter, sie ziehen ein Stück singend und tücherschwenkend mit. Es öffnen sich alle Fenster und Türen, Mädchenköpfe werden sichtbar, Blumen werden geworfen, Küsse getauscht, Stelldicheine vereinbart.

Den Abend verbringt der Wiener beim Heurigen. Alles, was Rang und Namen hat, trifft sich hier zu fröhlichem Treiben. Auch ich werde von meinen Gastgebern eingeführt.

Hier offenbart sich im höchsten Masse der Prunk der Wienerstadt. Während die Leute einfach, ja primitiv, wohnen und ebenso gekleidet sind, ist der Heurige überladen mit Luxus. Stühle und Tische aus Ebenholz stehen vor einer eleganten Tanzdiele, die Trinkgefässe sind aus Silber, edelste Weine werden ausgeschenkt. Das Publikum ist elegant gekleidet, die Herren in Smoking oder Uniform, die Damen in grosser Abendtoilette. Aber auch in höchster Eleganz bleibt der Wiener gemütlich. Immer wieder beginnt eine der Damen aus dem Publikum zu yodeln, und einer der Zigeuner, die typisch für den Wiener Heurigen sind, spielt ihr dabei mit seiner Geige ins Ohr und alle singen den Text mit: Hollodrio, hollodaro! Die Stimmung hat den Höhepunkt erreicht. Plötzlich flammen Scheinwerfer auf und beleuchten einen jungen Mann mit einer kühngeschwungenen Nase und einem buschigen Schnurrbart: es ist Johann Strauss, der Walzerkönig, der es sich nicht nehmen lässt, seinen Wienern allabendlich persönlidh seine unsterblichen Tänze vorzuzeigen. Nun gibt's kein Halten mehr. Alle, auch die Kellner, beginnen sich wie trunken im Kreise zu drehen, berauscht von der wundervollen, ins Blut gehenden Musik Johann Straussens. Es

gelingt mir ein kurzes Interview mit dem M
an einer grossen Ausstattungsrevue "Fle
Henry Ford und erklärt, nur auf Mans
können. Von der Bevölkerung Newpeeps h
und hofft, unserer Stadt einmal einen Be
muss er sich rasch verabschieden, er d
Wurstelprater, in Schönbrunn und vor der
umarmt er mich, ein Symbol echten Wiene
und immer gemütlich!

Am Tage, als diese Reportage in de
erschien, ereignete sich das grösste Wunde
zugestossen war: Ein ecbter Wiener hatte si
den Artikel gelesen und Gilly zornschna
aufgesucht.

"So einen Blödsinn habe ich mein gar
Gesicht bekommen," ereiferte er sich, "all
durcheinander und falsch!"

"Das verstehen Sie nicht!" erwidert
Wien! Ich werde doch besser wissen,
aussieht!"

"Lächerlich! Johann Strauss, zum Beis

"Das tut mir aber leid," sagte Gilly l
denn gestorben?"

"Das weiss ich nicht!" schrie der Wien

Gilly aber setzte sich an seine Masch
Nachricht für sein Blatt:

Heute rot — morgen
Johann Strauss — eine L

Der weltberühmte Musikant Johann
gestern in meiner Reportage über Wien
soeben drahtlos aus Wien erfahren, plötzl
ist umso mysteriöser, als seine Todesursa
Ein Selbstmord ist bei dem stets leb
anzunehmen. Vielleicht ein Mord. . .? Wir e
Details über diese sensationelle Kriminala
Leser auf dem Laufenden halten.

(*Mocca*, Vienna, December 1936)

ehem
Versc
ander
und ic
zu sto
und r
0skar
erfuh
Küste

mich
war.

Beflis
ist sel
die er
dasse
das is

"Zuers
folger
erhab
war u
sich e
Hirsc
Jahrh
erhalt
zerstö
(Fried
zweih
Kuns
Chors
dritte
sind a

Tonnen und zeigen dorische (jonische, korinthische) Stilelemente. Das Altarbild ist ein Meisterwerk Tizians..."

Ich unterbrach ihn. "Aber, um Himmelswillen, es kann doch nicht auf jeden Fall von Tizian ... !"

"Aber ja, glaub mir, es ist Tizian. Und wenn jemand Einwände erhebt, dann ist es ärgstenfalls ein Bild seiner Schüler." Er fuhr fort: "Die Augen sind so grossartig gemalt, dass sie den Beschauer immer anblicken, wo immer er sich im Raume aufhält.

Falls die Kirche eine Kuppel hat: Diese Kuppel, bitte beachten Sie, ist unter dem Einfluss der Kuppel des Petersdomes in Rom entstanden. Die Wölbung ist vollkommen. Falls sie bemalt ist: Das Fresko stammt von dem bekannten Künstler Francesco Piero della Caminato ..."

"Caminato? Den Namen hab ich noch nie im Leben ..."

"Glaubst du, einer wird sich blamieren nnd das sagen? Caminato ist ein Gelatoverkäufer in Triest, ein Freund von mir. Also in diesem Sinne geht es weiter, man besteigt meist auch den Turm, was mit einer Eintrittsgebühr verbunden ist. Hierbei ergibt sich die Gelegenheit, zunächst mitzuteilen, wieviel Stufen zur Glocke hinaufführen. 356 oder 415, oder sowas. Von oben erklärt man dann die Stadt. Die weitere Besichtigung führt dann zum Rathaus, Königspalast (Kronleuchter, Bilder, Gobelins etc.) und hierauf zu zwei bis drei Denkmälern. Für jede Art Gebäude habe ich einen Fahrplan, auch für Römerkastelle, Arenen, Kerker, Folterkammern, Kriegsdenkmäler, Stadtmauern, Festungswerke."

"Stellt man dir nie Fragen? Was sagst du, wenn ein Wissbegieriger dich nach dem Alter eines Bildes fragt?"

"Fünfzehntes Jahrhundert."

"Und wenn das falsch ist?"

"In neunzig von hundert Fällen merkt er's nicht; in den restlichen zehn kann ich mich meist mit dem Jahrhundert vorher oder nachher ausreden. Ist der Fremde unglückseligerweise Kunsthistoriker und hält das Bild für älter, dann sage ich, es könnte sein, dass es schon gegen Ende des vierzehnten Jahrhunderts entstanden ist; hält er es für jünger, sage ich, möglicherweise stammt es aus dem Anfang des sechzehnten Jahrhunderts. Die Fachleute streiten noch darüber. Neunzig Prozent aller alten Bilder, die man gewöhnlich zu sehen bekommt, stammen aus dem vierzehnten bis sechzehnten Jahrhundert."

Ich bin ein hartnäckiger Mensch. "Wenn aber das Bild doch älter oder jünger ist ..."

"Das ist eben Geschäftsrisiko. Seit ich Fremdenführer bin, hat sich niemand gegen mich getraut. Hab' ich gar keine Ahnung, sag' ich, das Bild ist vom Jahre 1486. Da rührt sich keiner. Man kann auch

1567 sagen."

Ich bewunderte das Genie Oskars. In der nächsten Stadt schloss ich mich einer Gesellschaft an, die von ihm durch die Stadt geführt wurde, benahm mich ganz als Fremder und liess nicht merken, dass ich in Oskars Methode eingeweiht war.

Zuerst ging alles gut. Wir besichtigten den Dom. "Dieses erhabene Kunstwerk der Gotik", erläuterte Oskar, "war ursprünglich ein winziges Kapellchen, das Ladislaus der Achte zur Erinnerung an seine Errettung aus Jagdgefahr erbaut hatte, als ihn ein Eber mit seinen erschrecklichen Hauern beinahe zu Tode gestossen hatte. Aber geistesgegenwärtig sprang Ladislaus der Zwölfte. . ."

"Der Achte", besserte ein Störenfried aus.

"Sprang also Ladislaus hinter ein Gebüsch, in dessen Geäst sich die Hauer des Ebers verfingen, und der König war gerettet."

Oskar klopfte an einen Quader in der Mauer. "Dieser Stein ist das einzige, was von der ersten Kapelle übriggeblieben ist, ausser diesem rostigen Nagel", setzte er mit einem Seitenblick auf mich hinzu, aus dem ich ersah, dass er dies aus dem Stegreif hinzufügte, "denn das Kirchlein wurde im siebzehnten Jahrhundert von den Türken dem Erdboden gleichgemacht und erst zweihundert Jahre später von Friedrich dem Frommen wiederhergestellt und mit reichen Kunstwerken bedacht. Ich mache Sie besonders auf die holzgeschnitzten Chorstühle aufmerksam; sie stammen aus dem vierzehnten Jahrhundert. . ."

"Wieso", sagte der Störenfried und zog eine Lupe hervor. "Das ist eine viel spätere Arbeit. Ich taxiere achtzehntes Jahr. . ."

"Herrr", unterbrach Oskar höhnisch, "wie kommen Sie auf diese absurde Idee! Das sind uralte Chorstühle und jeder Fachmann. . ."

"Ich kenne mich sehr genau aus", beharrte der andere widerspenstig. "Diese Stühle stammen aus dem Jahre 1770!"

Oskar wurde bleich. "Ich werde der Sache nachgehen und eine Expertise durchführen lassen. Gestatten die Herrschaften", er wandte sich formvollendet an das teils ungeduldige, teils ironisch lächelnde Publikum, "dass ich Sie weiterführe."

Wir kamen in das fürstliche Schloss. "Die Deckengemälde sind Meisterwerke des spanischen Renaissancekünstlers Jose Esteban da Gorgonzola . . ."

"Gorgonzola?" fing der Störer wieder an, "das ist ein Käse, soviel ich weiss."

Die übrigen lachten, Oskar grinste mit verzerrtem Gesicht: "Der Herr liebt Scherze, aber . . ."

"Was für Scherze? Dieses Bild ist ein ganz gewöhnlicher Baltassare Giacopo di Ferrari aus Turin!" brüllte der andere. "Das erkennt jedes Kind!"

"Ich habe die Geschichte der Stadt studiert", sagte Oskar nunmehr mit Würde, "und kenne ihre Sehenswürdigkeiten und deren Schöpfer. Wenn Sie Zweifel hegen. . ."

Er wandte sich mit herzoglicher Geste ab und benutzte die Handbewegung gleichzeitig, um die Besucher in den nächsten Raum zu weisen. Ich bewunderte ihn ausserordentlich.

"Hier ist das Spielzimmer des Bourbonenprinzen Charles, des nachmaligen Charles VII."

"Hehe", meckerte der alte Widersacher, "einen Charles VII hat es in Frankreich nie gegeben. Der höchste Charles war der Fünfte!"

"So", erwiderte Oskar. "Und was ist mit dem Charles, der im Alter von zwei Jahren von der schwarzen Pest dahingerafft wurde, in der modernen Geschichtswissenschaft aber nichtsdesto-weniger von jedem ernstzunehmenden Forscher als der Sechste gezählt wird? Und dann vergessen Sie seinen posthumen, in Orleans geborenen Sohn, den Isabella die Jähzornige nach der Schlacht von Cadillac. . ."

"Lächerlich!" fiel der andere wieder ein. "Wie kann ein Zweijähriger einen Sohn haben! Und ausserdem verwechseln Sie das mit Isabella der Abergläubischen, die aber keinen Charles, sondern einen Philipp ehelichte und nur einen nicht thron-berechtigten Sohn in die Ehe brachte, der zufällig Charles hiess."

Ich merkte, dass ich meinem Freunde beispringen musste, ehe ihm das ganze Geschäft verdorben wurde. Vorsichtig nahm ich den ewigen Widerspruchsgeist zur Seite.

"Ich bewundere Ihre überragenden Kenntnisse", sagte ich einschmeichelnd, "sind Sie Historiker?"

"Ach nein", sagte der Gelehrte lächelnd, "ich will dem Kerl nur auf den Zahn fühlen. Fremdenführer haben nämlich in dieser Gegend manchmal keine Ahnung von Kunstgeschichte und Historik. Wenn man etwas fragt, was ausserhalb ihres Programms steht, plappern sie irgend welche Namen und Jahreszahlen daher, die ihnen gerade einfallen. Ich selbst verstehe von der ganzen Sache auch nichts und alle Namen, die ich genannt habe, sind reine Erfindungen."

"Ja, was sind Sie denn eigentlich?" fragte ich.

"Fremdenführer", sagte der Mann und schneuzte sich.

(*Das Interessante Blatt,,* Vienna, June 24, 1937)

Der Mann mit dem Muttermal

"Nein, mein lieber Edgar P.," sagte der Verleger Baltimore zu dem jungen Autor von Kriminalgeschichten, "ich kann Ihr Buch nicht herausbringen. Es ist zu unwahrscheinlich, zu sehr am Schreibtisch zusammengezimmert. Es ist doch unmöglich, dass Ihr Held überall, an den unmöglichsten Stellen, geheimnisvolle Zettel und Warnungen findet. Wie sollen sie zum Beispiel in die Seife im Badezimmer gekommen sein? Oder eine andere Szene, die niemals im Leben vorkommen kann: Ihr Verbrecher hat die Manie, sich dauernd zu verkleiden, so dass ihn niemand erkennt. Er betritt das Zimmer als Elektromonteur, verlässt es fünf Minuten später als Zigeunerin, und taucht eine Viertelstunde danach im Hafenviertel als betrunkener Matrose auf. Oder gar die Schlusszene: der Verbrecher kündigt mit grossem Pomp an, er werde den Diebstahl am 13. November, Punkt halb vier nachmittags im Salon des Herzogs vollführen. Glauben Sie, ein Verbrecher wird so idiotisch handeln? Ich erkläre Ihnen, wenn sich die Handlung Ihres Romanes in Wirklichkeit abspielte, sässe der Verbrecher bereits auf Seite 5 hinter Schloss und Riegel. Auch ein Kriminalroman muss lebenswahr sein. Haben Sie den Mann gesehen, der wegging, als Sie kamen? Wissen Sie, wer das war? Jim Holly, der Einbrecherkönig, der eben seine fünf Jahre abgesessen hat. Ich veröffentliche seine Memoiren, die er im Kerker geschrieben hat. Da könnt Ihr jungen Autoren lernen! Keine geheimnisvollen Zettel, keine angekündigten Überfälle. Ganz einfach, eine gute Idee, ein einfacher Plan und eine schnurgerade Ausführung. Und das wollen auch unsere Leser. Sachen, die auch im Leben vorkommen, die jedem von uns passieren können. Das schreiben Sie einmal, mein lieber Edgar P., dann machen wir ein Bombengeschäft, denn schreiben können Sie, es geht Ihnen bloss die Phantasie durch. Also nichts für ungut, mein Junge, und auf ein andermal!"

Nachdem Edgar P. Billing gegangen war, verbrachte der Verleger einen anstrengenden Nachmittag und kam abends todmüde nach Hause. Er knipste das Licht an und erblickte auf seinem Polster einen Zettel. Neugierig nahm er ihn und las:

Dolch! Gift! Mitternacht! Nur noch drei Tage!
Der Mann mit dem Muttermal.

Baltimore klingelte der Haushälterin. Sie hatte keine Ahnung,
wie der Zettel auf den Polster gekommen war. Der Verleger dachte
sich seinen Teil und legte sich beruhigt schlafen. Am nächsten
Morgen fiel ihm beim Waschen die Hälfte der Seife aus den Hand.
Ein Zettel lag eingerollt darin, mit den Druckbuchstaben:

WEHE! WEHE! WEHE!,
DER ZWEITE TAG IST ANGEBROCHEN!
DER MANN MIT DEM MUTTERMAL.

Der Verleger lachte nur auf. Er hatte keine schlechten Einfälle,
der junge Edgar P. Wie hatte er nur den Zettel in die Seife
praktiziert? Er wollte offenbar beweisen, dass die unmöglichen
Szenen aus seinem abgelehnten Roman doch vorkommen konnten.
Baltimore wunderte sich nicht, als er in seinem Büro einen neuen
Zettel vorfand. Er war mit einem Dolch an den Türstock befestigt
und lautete in schwarzen Buchstaben:

4 oder 9? Grün oder schwarz?
Der Frosch hat gequakt!
Zittert vor dem Mann mit dem Muttermal!

Der Verleger konnte nicht arbeiten, da er umherspähte, ob er
nicht Billing oder einen Komplizen erwischen konnte, wie er gerade
einen Zettel hereinschwindelte. Er entdeckte aber keinen Menschen,
wohl aber noch einige Zettel im Kassabuch, unter der eingelaufenen
Korrespondenz und in seinem Zigarettenetui. Baltimore wurde
immer nervöser. Er durfte sich vor dem Lausejungen doch nicht so
blamieren! ! Er versteckte sich im Ankleideraum und guckte durchs
Schlüsselloch in sein Arbeitszimmer. Im Schlüsselloch steckte ein
Zettel. Der Verleger zerknüllte ihn wütend und schwor sich, er werde
Billing ertappen.
   Da öffnete sich die Tür zu seinem Arbeitszimmer. Baltimore
hielt den Atem an. Ein hagerer Mensch in einem blauen Arbeitsanzug
und mit einem roten Bart war eingetreten. Er näherte sich dem
Schreibtisch, aber der Verleger war rascher. Er stürzte auf ihn und
versuchte dem Einschleicher mit einem einzigen Griff den Bart
herunterzureissen.
   Der Mann schrie auf, denn der Bart war angewachsen.
   "Wer sind Sie?" rief Baltimore.

"Der Elektromonteur."

"Hinaus!" schrie der Verleger, "Aber vorher geben Sie die Zettel her!"

"Welche Zettel?" fragte der andere verwundert und strich sich über den Bart, der ihn noch schmerzte. "Ich bin herbestellt. Bei Ihnen soll die Leitung schadhaft sein," fügte er nicht ohne Zweideutigkeit hinzu.

Es blieb dem Verleger nichts übrig, als sich zu entschuldigen. An eine Arbeit war heute nicht mehr zu denken. Er ging ins Kino und zeitig zu Bett. Schlafen konnte er ohnehin nicht. Die ganze Nacht lauerte er auf Billing, wenn er eine neue Botschaft einschleichen sollte. Nichts rührte sich. Am Morgen lag ein Zettel im Käfig seines Kanarienvogels:

ACHTUNG! ACHTUNG!
HANSI, DER VOGEL, SAMT KÄFIG WIRD GERAUBT!
HEUTE PUNKT HALB VIER NACHMITTAGS!
DER MANN MIT DEM MUTTERMAL LÄSST GRÜSSEN.

Das war doch der Gipfel der Frechheit! Aber jetzt sollte der Kerl draufzahlen. Einen Augenblick überlegte er, ob er nicht die Polizei verständigen sollte. Er verwarf den Gedanken sofort, er hätte sich nur lächerlich gemacht. Wegen eines Kanarienvogels! Aber entgehen sollte ihm der Kerl nicht! Er versammelte alle seine Freunde, sein gesamtes Personal um sich und verteilte die Leute im ganzen Haus. Er selbst setzte sich in sein Zimmer, dem Käfig gegenüber. Er kam sich selbst lächerlich vor, als er den Revolver zu sich steckte. Ausserdem hatte er eine Alarmpfeife, die sofort alle anderen herbeirufen sollte. Es war zehn Minuten vor halb vier.

Minute um Minute verstrich. Nichts rührte sich. Keiner seiner Freunde oder seiner Angestellten gab das verabredete Zeichen eines unvorgesehenen Zwischenfalles. Drei Minuten vor halb. Zwei Minuten. Baltimore entsicherte den Revolver. Noch eine Minute. Gespannt verfolgte er den Sekundenzeiger seiner Armbanduhr. Halb vier!

Nichts. Ver Vogel, ungeachtet der ihm angedrohten Entführung, hatte soeben ausgiebig Mahlzeit gehalten, setzte sich auf die oberste Sprosse und schmetterte ein Lied. Zwei Minuten nach halb. Nichts war geschehen. Baltimore kam sich plötzlich sehr dumm vor, dass er sich bluffen hatte lassen. Diese verdammten Zettel hatten ihn nervös gemacht. Na schön, hatte er eben zwei Arbeitstage verloren. Aber sonst war der Spass doch recht gut gewesen. Der junge Edgar P. war ein Hauptkerl! Dass er doch nicht gewagt hatte, den Vogel vor seiner Nase zu stehlen, stimmte den Verleger fröhlich.

Er nahm den Hörer und rief ihn an.

"Edgar P.?" rief er wohlgelaunt in die Muschel. "Der Mann mit dem Muttermal, wie ? Nun, was macht der Vogel? Er singt hier ganz gemütlich. Der Frosch hat gequakt, haha! Was? Ach, stellen Sie sich doch nicht so. . . Na, schicken Sie mir jedenfalls Ihr Manuskript, ich werde es mir noch einmal ansehen."

"Er leugnet," sagte er zu seinen Freunden, als er sich für ihre Hilfe bedankte. "Edgar P. leugnet, haha!" Vergnügt fuhr er mit seinem Personal ins Büro zurück. Dort fand er eine gewaltsam geöffnete Kassa vor. Sie war vollkommen leer, bis auf einen Zettel:

TAUSEND DANK FÜR LEERES BÜRO!
GELD HABE ICH. VOGEL HABEN SIE!
SO ARBEITET DER MANN MIT DEM MUTTERMAL!

Erst als die Polizei eintraf, hatte sich Baltimore soweit von seinem Wutanfall erholt, dass er sich einigermassen verständlich machen konnte. "Jim Holly!" stammelte er. "Er hat uns belauscht, Billing und mich. Er war es, der diese Zettel. . .Um mich abzulenken. . ."

Plötzlich heiterte sich sein Gesicht etwas, er wandte sich an Billing: "Das schreiben Sie, Edgar P., das ist ein Einfall, schnurgerade und lebenswahr, ach, so lebenswahr!"

(*Mocca*, Vienna, April 1937)

Ein Lord macht Geschäfte

"Monsieur Lavertaine lässt bestellen, dass er Eure Lordschaft für heute abends um acht in sein Büro zur Besprechung bittet," sagte der Diener. "Bis dahin dauert leider die Modevorführung."

Den jungen, sehr eleganten Mann schien diese Nachricht zu freuen. War doch diese leidige geschäftliche Besprechung, wiederum mehr als zwei Stunden aufgeschoben.

Zwei Stunden in Paris! In gehobener Stimmung, den Hut unternehmungslustig schief über dem Ohr, durchschritt er die breiten, teppichbelegten Gänge des Modehauses Lavertaine.

Plötzlich blieb er stehen. Eine Gruppe herrlich gewachsener Mannequins in erlesenen Nachmittagstoiletten kam ihm ent-gegen. Eines der Mädchen war das reizendste, das er in seinem an Frauen reichen Leben gesehen hatte.

Percy hatte eine sehr sorgfältige Erziehung genossen, aber nun stand er und starrte sie an. "Wünschen Sie etwas?" fragte das Mädchen freundlich.

"Ja," sagte er rasch. "Ich wünsche die nächsten zwei Stunden in Ihrer Gesellschaft zu verbringen." Und da er ihre aufsteigende Entrüstung sah, stellte er sich vor: " Lord Percival Hunnington."

Statt jeder Antwort brach sie in ein Lachen aus, das er entzückend fand. Die übrigen Mannequins waren bereits verschwunden. Er und sie standen allein im Treppenhaus.

"Wissen Sie was," schlug er ihr eifrig vor, "brennen wir auf zwei Stunden durch. So rasch werden Sie Ihren Posten nicht verlieren. Ich habe heute abends eine Konferenz mit Ihrem Chef, da werde ich schon dafür sorgen, dass Ihnen die Stelle nicht verloren geht." Als er sah, dass sie ihn zögernd anblickte, wurde er redseliger. "Sollten Sie wirklich Ihren Posten verlieren, nehme ich Sie mit nach London ins Middleton-House. Dort bekommen Sie das doppelte Gehalt als hier bei dem alten Knicker. Ich habe nämlich die Ehre, das Middleton-House zu vertreten."

Sie nahmen den Tee bei Gerron und, da ihre Zeit kurz bemessen war, gingen sie gleich anschliessend zu Marloque soupieren. Nach dem dritten Glas Sekt war Percy verliebt wie ein Sechzehnjähriger. Zweifellos gefiel auch er dem Mädchen. Er küsste ihre Hände und wollte unbedingt Bruderschaft trinken. "Nun," meinte Jacqueline, "wenn sich unsere Bekanntschaft bereits in diesem Stadium befindet, möchte ich ein paar Erkundigungen über Sie einziehen, junger Mann. Wer sind Sie also? Sagen Sie die Wahrheit und nichts als die Wahrheit!"

"Meine Familie", begann Percy, "stammt in direkter Linie von jenem William P. Hunnington ab, der unter Oliver Cromwell in der Schlacht bei Mars-la-Tour . . ."

"In Anbetracht der vorgeschrittenen Zeit unserer Bekanntschaft dürfen Sie die nächsten fünfhundert Jahre überspringen."

"Danke." Percy nippte an dem vierten Glas. "Ich wurde als das vorläufige Schlussglied einer endlosen Ahnenreihe als der Sohn des Duke und der Marquise von Hunnington geboren. Ich habe eine ganze Menge von Fähigkeiten. Ich bin der Gründer des 'Klubs der Klubtiger', dessen Mitglied man nur werden kann, wenn man nachweist, dass man zwölf anderen Klubs angehört. Ich spiele Bridge nach 15 Ansagesystemen und mehrere Quadrat-sporte: Eistennis, das ist Tennisspielen auf Schlittschuhen, ferner Motorrad-Golf und Segelflug-Baseball. Cocktail mische ich auf 94 verschiedene Arten und auch der Einfall, zu einer blaulila Weste getupfte Socken zu tragen, geht auf mich zurück - nur eines bringe ich nicht fertig: ich habe noch nie in meinem Leben gearbeitet. Das ist es, was mir mein zukünftiger Schwiegervater übelnimmt."

"Wer?" fragte Jacqueline, und es klang, als hätte man eine brennende Kerze in Eiswasser getaucht.

"Mein zukünftiger Schwiegervater. Ich habe mich in einer schwachen Stunde mit Jane Middleton verlobt. Es ging alles so rasch. Ein Abend in ihrem Park, ein bisschen Duft von Rosenhecken, ein Mond, nein, nicht einmal: ein Halbmond, und hups, schwups – Sie wissen ja, wie das geht."

"Bei Ihnen scheint überhaupt alles hups, schwups zu gehen", bemerkte Jacqueline.

"Ich will nicht sagen, dass Jane mir nicht gefällt. Bis vor einer Stunde hielt ich sie für das prachtvollste Mädel. Ihr einziger Fehler war die fixe Idee ihres Vaters, dass ein junger Mann wie ich arbeiten müsse. Deshalb bin ich hier in Paris und in einer halben Stunde sitze ich beim alten Lavertaine, um für Middleton einen Vertrag abzuschliessen. Das soll so eine Art Probe sein. Wenn ich Lavertaine hineinlege, dann ist der Beweis erbracht, dass ich für die Arbeit tauge und ich bekomme Jane. Legt Lavertaine mich hinein, wird Jane einen anderen heiraten, der mit Schmerzen wartet. Gelungen, was?"

"Sie haben einen Schwips," sagte das Mädchen kühl.

"Ich weiss ganz genau, was ich tun werde", blinzelte Percy ihr zu und gab ihr einen raschen Kuss auf den kleinen Finger, "ich werde mich von Lavertaine hineinlegen lassen!"

Jacqueline erhob sich. "Das werden Sie nicht tun! Sie werden mich jetzt ins Geschäft bringen, ich habe abends noch eine Vorführung. Und dann werden Sie mit Monsieur Lavertaine verhandeln, so gut Sie es können."

"S-Sie haben eine g-ganz falsche Meinung von mir", stotterte Percy.

"Ich habe ganz genau die richtige Meinung von Ihnen, Mylord," sagte Jacqueline mit fester Stimme. "Und jetzt bringen Sie mich augenblicklich ins Modenhaus Lavertaine zurück."

Die Rückfahrt verlief einsilbig. Percy musste sich gestehen, dass sie das entzückendste Geschöpf war, das er jemals angetroffen und dass er sich wie ein Esel benommen hatte.

Der Abschied war kurz. Jacqueline reichte ihm die Hand und verschwand im Aufgang für Angestellte, während Percy nachdenklich die Haupttreppe emporschritt.

Es kam ihm nicht ungelegen, dass er einige Minuten auf Lavertaine warten musste, denn der Entschluss, den er fasste, war der schwerwiegendste seines sorglosen Lebens.

Lavertaine trat ein, ein liebenswürdiger, grauhaariger, jugendlich lebhafter Mann. Percy hatte sich Geschäfts-kontrahenten als alte, vertrocknete Männchen vorgestellt, mit verkniffenen Lippen, einem an einer Schnur baumelnden Kneifer und einem Sprachschatz, der nur aus den Worten Kartell, Dollar und Krise besteht. Er war angenehm überrascht, mit Lavertaine in höchst natürlicher Weise über den nächsten Derbytip und das Tennisturnier in Wimbledon plaudern zu können.

"Nun," sagte der Franzose schliesslich, "und jetzt wollen wir noch rasch das Geschäftliche erledigen. Ich will bloss die wichtigsten Punkte zu Papier bringen." Er klingelte. Ein Mädchen mit einem Stenogrammblock erschien. Percy klapperte erschrocken mit den Augenlidern. Es war Jacqueline.

"Im wesentlichen habe ich unsere Geschäftsverbindung bereits mit Mister Middleton besprochen," setzte Lavertaine fort. "Wir beziehen die englischen Stoffe ausschliesslich von seinem Hause, dafür kauft er Pariser Modelle nur von uns. Es handelt sich jetzt bloss darum, Zahlen festzusetzen, insbesondere den Betrag des garantierten Mindestumsatzes. Ich glaube, ich kann mich bei Ihrer Firma mit 10.000 Pfund begnügen."

Percy wusste, dass dies ein sehr anständiges Anbot war. Middleton wäre sogar bis auf 15.000 gegangen.

"Nein," sagte er, "wir müssen Ihnen grössere Sicherheiten bieten. Wir garantieren Ihnen für 20.000 Pfund."

"Aber," protestierte Lavertaine, "das ist doch viel zu hoch."

"Ach was," machte Percy und blinzelte dem Mädchen, das rot

geworden war, freundlich zu, "der alte Middleton kann's schon vertragen. Warum sollen Sie ein Risiko eingehen? Sagen wir sicherheitshalber 25.000 Pfund."

Der Franzose starrte Percy verständnislos an. "Aber Sie müssen doch die Interessen Ihres Schwiegervaters wahren."

"Zuerst werde ich meine Interessen wahren. Und ich sage, Middleton wird für 25.000 Pfund garantieren. Wenn's ihm nicht passt, soll er mich rauswerfen."

"Das wird er zweifellos tun," meinte der Franzose.

"Ich bin nicht so sicher," erwiderte Percy. "Er möchte gerne einen Lord in seiner Familie und im Geschäft haben. Schreiben Sie, bitte, Fräulein," wandte er sich an Jacqueline, "dass er die englischen Stoffe zum Selbstkostenpreis liefern wird, dagegen wird er für Ihre Modelle das Doppelte des Normalpreises zahlen. So!" seufzte er erleichtert und wandte sich dem Buffet zu, "und nun werde ich mir, mit Ihrer Erlaubnis, einen Cocktail mixen. Ich kenne 94 Arten."

"Sagen Sie," erklang die Stimme des Franzosen hinter ihm, "haben Sie Jacqueline in dieser kurzen Zeit wirklich so lieb gewonnen?" Percy fuhr mit einem Ruck herum. "Sie hat mir alles erzählt. Sie haben aber ein Eilzugstempo!"

"Hups, schwups," sagte Jacqueline.

"Und in der Eile haben Sie noch nicht erfahren," setzte Lavertaine fort, "dass Jacqueline meine Tochter ist. Sie hilft heute aus, unsere Mannequinvorführungen zu leiten."

Percy liess sich vor Überraschung in einen Stuhl fallen. "Und da soll noch einer sagen, dass ich kein tüchtiger Geschäftsmann bin! Finden Sie nicht, dass ich die Interessen meines künftigen Schwiegervaters vortrefflich gewahrt habe?"

(*Telegraf*, Vienna, November 20, 1936)

Ein Dieb hat Pech

Jimmys Methode, Einbrüche zu begehen, war höchst einfach und erfolgversprechend. Seine Ausrüstung bestand aus einer Pistole, einer Taschenlampe und einem Gummiball. Diesen warf er, wenn er durch entlegene Gassen spazierte, in offenstehende, ebenerdige Fenster. Zeigte sich eine schimpfende Gestalt, entschuldigte er sich, dass ihm der Ball beim Spiel durchs Fenster gefallen war. Zeigte sich niemand, dann schwang sich über die Brüstung. Mit dieser Methode hatte er die besten Erfahrungen gemacht. Nicht einmal einen neuen Ball hatte er kaufen müssen.

Eines Abends entdeckte er eine kleine Villa am Rande der Stadt. Weit und breit war kein Mensch zu sehen und ein ebenerdiges Fenster stand einladend offen. Kurz entschlossen köpfte Jimmy seinen Ball hinein und, da sich niemand zeigte, folgte er selbst nach. Das Zimmer war gross, elegant eingerichtet, und in der Ecke stand ein Schrank. Er öffnete eine Lade: einige Ringe und eine Krawattennadel blinkten ihm entgegen.

Bevor Jimmy diese Gegenstände noch an sich nehmen konnte, öffnete sich eine Tür und ein kleiner, etwa vierzigjahriger Mann wurde sichtbar. "Hallo?" fragte er überrascht

"Verzeihung, Herr." erklärte Jimmy, "mir ist ein Ball hier ins Zimmer gefallen und ich bin eben dabei, ihn zu suchen."

"In einer geschlossenen Lade, he?"

Für solch unangenehme Fälle hatte Jimmy seinen Revolver vorbereitet. Er hasste rohe Gewalt, aber die blitzenden Ringe in der Lade waren verlockend. In weniger als fünf Minuten hatte er den kleinen Mann sorgfältig an Händen und Füssen gefesselt und ihm einen Knebel in den Mund gesteckt, so dass er als ohnmächtiges Bündel auf dem Sofa lag und weder reden noch sich bewegen konnte. Dann versperrte Jimmy die Tür, schloss die Fenster und wandte sich in aller Seelenruhe den Laden zu, von denen er mit Recht vermutete, dass sie mehr enthielten als einige Ringe.

Er war mitten im besten Aufräumen, als hinter ihm eine schrille, keinen Widerspruch duldende Stimme befal: "Hände hoch oder ich schiesse!" Jimmys Arme fuhren in die Höhe. Er wollte sich umsehen, aber augenblicklich ertönte wieder die Stimme: "Keine Bewegung oder du bist eine Leiche!"

Etwas lag in der Stimme, das Jimmy lähmte. Er konnte sich auch nicht erklären, was geschehen war. Denn dass sich der Geknebelte befreit hatte, schien ebenso undenkbar wie die Dazwischenkunft eines Dritten bei geschlossenen Türen. Dieses Rätsel verwirrte Jimmys Geist. "Drücke auf den Knopf vor dir!" befahl die Stimme. Als Jimmy sich nicht rührte, wiederholte sie kurz und kreischend: "Läute, oder ich schiesse!"

Nun gab Jimmy jeden Widerstand auf. Zitternd gehorchte er. Das helle Klingeln, das sein eigener Finger auslöste, liess ihn zusammenfahren.

Draussen wurden Schritte laut. "Tür einbrechen!" befahl es hinter Jimmy. "Wie bitte?" fragte man draussen. "Tür einbrechen! Ein Dieb ist hier!"

Einige Fusstritte sprengten die Tür. Ein Diener, mit einem Schürhaken bewaffnet, drang herein. Was er erblickte, war seltsam genug. Vor dem Schrank, mit dem Gesicht zur Wand, stand mit erhobenen Händen, zitternd und bleich, Jimmy. Hinter ihm, auf dem Sofa, lag gefesselt, geknebelt und hilflos, der Hausherr. Sonst war niemand im Zimmer.

Jimmy leistete keinen Widerstand. Bald lag er selbst als hilfloses Bündel auf dem Sofa, während der kleine Mann, von seinem Diener befreit, die Polizei anrief.

"Ein Überfall hat stattgefunden?" fragte der Wachebeamte, der wenige Augenblicke später auf dem Tatort eintraf. "Der Bursche hier, mit dem Gummiball! Wir suchen ihn schon lange. Ich werde gleich die Daten für die Strafanzeige aufnehmen." Er wandte sich zuerst an den Überfallenen:

"Sie heissen?"

"Marcell Bovatti."

"Alter?"

"Zweiundvierzig."

"Beruf?"

"Künstler," sagte der Kleine lächelnd, "Bauchredner."

(*Neues Wiener Journal,* Vienna, Oct. 4, 1936)

Landstrasse

Ich bin ein Vagabund gewesen und durch Europas Länder gezogen. Ich hatte kein Gepäck, bloss einen Rucksack, ich hatte kein Geld und keine Begleitung. Aber ich hatte Zeit, und das ist das wichtigste, was ein Landstreicher haben muss.

In einem Reisebureau erscheint ein gut gekleideter Mann und verlangt eine Fahrkarte nach einem bekannten Kurort.

"Wie lange wünschen Sie dort zu bleiben?" fragt der Angestellte.

"Drei Wochen."

"Wenn Sie so lange bleiben, können Sie sogar ein um 30 Prozent ermässigtes Retourbillet nehmen." Der Angestellte freut sich, seinem Kunden einen Dienst erwiesen zu haben, und dieser, ebenfalls erfreut, nimmt die Retourfahrkarte.

Nimm in jeder Einzelheit das Gegenteil dieses Mannes, dann weisst du, wie der Landstreicher reist. Er hat nie eine bezahlte Fahrkarte, wird sich nie drei Wochen an einem Ort aufhalten und wird sich nie an einen Rückweg binden. Dieser Gedanke allein vermag der ganzen Fahrt ihren Sinn zu rauben, weil er die Freizügigkeit, diesen reinsten Quell der Freude, stört.

Da ist sie, die grosse, weite Landstrasse, sie liegt vor mir, nein, sie läuft unter mir weg, und in mir singt das grosse Lied der Strasse, das keine Worte hat und keine Strophen. Und der Kehrreim dieses Liedes ist: Hab' Freude am Augenblick!

Ich weiss nicht, wohin die Strasse führt. Wohl stehen Tafeln am Wegrand, mit Namen von Orten. Aber diese Orte könnten ebensogut anders heissen, die Namen sagen mir nichts, ich bin in einem fremden Land, und kenne nur aus der Schulzeit die Namen der grössten Städte.

Es kommt mir nicht darauf an, wohin und wie weit ich komme. Ich suche nicht diesen oder jenen Ort und muss nicht täglich soundso viele Kilometer "zurücklegen". Ich wandere, und plötzlich stehe ich auf einer Anhöhe, und tief unter mir fliesst ein Fluss, und ich steige hinunter und das Ufer ist ganz aus feinem Sand. Und ich lege meinen Rucksack ab und meine Kleider, und das Wasser ist kühl und frisch, und die Sonne ist warm und trocknend wenn man im Sande liegt. Das suche ich.

Ich weiss nicht, wo ich heute nachts schlafen werde, ich weiss nicht, wo ich morgen sein werde. Heute bin ich nur 10 Kilometer weiter gekommen; wenn ich umkehre, kann ich in zwei Stunden wieder dort schlafen, wo ich gestern schlief. Morgen werde ich vielleicht 200 Kilometer von hier weg sein, wenn mich ein Wagen mitnimmt.

Ich bin ein winziger Punkt, mitten hineingestellt in Europa. Ich bin unendlich frei. Alles, was ich brauche, trage ich bei mir, ich habe nicht Frau und Kinder, und habe kein Mädchen, das ich liebe. Wenn das Wetter schön ist und ich bleibe, dann gehört alles mir, die Berge sind für mich gemacht, das Meer und der Wald.

Wochenlang bin ich durchs Land gezogen. Am Strassenrand lag einer in der Sonne mit einem lustigen Hut.

"Hallo, Kamerad," rief er, als er mich sah.

"Hallo," rief ich. "Wohin?"

"Zum Meer."

"Ist es noch weit?"

"Zwei, drei Tage. Weiss nicht."

Er gefiel mir, wir zogen gemeinsam zum Meer. Wir kamen durch einen grösseren Ort. Im Postgebäude hing eine Landkarte an der Wand, ich zeichnete die Strasse bis zum Meer in mein Notizbuch. Nun hatten wir eine feine Landkarte.

Ein Lastauto kam vorbei, hoch beladen mit Stroh. Mein Begleiter schwenkte seinen Hut, der Wagen blieb stehen, wir durften aufsitzen.

Die einen teilen die Autos ein nach ihrer Marke in Rolls-Royce und Ford, die andern nach ihrer Grösse in Limousine und Kabriolett, die dritten nach Leistungsfähigkeit und Pferdekräften.

Wir teilen die Autos ein in Lastwagen, Geschäftswagen und Luxuswagen. Die Lastwagen führen Fässer, Holz und Flaschen; jeder dritte nimmt dich mit. Die Geschäftswagen führen Musterkollektionen in Stoffen, Uhren oder Spielwaren und werden von Geschäftsreisenden gelenkt; jeder zehnte nimmt dich mit. Die Luxuswagen sind farbig gestrichen, die Menschen darin tragen Autohauben und weisse Mäntel. Sie fahren rasch und weit. Dreissig müssen vorbeifahren, ehe dich einer mitnimmt.

Wir sassen hoch oben auf dem Strohwagen, wir thronten wie Könige und jubelten. Die Sonne schien, wir zogen unser Hemd aus, und der Wind wühlte in unserm Haar. Ich blickte zurück in die Landschaft, die Strasse lief wie ein abspulendes Band.

Plötzlich fühlte ich eine derbe Hand im Nacken, mein Gesicht wurde roh ins Stroh gepresst, dass mir fast der Atem verging. Ich wollte mich wehren aber die Hand liess erst nach einigen Augenblicken locker. Als ich aufsprang, lag mein Gefährte blass im Stroh, aber er lächelte: "Es war der letzte Augenblick. Du hast mich nicht gehört, das Auto rattert zu stark." Hinter uns lag ein Bahnviadukt, handbreit über dem hochgetürmten Wagen.

Es war abends als wir ans Meer kamen. Flach legten sich die Wellen an den Sand und zogen sich wieder zurück. Palmen zeichneten dunkle Silhouetten gegen den dunklen Himmel. Wir sassen nebeneinander, die Hände um die angezogenen Knie gelegt, und blickten hinaus.

Unsere Herzen schlugen im gleichen Rhythmus, und wir kannten einander nicht, wussten nicht den Namen des andern, obwohl wir schon den dritten Tag Brot und Lager teilten.

Der Strand war ruhig und menschenleer um diese Zeit.

Diese Nacht schliefen wir im Sande.

Wir wanderten von einer Palmenstadt zur andern und badeten uns durch die ganze herrliche Küste durch. Blau waren Himmel und Meer, man sah die Linie nicht, die beide trennte: Cote d'Azur.

Vor der Grenze sagten wir einander Lebewohl. "Ich bleibe in Frankreich," sagte er. "Ich gehe nach Italien," sagte ich.

Am Schlagbaum erfuhr ich, dass Fussgänger die Grenze nicht überschreiten dürfen. "Ich will mit meinem gültigen Pass über die Grenze," rief ich erbost.

"Ja, aber per Bahn," sagte der Beamte, "das ist Vorschrift. Halten Sie uns nicht auf."

Ich musste – Schmach für den Landstreicher! – mit einigen meiner Notpfennige eine Bahnkarte kaufen.

Ich stieg aus und ging zum Strand. Ich blickte hinüber zur französischen Küste, wie ich vor einigen Wochen zur englischen geblickt hatte. Das Land war schön und die Nächte waren warm. Ich kam in die Hafenstadt und sah viele Schiffe. Da lag eine Barke, viel Gerät darauf; Taue, Kisten, Decken. Ich hatte noch kein Nachtlager, es war spät, ich kroch in einen Winkel, und schlief ein. Niemand störte mich. Das Wasser schlug leicht gegen die Schiffswand. Ich träumte, ich wäre am Weg nach Brasilien.

Als ich aufwachte, löste ein schmieriger Matrose die Taue. "Sir," sagte ich höflich, "darf ich hier bleiben?" Er taxierte mich kurz mit einem Auge, dann nickte er. Ich wusste nicht, wohin die Fahrt ging und ich fragte nicht.

Drei Tage kreuzte das kleine Schiff längs der Küste und verkaufte Obst. Einmal besuchte es auch eine Insel, die weiter im Meer lag. Es war eine herrliche Zeit, ich lebte von Obst, und ich sperrte die Augen auf. Aber nach drei Tagen packte mich wieder die Lust nach der Landstrasse, ich wollte nicht stillsitzen.

Als wir in irgend einer Bucht lagen, stahl ich mich fort.

Es war an einem grünblauen See, als ich zum erstenmal in der Ferne weisse Bergspitzen sah.

"Das sind die Schweizer Berge," sagte einer.

Da zog ich zur Schweizer Grenze, den weissen Bergen entgegen. Noch war alles südlich. Ich kam an einem Garten vorbei, in dem reife Feigen hingen. Eine Frau stand darinnen. "Habt Ihr was für einen hungrigen Wanderburschen?" rief ich.

"Ich bin nur die Wirtschafterin," sagte die Frau zögernd.

"Sind die Feigen gezählt?" fragte ich und lachte.

Sie verschwand im Haus und kam mit einem grossen Papiersack zurück, der war bis oben mit Feigen gefüllt. Ich dankte und ging. Als ich die Feigen in meinen Rucksack leerte, fand ich dick belegte Brote am Grunde des Papiersacks.

An der italienischen Seite der italienisch-schweizer Grenze war ein Zollwächter aus Meran, der sprach deutsch.

"Eigentlich sind wir Landsleute," sagte ich. "Sie müssen mir zu einem Wagen in die Schweiz verhelfen, zufuss komme ich heute nicht mehr über den Pass." Am Zollschranken müssen alle Wagen halten.

Eine Stunde später sass ich in einem weichgepolsterten Wagen auf dem Wege nach St. Moritz. Rechts und links ragten die weissen Berge, nach denen ich mich gesehnt hatte. 'Ich will ganz nah hinkommen zu den weissen Bergen,' dachte ich.

Ich kam in den grossen Kurort. Herrlich lag er da in seiner internationalen Würde. Gewaltig war das Panorama, gewaltig die Hotels und gewaltig die Preise.

Ich war 1800 Meter hoch, zu kalt zum Übernachten im Freien. Das billigste Zimmer war zu viel für meine Notpfennige.

Ein Mädchen kam vorbei, braungebrannt, in Hosen, ein Seil über der Schulter. Man sah, sie kam aus den Bergen.

"Grüetsi," sagte ich; das hatte ich schon gelernt.

Ich fragte sie, wo ein Wanderer hier übernachten könne.

"In der Herberg natürlich. Komm nur mit."

Damals lernte ich diese wunderbare Einrichtung kennen, dass in allen grösseren Orten der Schweiz jungen Leuten reine Herbergen zur Verfügung stehen.

Als wir eintraten, fragte mich niemand nach meinem Namen und ob ich irgendein Mitglied sei. Um ein paar Rappen durfte ich bleiben.

Als es dunkel wurde, setzten wir Wanderer, Jungen und Mädchen, uns rund um den Tisch und sangen Berglieder. Die Mädchen schenkten mitgebrachten Tee aus.

Ich war glücklich an diesem Abend und ein heimisches Gefühl überkam mich. Ich glühte von der Sonne, die untertags gebrannt hatte. Eine Welle ging über mich hinweg, ich hätte sie umarmen mögen, diese lieben Menschen, wie sie geschwisterlich um den Tisch sassen, reine Kinder der Landstrasse.

Drei Tage blieb ich in der Herberge. Wir machten von hier aus gemeinsame Touren in die weissen Berge, über Schneefelder und Gletscher. Dann rief die Landstrasse wieder.

"Ich muss fort," sagte ich. "Wo ist es am schönsten?"

Sie zeigten nach Osten. "Dort sind die Dolomiten," sagten sie. Ich ging auf die Strasse hinaus, die nach Osten führte. Das Schweizer Mädchen gab mir das Geleit.

Wir schritten kräftig aus. Es war ein strahlender Morgen und ich fühlte mich jung und frei. Mädchen, du bist schön, dachte ich, aber die Landstrasse ist schöner.

"Hier auf der geraden Strasse hat es keinen Sinn einem Auto zuzuwinken," prahlte ich mit meiner Wissenschaft. "Hier bleibt keines stehen. Wir wollen es an einer Biegung versuchen, die bergauf führt, da muss der Fahrer den Gang wechseln."

Wir kamen an eine steil bergauf führende Kurve, die eine vollkommene Schleife bildete. Ich stieg so weit hinauf, dass ich auf den unteren Teil der Strasse hinabblicken konnte. Das ist eine gute Stelle, schätzte ich, von hier kann man sehen ob Platz im Wagen ist, wer drin sitzt, und welche Staatentafel er hat.

"Warum gehst du weiter?" fragte sie.

"Nur ein paar Schritte. Man darf nicht unmittelbar hinter der Kurve stehen, sonst wird man vom Fahrer erst im letzten Augenblick gesehen. Er muss etwas Zeit zur Überlegung haben, ob er einen fremden Menschen als Begleiter mitnehmen will. Man muss auch entsprechend zivilisiert aussehen," fügte ich hinzu.

Sie lächelte. "Also deshalb hast du dich heute rasiert?"

"Ja," gestand ich. "Das tue ich immer an den Tagen an denen ich versuche per Auto weiterzukommen."

Ein dumpfes Knattern war in der Ferne vernehmbar.

"Es kommt eines," rief sie. Es klang eher enttäuscht als freudig.

"Nein," sagte ich. "Das ist ein Motorrad."

Wir warteten eine Weile. Sprich nichts, Mädchen, sprich nichts, die Landstrasse ruft und du kannst mich nicht halten.

"Warum legst du den Rucksack nicht ab?" fragte sie.

"Ich will nicht scheinen, als hätte ich auf das Mitnehmen gewartet." Plötzlich spitzte ich die Ohren. "Jetzt," sagte ich. Ich beugte mich über das Strassengeländer und blickte scharf gegen eine herankommende Staubwolke. "Es ist ein Privatwagen," sagte ich. "Ein Ausländer!" Er kam rasch heran.

"Er ist aber ganz besetzt," sagte sie, als er näher kam.

Nun war das Auto genau in der Kurve unter uns . . . schon sah ich es von der Rückseite.

"Es ist ein Engländer!" rief ich aufgeregt. "Siehst du das GB an der Autotafel?"

"Freut dich das so?" fragte sie etwas verständnislos.

"Freilich. Pass auf, er bleibt bestimmt stehen, auch wenn er mich nicht mitnehmen kann. Alle Engländer tun das, wenigstens um ein bedauerndes Wort zu sagen. Sie sind die freundlichsten Autofahrer."

Ich trat einen halben Schritt vor, hob die Hand, schwenkte lebhaft mein Taschentuch. Am Steuer sass ein junger, bar-häuptiger Mann. Er hatte mich erreicht . . . ein paar Griffe . . . ein schwacher, ächzender Laut. Der Wagen stand.

Das Mädchen hörte nicht, was der Fahrer zu mir sagte, es sah nur das bedauernde Achselzucken, das der junge Engländer mit einer Geste verband, die auf das vollbesetzte Auto hinwies.

Aber dann fiel dem Landstreicher offenbar etwas ein, der Mann am Steuer lachte und rief etwas, "hop on!" Dann schwang sich der junge Vagabund auf das Trittbrett, der Fahrer legte den Fuss auf den Gashebel, Staub wirbelte auf . . .

Immer kleiner wurde das liebe Schweizer Mädchen an der Kurve.

(*Neues Wiener Tagblatt,,* February 21, 1935).

Transition

Exilia
Features

Exilia

The Refugees in a Vagrants' Camp

In a kitchen, three men are at work: one is bending over a wooden tub stacked with mountains of plates, the other two are busy with towels. The floor is wet and greasy. Huge buckets full of scraps are grouped in a corner. A pile of knives and forks is waiting to be washed. The men wear wooden clogs, their shirt sleeves are rolled up to the shoulders. The washed and dried plates are neatly stacked.

They chat while working. One of them is complaining about back pain since he was knocked down by a car a few weeks ago. He describes the accident in technical details, for he is an engineer. The second man fingers the sensitive spot and diagnoses a slight crack in a rib; he is a physician. The third discusses the damages that could be claimed from the motorist; he is an attorney.

The scene is the refugee camp at Merxplas in Belgium where German Jewish emigrants have found shelter. The arrangement was made by the Belgian government, in cooperation with the Jewish Relief Committee in Brussels, to save the refugees from the worst fate of all – a forced return to Nazi Germany – and prepare them for manual work in a hoped-for future life overseas. They are professionals, businessmen, also craftsmen and workers. Here, the professors go to classes taught by workmen. Courses are offered in agriculture, carpentry, electrical work, auto mechanics, plumbing, tailoring, house painting, and other possibly useful crafts. The youngest pupil is 16, the oldest 62. The latter was a noted sculptor, a professor in Vienna. He had made a name for himself even before the war, and members of the old Austrian court had sat for him. After the war he had made busts of the Austrian chancellor Engelbert Dollfuss and other party leaders of the anti-Nazi *Vaterländische Front* , which caused his persecution and exile.

At present, 250 men are in the camp; before long there will be 650. Every one of them has gone through traumatic experiences. Ordinary, humdrum citizens have gone through persecutions, flights, imprisonments, and adventures found in trashy novels.

Many have been hounded from country to country, fled through forests, waded through rivers. For example: one young man had, with great trouble and bribery, obtained a three-month transit visa for Cyprus. When he arrived, the regulations had been tightened and he was asked to furnish proof that he could further emigrate to another country. He was not allowed to land and had to stay on the boat that went on to Palestine. Here, too, he could not land as he had no certificate. He wandered through half of Europe, passing through Greece, Yugoslavia, Switzerland, Luxembourg, and Belgium where he found shelter in Merxplas. His story is not exceptional. Most internees have an odyssey to relate, tales of wanderings by land and sea before they found protection from imminent persecution.

Many have wives in Brussels. The Belgian government agreed to protect female dependents of the interned. One man with a still-valid two-month permit to stay in Belgium, had himself interned to legalize the position of his visa-less daughter.

The camp at Merxplas has been in existence since 1905 and, as "vagrant camp", is known to social workers over the world. Here, tramps, the homeless, the work-shy, learn to do useful work. The camp spreads over 600 hectares and accommodates up to 3,000 inmates. It forms a model state within the state of Belgium and produces all its own necessities. Two farms are run on model lines. The camp has brick-kilns, a weaving mill, a shoe factory, a bakery, and every kind of workshop needed by a self-supporting community. There is a hospital, a church, a cemetery, a school, a swimming pool, a slaughterhouse, a quarantine for animals, and a small field railway to connect the various parts.

The Jewish refugees have been assigned two buildings in this self-supporting state; these they have to manage for themselves. The rule, strictly enforced, forbids them to make any contact with the vagrants. The refugees form a separate small community within the vagrant state. They keep their buildings clean, stoke the fire, cook their meals, wash their clothes, have their training courses. They are restricted to a small area. Only the agricultural workers are allowed outside this enclosure, to learn agricultural skills. A small farm, with four horses, 34 cows, and 40 pigs, has been turned over to them.

The boys under 20 form a community in which private property, to all intents, is unknown. They take their meals together, and no one asks who contributed those sardines or sausages which inmates sometimes get from their relatives in Brussels. The better-off members help the poorer ones. A card index records the qualifications of each inmate, and everyone uses his talents for the good of the community. They are sure that any member who will succeed in getting settled overseas, will remember his friends.

In the evening, when the doctors, civil servants, and former business leaders come back from their unaccustomed labors, the artists take over. An accordion player is acclaimed joyfully; singers and comedians show their, now unused, talents; a young artist amazes the inmates with his stunning caricatures. A former film technician, who owned a chain of cinemas, uses his connections to obtain films for the amusement of his fellow-sufferers. No sound apparatus is available but films are popular that show the scenery and life in countries the refugees hope to reach some day.

A camp newspaper is soon to be produced by a former editor of three Vienna magazines who has a precious portable typewriter. But all the occasional waves of laughter and activities cannot drown out the tragedy that lies in the fate of these uprooted strangers, the despair that at times overcomes them, and the anxiety about their relatives still in Germany, news of whom is rare and usually bad.

But they are aware that it is their own future for which they are working so tirelessly. Then they clench their teeth, grasp with unpracticed hands the spade, the awl, or the plane, turn their thoughts from the sad and dreary present, and look forward to what the future may bring.

(*Jewish Chronicle*, London, February 24, 1939)

The First Swallow

When Kurt Schuschnigg announced on the radio his resignation as chancellor, our family was having dinner. He concluded with the words, "May God save Austria." I dropped my spoon without finishing the food. I said, "This is the end," walked into my room where my suitcase was packed but not closed, and called to my mother to telephone the Western Railroad and ask when the next train was leaving for London. I heard her say on the phone: "Nine thirty-five? That's too soon, when is the next one?"

"It isn't," I called back. "I'll catch it." I closed the suitcase.

I hurriedly kissed my mother. I was getting out. Unattached and unencumbered, I was the one in the family best qualified to try and get them all out eventually. My father called for a taxi and drove with me toward the railroad station. The streets were crammed with shouting people and we had trouble getting through. My father promised the taxi driver a reward if he reached the station in time. At one crossroad the way was blocked by a long column of Nazi motorcyclists preceded by an open automobile with two men in it, one driving, the other holding aloft a large red banner with a glaring swastika.

My heart was feverish with impatience as we waited for the cyclists to pass. Every moment counted. At a break between two sections in the procession our driver shot through.

We got to the station minutes before the train was to depart. Only three people were in line at the ticket window, but even they seemed too many. I had my eyes glued on my wrist watch. "Plenty of time," I said to my ashen-faced father, pretending to be calm.

My hands trembled as I received the ticket. We rushed to the train and I got on. Mercifully, the leave-taking was short. The train pulled out almost immediately. As we began to move I heard ear-splitting yells from the plaza next to the station: "Heil Hit-ler! Sieg Heil!" There must have been thousands shouting. It seemed like the howling of wolves. The yelling, reverberating, was the last sound I heard as I left my home town, my country, forever.

But, of course, I was still eight hours from the Swiss border. Every station along the route was patrolled by swastika-bearing guards. Illegal and underground only hours ago, they had been prepared for the takeover.

I shared the compartment with three silent men who tried to appear calm. One was visibly shaking, the second, sitting by the window, gave the Nazi salute whenever a guard passed on the platform in the stations, a primitive attempt at camouflage; I had no doubt he was a refugee. The third huddled in his corner.

In Salzburg we stopped for an uncomfortably long time. I did not know it then but as we were crossing Austria from east to west, the first Nazi troops were on their way from Germany in the north and would reach Salzburg during the night. We must have missed them by hours. That was the closest shave I had with the Nazis.

Well, not quite. The hours crept by slowly as we approached the border, and the temperature in the compartment seemed to be rising.

At dawn we stopped close to the border. A man with a swastika armband stepped into our compartment.

He collected our passports and asked each of us where we were going. The saluting man said London, and so did I; the other two said Paris. The Nazi returned the passports and left. We breathed a sigh of relief. Was it that easy?

It wasn't. He came back within minutes, this time with a man in a leather jacket. The new man pointed at the two going to Paris. "Come with me." The shaking man could hardly stand up, but they both followed the leather jacket, and I saw them being marched to the station building. The leather jacket returned and pointed his finger at the saluting man.

"Out," he said gruffly. The two disappeared in the same direction as the others.

My turn was next. I was sitting on hot coals but no one came. After what seemed like an endless time, the train started on the last kilometers to the border. I was alone in the compartment.

Then the door opened again. This time it was the shaking man who entered. I was glad to see him, but asked nothing and he said nothing. He sat down and smoked furiously. The door opened again, and the saluting man entered. He too was silent. But the door did not open a third time.

We were not checked at the border itself. We rolled over it. Nobody spoke until we reached the station of Buchs on the Swiss side.

Railroad officials in Swiss uniforms walked the platform. It is impossible to describe our relief at the sight of those uniforms after eight hours of tension.

Now the two men came alive and gushed out their stories. The shaking one, an artist, had been taken to the stationmaster and briefly interrogated. The other man, who was beside himself with elation, told us that all his life savings had been hidden in his shoe in large denomination bills. He had pretended to tie his laces as he was being taken to the stationmaster, rested his shoe at the base of a pillar of the building, and hid the money behind the pillar. When they searched him for money, they found nothing.

"I got rid of it, I got rid of it," rejoiced the man, who had just lost all his earthly fortune, the money he had hoped to use to build a new life abroad. I fantasized a cleaning woman, wielding a broom routinely tidying up the yard of the station, finding this treasure .

Two obvious questions remained: What happened to the third man , and why was I spared? There was no one to ask.

And I? As I later tried to understand it, the Nazis at borders close to Vienna, at Hungary and Czechoslovakia, were trying to catch political refugees, those who had the most to fear, those closest to an exit. The guards at the Swiss border primarily looked for refugees smuggling money out of Austria. I was a young student, less likely than the others to be a plutocrat. In those very first hours of the takeover, the Nazis had their hands full, and perhaps concentrated on the most likely targets. Besides, the three others were visibly seething with fear. I was just as scared, but may have shown it less.

Actually, the Nazis were right. I carried no more cash than the equivalent of 50 dollars, in British pound notes. With that amount I was to start my new life.

The train stopped in Basel, long enough for me to make a telephone call from the rail station to the editorial office of the *Basler National-Zeitung to* which Joe and I had contributed short stories. I was lucky to catch "our" editor, the man with whom we had corresponded. Though in safe Switzerland, he was shaken by the events in Austria and was receptive to my plea to accept as many contributions as possible from now on. He understood that 50 dollars would not last long.

In Paris the passenger who had said he was going to Paris got off. The other traveler continued on with me. We reached the coast and took the Channel boat to Folkestone.

There we were grilled by an immigration officer. British policy required foreign travelers to stay no longer than three months, to have enough money to maintain themselves during that time, and not to take jobs. A specific permit or visa was not required in early 1938. I had to play the role of a visitor. I was not "immigrating."

The officer asked how long I intended to stay, and I said three months. Did I have money? I showed him my pathetic amount. But this would certainly not last for three months. What was I to do when they were spent, he asked.

I said I was a journalist. I would write articles for British newspapers and live on the fees. I showed him some Fabrizius manuscripts in English translation I had brought with me.

It was the wrong thing to say. The officer, up to now coolly correct, turned tense. No, I was not to do any such thing. In writing for British newspapers I would be taking away space from British journalists. He was not going to admit me into England.

The world seemed to fall apart. I had caught the first train leaving Vienna after the Nazi takeover, slipped through the border control, and now, at the gate, the door slammed shut.

I said I had done the same thing only three months ago. I had been in England, sold stories, and returned to Austria. I planned to do the same now. I showed him my passport with the British entry and exit stamps and thought this should be convincing.

But that was three months ago. Something had happened yesterday that alerted the immigration officers to be especially careful with "visitors" who could become a burden to the already precarious British employment situation.

While he inspected my passport, I had a few precious moments to think of a better answer. It is not too much to say that life depended on it. The answer had to be convincing and given in a calm, self-assured way, not by a frantic refugee, but by a contributor to British papers, traveling between England and the Continent.

And so I said, and tried to be almost ironical without being offensive that, as a freelance writer, I could write stories anywhere, for example in France, if he chose to send me back. I would be free to mail my articles to England from there or anywhere else; the payment I would receive from the British newspapers I would then spend in France, instead of in England where the country at large would benefit from it.

The answer was an inspiration. The man bought the story. He did not discover the big hole in it – that I could *not* send stories from France. If the British sent me back to France, the French would either ship me back to Austria or lock me up in a refugee camp.

The officer waved me on. As I walked through the gate, I could just make out another officer refusing admission to my remaining companion. I never saw him again and know nothing about his fate.

Gerda had remained in London when I returned to Vienna the previous December. Now she received me with open arms. She had expected me and had taken a tiny room for me at Swiss Cottage, around the corner from where she lived. It was a miserable attic but it looked glorious. Exhausted, I dumped my suitcase and opened it. On top lay a spoon. I had dropped it there inadvertently in closing the suitcase when I rushed from our last family dinner.

*

The next morning I sat opposite a distinguished-looking, mild-mannered gentleman, Leonard Montefiore, head of a committee that had been established five years earlier to assist refugees from Germany. I assumed that this committee would be the right group to approach now, although I was from Austria.

"Do you realize," he said, "that you are the first swallow?"

Indeed, of the four on that first train out of Vienna, one was taken off at the border, one left in Paris, and one was turned back at Folkestone. I was the first refugee from Austria in England – the first of thousands.

(*The Cornhill Magazine,,* London, May 1939)

Erste Lektion

Mr. Finn und ich sind Kollegen. Mr. Finn ist ein grosser Dichter. Ich bin ein kleiner Dichter und da ich auch so berühmt werden wollte wie Mr. Finn ging ich zu ihm und fragte ihn, ob er nicht einen Gehilfen brauchen könnte. Ich sagte, ich könnte sehr schöne Gedichte machen. Molly sagt, sie sind schöner als von Wordsworth, auch schwärmte ich sehr für die Natur, Mondschein, säuselndes Laub und Segelboote am Horizont.

Mr. Finn dachte eine Weile nach und sein Blick schwebte in die Ferne. Ich war nicht sicher, ob er mir zugehört hatte und wollte ihm gerade nochmals alles sagen, da fragte er:

"Können Sie Irish Stew machen?"

Ich sagte, ich hätte gemeint, ich könnte *Gedichte* machen, aber nicht Irish Stew, leider.

"Schade,",sagte Mr. Finn. "Das ess ich nämlich so gern."

Ich war betrübt, dass ich so ungebildet war, und ich bewunderte Mr. Finn sehr, der ein so grosser Genius war, dass er selbst bei so einfachen Gesprächen offenbar in anderen Welten schwebte und vielleicht an seinen nächsten Roman dachte.

Das war aber ein Irrtum, Mr. Finn schwebte in dieser Welt.

"Ich kann Ihnen nämlich leider keinen job als Gehilfe anbieten," sagte er, "aber unser Stubenmädchen hat uns gestern Knall und Fall verlassen und nun haben wir niemanden, der kochen und aufräumen kann. Wenn Sie wollen, könnten Sie bei uns Hausknecht werden."

Ich dachte, es wäre sehr schön bei Mr. Finn zu sein, selbst als Hausknecht, denn vielleicht würde er sich's später überlegen und mich doch als Gehilfen nehmen. Aber wie sollte das gehen, wenn ich nichts von diesem plötzlich angebotenen Geschäft verstand ?

Ich sagte Mr. Finn freimütig meine Bedenken, aber er sagte, das mache gar nichts, denn seine Frau, würde mir alles genau erklären. Da sagte ich, das wäre allerdings grossartig und ich nähme sehr gerne an.

So wurde ich statt Dichter Hausknecht.

"Das Wichtigste, was jeder Hausknecht wissen muss, ist Staubwischen," sagte Mrs. Finn am nächsten Tag. "Also werden wir als erste Lektion das Staubwischen durchnehmen."

Ich sagte, ich könnte nirgends irgendwelchen Staub sehen und meiner Meinung nach gäbe es Staub überhaupt nur auf der Strasse und auch dort nur, wenn ein Auto drüberfuhr. Aber Mrs. Finn sagte lächerlich, das ganze Haus sei voller Staub. "Schau doch einmal auf diesen Tisch zum Beispiel." Sie deutete auf einen vollkommen sauberen Tisch und ich sagte zaghaft, dass ich leider gar keinen Staub bemerken könnte.

Da schrieb Mrs. Finn mit dem Finger auf den Tisch das Wort Idiot und ich bin bis heute nicht sicher, ob sie damit etwas Persönliches andeuten wollte, und selbstverständlich war dann Staub rundherum um das Wort Idiot. Man kann über solche Dinge denken, wie man will, in meinen Augen ist das einfach ein unfairer Trick. Niemand hat ihr geschafft auf dem Tisch zu schreiben, und wenn sie nicht geschrieben hätte, wäre keine Rede von einem Staub gewesen. Das kommt mir so vor, wie wenn man erst den Indianern Feuerwasser zu trinken gibt und sich dann wundert, wenn sie betrunken sind. Ich glaube, ich werde über dieses Thema einmal ausführlich schreiben, mehr philosophisch und psychologisch, wenn ich nicht mehr Hausknecht bin.

Mrs. Finn ging im ganzen Haus herum und wischte alles ab, was sie nur erreichen konnte, es war direkt lächerlich. Um allem die Krone aufzusetzen, stieg sie noch auf eine Leiter um irgendwo in der Höhe abzuwischen, in Gegenden, wo ich, wenn ich Staub wäre, nicht träumen würde hinzufliegen. Dort kann schon deshalb kein Staub sein, weil dort niemand im Leben Worte hinschreiben wird.

Ich liesse mir alles gefallen, aber Mrs. Finn schob noch die Betten, Tische und Stühle zur Seite, um darunter herum-zuwischen. Ich habe mir vorgenommen, alles wahrheitsmässig zu erzählen, auch wenn es unwahrscheinlich klingt. Ich sage also, dass Mrs. Finn alles das wirklich tat, um einem unsinnigen Aberglauben zu frönen. Ich betrachtete mir das Zimmer nach dem Staubwischen und alles sah genau so aus wie früher, und ich bin überzeugt, wenn ich Mrs. Finn geprüft hätte und gefragt hätte (ohne dass sie wusste, ob ich Staub gewischt hätte oder nicht): "Nun, ist der Staub weg oder nicht?" Sie hätte diese Prüfung nie bestanden, ausser durch solche Tricks wie Worte schreiben.

Mrs. Finn gab mir also einen Fetzen und sagte, ich sollte nun im nächsten Zimmer Staub wischen. Der Fetzen hatte eine rosa Farbe und als ich ihn in meinem Studenteneifer genauer auseinanderfaltete und betrachtete, war es ein Höschen von Mrs. Finn mit einigen Löchern drin, die sie nicht geflickt hatte. Ich fragte Mrs. Finn, weil ich doch lernen will, warum sie die Löcher nicht gestopft hat, aber Mrs. Finn riss mir das Höschen weg, regte sich unnötig auf und sagte, ich hätte nicht jeden Fetzen zu untersuchen, den sie mir zum Staubwischen gäbe und ich sollte mich um meine eigenen Angelegenheiten kümmern. Sie gab mir einen anderen Fetzen und als ich ihn später heimlich ansah, bemerkte ich dass es ein früheres Hemd von Mr. Flinn war, aber mir war schon alles ganz egal und ich dachte, es hätte gar keinen Sinn tiefer in die Dinge einzudringen. Ich würde einfach oberflächlich sein und nichts mehr fragen, denn wenn ich mich all diesen Themen philosophisch nähern würde, käme ich ohnehin nur auf solche Schlussfolgerungen, wie dass das Staubwischen ein Aberglauben sei, der erstens unnötig ist und zweitens gar nichts hilft, weil am nächsten Tag der Staub ohnehin wieder da ist, also wozu?

Ich könnte mich dem Thema auch von der physikalischen Seite nähern und etwa fragen, wieso denn Staub auf senkrechten Flächen überhaupt hängen könnte, zum Beispiel auf einem Spiegel, das widerspricht doch allen Gesetzen der Schwerkraft und führt schon deswegen den Aberglauben ad absurdum. Aber ein Hausknecht hat nichts zu fragen, sondern muss überall Staub wischen oder zumindest so tun. Selbst wenn gar keiner da ist, so wie bei der Geschichte vom Kaiser, der keine Kleider anhatte und alle so taten als hätte er die wunderbarsten Gewänder.

Es gibt noch eine zweite Stufe des Staubwischens, nämlich den Mop, der für den Fussboden reserviert ist. Um dem Fass den Boden auszuschlagen, sagte Mrs. Finn, ich solle erst den Staub wischen und dann mit dem Mop auf dem Boden auf- und abfahren! Sie selbst gab also zu, dass selbst theoretisch gar kein Staub da sein könnte im Augenblick wo der Mop in Aktion gesetzt wird. Der Mop besteht aus einem unfrisierten Büschel von Schnüren und ist zwecklos. Psychoanalytiker werden einmal entdecken zur Befriedigung welcher hausfraulicher Triebe der Mop dient.

Ein Spezialinstrument, um Teppiche zu "reinigen" ist der carpet sweeper. Ich setze reinigen unter Anführungszeichen, weil all meine männlichen Freunde bestätigen werden, dass ein Teppich niemals schmutzig ist, es schon aus logischen Gründen niemals sein kann, da doch der Schmutz zwischen den Haaren des Teppichs verschwindet und daher unsichtbar ist. Manchmal fällt allerdings etwas auf den Boden, ein Hemdknopf oder eine Münze u. dgl. und jeder Mensch weiss, wie beinahe unmöglich es ist, solche Gegenstände auf einem Teppich wiederzufinden, geschweige denn winzige Staubkörner, die man auf Teppichen nicht einmal durch Tricks sichtbar machen kann.

Der einzige Gegenstand, in Wirklichkeit, der tatsächlich einer Reinigung bedarf, ist der carpet sweeper selbst. Man möchte es nicht für möglich halten, was für ein staubiges und schmutziges Instrument das ist. Ich erwähne das schon deshalb, damit man nicht etwa glaubt, ich sei ein Mensch mit Vorurteilen und fände nirgends Schmutz, um mich von der Arbeit zu drücken. Dem ist durchaus nicht so. Der carpet sweeper besteht aus zwei Rollbürsten, die in einem kleinen Käfig sitzen. Dieser Käfig, den ich natürlich aufmachte, um zu sehen, was drin ist, war voll von ekelhaftem Schmutz, den ich sofort herausschüttelte und unter einen Schrank kehrte, denn ich hatte schon etwas Hauswirtschaft gelernt und wollte auf dem Teppich keinen Schmutz machen.

Aber es ist kaum vorzustellen, wie rasch diese carpet sweeper schmutzen. Kaum hatte ich eine Weile den Hokuspokus mitgemacht und den carpet sweeper auf dem Teppich hin- und hergerutscht, war er wieder voller Schmutz.

Um die Staubwischapparate wissenschaftlich zu erforschen und ihre Wirkung festzustellen, verwendete ich sie experimentell in umgekehrter Form, als Mrs. Finn nicht im Zimmer war. Ich pinselte den Teppich mit dem Mop und rutschte den carpet sweeper auf dem Parkett und, wie erwartet, war die Wirkung vollkommen dieselbe, es änderte sich am Aussehen des Bodens und Teppiche gar nichts.

Ich staubte zuletzt gottergeben, und von der Überflüssigkeit überzeugt, alles noch sehr ordentlich mit Mr. Finns Hemd, aber plötzlich erschien Mrs. Finn, der man nie etwas recht machen kann und sagte, ich sei nicht talentiert, weil ich die Bücher gründlich abstaubte. Sie sagte, die Seiten innen brauchte man nicht abstauben. Natürlich nicht ! Das wusste ich ja auch. Aber kann ich wissen, auf was sich der Aberglauben einer solchen Hausfrau bezieht und auf was nicht ?

(Unpublished opening pages of a planned story, 1941)

Storyteller of the Hong List

My emigration odyssey included a year in Shanghai.
During that time I became an editor of the British-owned
North China Daily News. *As a sort of apprenticeship I was*
to work on a commercial directory, called Hong List.

M.K.

The Hong List contains hundreds of streets and thousands of names. Once a year a new edition comes out and the thousands of names must be read and re-read to make the changes. Can you imagine a job more monotonous than checking these names on endless lists?

It was my job.

The first day was a trial. I checked 13 proofs which was much less than my lady-colleague did. And yet, each proof contained about 200 names - about 2,600 after the first day. When I came home I thought I wouldn't be able to carry on; my eyes were sore.

The next morning I had to insert the letters "& Mrs." to one of the names. I had done that many times the day before, but it was only on this morning that I began to think about it. Of course, there had been a young man, unmarried last year, and now, here you are: "Mr. & Mrs. H. L. Somebody." I caught myself looking out for more additional " & Mrs." and before long I found out that all the town seemed to have been full of romance during the past year. I had my own thoughts now, when here and there a "Miss" had to be taken out from the former year's list. Naturally, I could not know whether and which of those disappearing "Misses" might turn up inconspicuously at some other place as "Mrs."

Now and then I had to take out the "Mr." A still mourning "Mrs." remained and that lady hardly imagined that somebody whom she had never seen was lending a thought of sympathy to her. I imagined her looking up her name in the new edition, finding out the difference between this year's and last year's insertion in the list and quietly closing the book again.

By and by the dead and boring lists began to live and tell stories. I saw children joining their parents: from the names you could easily guess they were refugee youngsters who had managed to cross the seas. I saw new firms being founded and old ones disappearing. I watched people moving into better neighborhoods; and, of course, I had to register the opposite, as well.

I noticed entire houses being pulled down, and new buildings being rented to new tenants. I saw how members of the same nationalities lived together, in small clusters, in the same buildings, in this international city. The Chinese, Anglo-Saxons, Japanese, Greeks (Mr. –oulos and Mrs. –ides), the Portuguese (those scores of Remedios), the Russians (–ieff, –off), the Germans (Nazis and exiles), the Armenians, Turks, Persians. You could tell most of them by their names, and many of them lived together.

I pondered about the question what the closest relationship could be between two "Mrs. O." who lived in the same flat; probably sisters-in-law if related at all. I speculated about a bare line "Marcelle" without "Miss" or Mrs. and came to the conclusion that this might even be more illuminating than with those personal additions. I found that a "Mrs. H." was living now at the place which in last year's issue was marked "British Defence Force." I had to take out many names of one nationality replacing them by many of another. It was exciting business.

My pencil ran from one name to another, from one proof to the next. I was no longer correcting names, I was reading stories and tales, real ones, written by life itself. On the evening of the third day I noticed I had checked 32 proofs on that day.

One day I suddenly stopped when a name struck me; a name which I didn't expect, somehow.

It was my own name. I had met myself, officially. I checked my name. Correct.

(*North China Daily News,*, Shanghai, Feb. 2, 1941)

Today's Foreigner - Tomorrow's Ancestor

This is the story of an American who came to this country 318 years after the Mayflower. He has no forefathers here. He himself is a forefather, the ancestor of future generations. His descendants will say: "Our forefather immigrated during the Great War, just before the Atomic Era." They will be as proud of him as everybody is proud of the forefather. They won't speak of him as "refugee," just as today we do not call the Pilgrims "refugees."

But our friend's contemporaries don't show him the reverence which should be accorded a future forefather. Every time he opens his mouth a heavy accent pops out, and people ask where he is from. They mean well, but our friend is touchy on this subject. He should not feel that way. Vienna is popular in this country. Americans remember Strauss rather than Hitler, and see the Danube blue, not red from the blood of Hitler's victims. But then people inquire how long our friend has been in this country? Since 1938? Oh, a refugee?

This annoys him. After all, he passed his citizenship examination and was sworn in. He knows the three ways a bill can become law, the 21 amendments, and that all men are created equal. He knows also that a naturalized citizen can hold any office except the presidency and vice-presidency.

But knowledge of the Constitution doesn't make him an American. There is more to it. He goes to baseball games, reads the comics, listens to the radio programs, commercials and all. He is a master of the spelling bee. On Thanksgiving Day he eats turkey and on Hallowe'en he hides his face behind a mask and scares his neighbors. And he is for free enterprise lock, stock, and barrel.

But still he isn't an American. Not only in the eyes of the DAR, but in his own. He doesn't belong yet. He hasn't taken root.

That leaves the $64 question: when does a recent immigrant cease being a refugee and start becoming an American?

Here is the answer: when one day his three-year-old comes home from nursery and says, "Daddy, sing 'Baa baa, black sheep'!"

Daddy has never heard of "Baa baa, black sheep." But he can't admit it. He can't disillusion the child. He says, "*You* sing it," he says.

The child sings something which doesn't make sense to Daddy at all. And every day the child comes home with another song. One day it is "Pop goes the weasel"; the next, "Jack and Jill." He is unhappy to see his own child live in a world where he is a foreigner. He buys *Fifty Favorite Nursery Songs* and practices them on the piano while the child is at the nursery. He learns them by heart although they don't seem to make much sense. But the child's eyes light up when Daddy, one day, joins in:

Hickory, dickory dock!
The mouse ran up the clock.
The clock struck one,
the mouse ran down . . .
hickory, dickory dock!

Once in a while he recognizes a tune from his childhood. "Trot, trot, trot! Trot, my pony, trot," used to be *"Hop, hop, hop! Pferdchen, lauf Galopp!"* It's like meeting an old Viennese acquaintance who – surprise! – talks English.

But singing is not everything. The child learns games in the nursery and expects Daddy to play them at home. Pat-a-cake, pat-a-cake. Now clap, Daddy. First your hands, then mine. Easy, see?

When he sits on the floor next to the three-year-old, takes the little fingers and says, "This little pig went to market," he starts thinking. 'That's how my child is growing up. An American child. Not because the law says so, but because she goes to an American school. She grows up an American. And I will be with her when she goes from elementary school through high school. I will meet her friends. I will do homework with her. Not so much to help as to learn from her. Today I am, like my child, a beginning American. But just as my child grows up to become a grown-up American, I will become an American, too. For my child, and through my child, I will cease being a 'foreigner'.

So the American who came to this country 318 years after the Mayflower and who has no forefathers here, is now one himself. A modest beginning of his future ancestry has already been made.

(*Common Ground*, New York, Summer 1946)

From Emigrant to Immigrant

For many Hitler refugees, 1945 was the year of decision whether to remain in their new homeland or return to their native countries. Political refugees live by the illusion that the nightmare that had driven them from their country would dissipate, allowing them to return to the old conditions. That is still true today for the refugees from Cuba, Vietnam, China, and all the other dictatorships which prompt the political mass migration of our cruel century.

This was also true for the Hitler emigrants But after the war, most of them in the United States didn't return to Austria or Germany. The wounds of the holocaust were too painful.

The situation was different for writers with a tie to the German language. Some, like Thomas Mann or Franz Werfel, were well-known enough in America to be successful there. Others, like Josef Wechsberg, had learned to write and publish in English. Still others, like Friedrich Torberg and Bert Brecht, failed to succeed in the United States, although they had been famous in Europe. For them, there was a conflict.

For me, there was no conflict. My fame as writer in Europe had been modest. I had published short stories, written cabaret sketches, edited for three Viennese magazines. None of the magazines, newspapers, and cabarets still existed. My play had been performed in Vienna, but under the name of a co-author who had two guaranteed Aryan grandmothers, a precondition of production in Nazi Austria. There wasn't much to lure me back.

More important, by 1945 I was able to make a living by writing in English. My wife came from Austrian parents but was born in New York and spoke English without an accent. Judith was an important part of my Americanization. Another part was my survival work in factories and shipyards where I soaked up all sorts of American accents and idioms. In 1943, I had my first writing job as scriptwriter for the Office of War Information (later the Voice of America). My reports were shortwaved to China and my English didn't have to be faultless because my scripts were translated and voiced in Chinese.

But beyond the Atlantic, Europe was calling. Austria. Vienna. It was not homesickness, it was "unfinished business," a sickness of the soul. I postponed the visit. I knew it would cause pain. But it was like an operation I had to undergo if I wanted to really get well.

In 1965 I was ready. Our three children were old enough to be left by themselves. We had enough financial security through my work at the University of California. And I wanted to go to Vienna to discuss with Viktor Frankl a book I planned to write.

After an absence of 27 years, Vienna was a ghost town. The streets were familiar, the buildings, restaurants, coffee houses, and stores were pretty much the same, but the people were strangers. I never saw a familiar face on the street, in the theater, or on streetcars. I was Rip Van Winkle wandering through the well-known, yet strange city. Actors whom I had asked for autographs at the stage door were now busts in the foyer of the theater. (Several years later it became still more absurd: Sigmund Freud's apartment where, as a high-school student, I had sipped hot chocolate [he was the uncle of a school mate] was now a museum. His face was on a postage stamp. Hans Kelsen, my professor at the Vienna University, also was a stamp. Robert Stolz, whom I met in my cabaret work, was a statue in a park.)

Back to 1965. I had the unexplainable need to visit all the places where I had suffered so many humiliations. I went to the apartment from which we were thrown out; the university where I was beaten up; the street where I was spat at while being forced to clean up anti-Nazi graffitti. I met my high-school mates who had swastikas in their buttonholes and looked the other way on the street. One could think my desire to revisit painful places was masochism. Today I know it was therapy.

Meeting with my "Aryan" school mates was especially revealing. Their reactions were varied: they ignored, trivialized, rationalized. One of them tried to convince me how lucky we emigrants were to sit in rich America while the Viennese suffered bombardment and starvation. When I mentioned that those in Vienna at least did not have their parents murdered, he allowed that, regretfully, some excesses did happen. A second schoolmate reminded me that he always had been in favor of Austria's joining Germany which he supported at any price, even if the price included (this he didn't say explicitly but it was understood) the lives of a few million Jews. Another school mate explained why he joined the Austrian Nazi party during the 1930 depression when no one could foresee what would happen later. But then there was a forth, a high functionary in the new Austrian government, who came to thank me for having helped him at the all-important high-school finals. Failure at these finals, in his mind, would have been a black mark against his steep career. This last meeting did much to reconcile me with my Austrian past, although I realized that none of my colleagues even hinted at feeling in any way responsible for anything that happened during the Nazi period, except one who said: "If we Austrians are proud of Mozart, we also must share the blame for Hitler."

My first revisit of Vienna in 1965 was therapy and an eye opener. Also about language. By then I had begun to translate German-writing authors like Johann Nestroy, Karl Kraus, and Bert Brecht. My accent didn't show in print. But in Vienna it often happened that my German sentences had an English construction, or that I suddenly couldn't think of the proper German word. I expressed my dilemma in a poem that, unfortunately, can be understood only by those who speak both languages.

Der Doppelrefugee

Ein Refugee der Doppelsorte
bin ich hier am Kontinent.
Im Deutschen fehlen mir die Worte
mein Englisch hat einen Akzent.
Mein Deutsch und Englisch live in wedlock,
commuting between Sprach und Sprach.
Both languages are sick from jetlag –
die Reime sind denn auch danach.
As writer earn ich Mark und Schilling,
auch Pfunds und Dollars freu'n mein Herz.
My feeling reimet sich auf Frühling,
my Lust auf boost, my Schmerz auf hurts.
Hier sitz ich nun, ein alter Gaul
am Ort, den ich verliess als Jüngel –
nicht Fisch, nicht Fleisch, not fish nor fowl:
my ignorance is now bilingual.

It required more visits to Vienna to sort out my inner conflicts. My evolution from emigrant to immigrant led me through the same stages as it did to most of the other refugees. First, we compared everything American with "how it was at home," and found the customs of the old country superior, despite the Nazi persecutions (which we considered a passing aberration). Next came the stage of enthusiasm for everything in the adopted country where we made new friends, started families, and which had become home. Eventually the time came when we were able to combine the best of Europe with the best of America.

This happened in my case. I translated some of my favorite German authors unavailable in English. I started the Institute of

Logotherapy to familiarize Americans with the "Third Viennese School of Psychotherapy" Dr. Frankl's.

These efforts went far toward healing the wounds of the past. Many immigrants remained stuck in the first two stages. They could not adjust and kept dreaming of the good, old times of their youth. Others were bitter toward the land that had treated them so cruelly. They avoided everything that reminded them of the old country. The wounds did not heal.

I tried for reconciliation. Here lies the way to healing; this, too, I learned from Frankl's logotherapy. It's not a depth psychology trying to dig up past traumas but a "height" psychology, reaching out for present and future meanings.

There are many meanings I can find today that have their roots in the unmeanings of yesterday. I can fight nationalism, racial hatred, dictatorships, and economic crises that breed these evils. There are many ways to discover meaningful possibilities in the meaningless suffering during the Nazi period. I know Hitler emigrants who help the homeless in America because they remember how their parents lost their homes in Austria. I know many who went into social work to help those suffering as they had suffered. I know a man who for 40 years has been sending monthly support to a family that hid him and his children.

My son tells me I still have a refugee mentality, for example, not wasting food, bending down to pick up a penny, my strong support of Israel. He is probably right. I have no wish to change that. But when I recently watched the graduation of my granddaughter, I realized happily that the former emigrant is now the ancestor of a new generation.

(Adult Education Center 'Urania,' Vienna, Oct. 3. 1977, translated)

I Become One of Them

My shipyard memories were written as if authored by an American.   JF

One day I was walking through a gate under a huge sign: REMEMBER PEARL HARBOR. I didn't need to be reminded, for on that day I had been bombed out of home and business. Not in Hawaii but right off the main street in Omaha, Nebraska. I was a salesman of vacuum cleaners. It was a job I liked, traveling all over, seeing the country, talking to people, listening to their stories. Suddenly, all what was left of the vacuum cleaner business was the vacuum.

Then I learned they were building ships on the coast in a new way, preassembling them as you do cars. They needed workers, lots of them, and it wasn't necessary to know anything about ships. All you needed were two hands. If you had only one, they'd find a job for that one, too. So I packed up and headed out. Sunny California, here I come.

At the Richmond hiring office a couple of hundred guys stood in line. Some had white collars and some had no collars at all. Some looked as if they had been waiting in hiring offices all their lives, and some looked lost like rookies.

When my turn came up, a guy asked me what kind of a job a wanted. I told him I wantd to build a ship.

"Take it easy now," he said. "It takes 60 trades to build a boat. How about becoming a flanger?"

"Okay with me. What does he do?"

"Beats me," he said. "Just report to work. They'll tell you."

Next morning at 6 A.M. I rolled in merrily. It was still pitch-dark and the highways were dotted with headlights. You could see the dandiest limousines next to the oldest jalopies and trucks still marked with the name of a firm which had given up for the duration. It was a good feeling to belong to this stream of workers.

And so I was walking through the gate under that REMEMBER PEARL HARBOR sign. A procession of tin hats, overalls, and lunch boxes, crowding into a new world: piles of steel plates of all shapes and sizes, shacks and booths, ladders and scaffolds, posters like the one reminding you that the guy who relaxes is helping the axis. The

62

yard was arranged city-like: F, G, H streets running in one direction, 9th, 10th, 11th streets in another. It was a city without houses, but the traffic was heavy with cranes, trucks, trains. Finally I came to the edge of the water. There were the ships, or rather halves, thirds, and tenths of ships. A piece of ship here and a piece there, and a hole in between. Then, out of a clear sky, a crane dropped a missing piece of ship, big as a house, into that hole.

I was assigned to the gang on Assembly Way Five. I got a couple of wrist-breaking handshakes but most of the guys didn't bother to look up from their hammering and welding. They all looked as though they had dug coal with their bare hands and wiped their hands on their faces.

It took me just half an hour to become as dirty as they. I gave a hand to one of them, puzzled over a blueprint with another, swapped jokes with a third, and soon they ceased to be a bunch of guys with dirty hands and rough language. I shared with them the great adventure of helping to build ships for victory.

*

I worked with them for two years and often wondered how people with such different backgrounds could have gotten along together so well. How could the gang on Assembly Way Five click? For two reasons, I think. First, we had a common purpose. Second, we got to know each other's stories. Stories beginning on a Montana ranch, an Oklahoma laundry, a California college, a garage in Michigan, a tamale stand, a mine – all flowing together on Assembly Way Five, tying us all together.

While working in this new world where you don't say Left and Right but Port and Starboard, where your nose is on your forward end and you sit on your afterpeak, I listened to those stories, and saw them develop, especially when women workers joined us. And when I look aft now, it's not so much the records we broke but the stories I heard that I want to talk about. Taken together, it's the story of a little melting pot within the big melting pot, America.

(*Swing Shift: Building the Liberty Ships,* San Francisco: Strawberry Hill Press, 1982)

Building Language Bridges

I am honored to have been invited into this circle of Germanists, as something like a chameleon. It required a generous interpretation of the term "Germanist" to include me.

True, until retirement the university was my professional home – not as Germanist but as editor. True, I contributed my share to students learning German – not as teacher, but as author of text books. And when I was addressed in the classroom as *Herr Professor*, it was not by students of German literature but by students of the philosophy of the Viennese psychotherapist Viktor Frankl.

There is an American saying: "If a bird quacks like a duck, waddles like a duck, and looks like a duck – it *is* a duck."

And so, whether as chameleon or duck, I would like to contribute the following to this symposium:

When I came to America in 1940, I was 30, not old enough to be known in America as a writer, and too old to go to an American university and become a Germanist. My first problem was to learn the new language. I discovered a method I can recommend to all who wish to learn a language. During my stay in London I had an English girl friend who didn't speak a word of German. As a supplement, I went to movie theaters and saw an American film three times all afternoon.

After the usual apprenticeship of the penniless refugee as factory worker, male charwoman, and gardener, I made up my mind to become an American author. I would never be able to speak English without an accent, but I could write accent-free. After the war my English was good enough to become editor of scientific publications at the University of California in Berkeley. I loved America and still was steeped in the culture of Europe. I wanted to build bridges of understanding.

I didn't know how. But in the course of the years three important opportunities for such bridge-building turned up: our Peter Fabrizius short stories were used as text books for German-language students. We translated German-writing authors into English. And I gave courses about a Viennese school of psychotherapy at American universities and seminars at American colleges.

Our humorous short stories were published for American classrooms and used at Harvard, Princeton, and Stanford. We were delighted that our old stories, too, had succeeded in emigrating.

At that time my Peter-Fabrizius-partner, started to translate Christian Morgenstern's *Galgenlieder* into English. We spent many lunch hours working on the language somersaults Morgenstern invented in German. Morgenstern phantasized about "ein Wiesel/ [that] sass auf einem Kiesel/ inmitten Bachgeriesel" (literally: "A weasel sat on a pebble in the ripple of a brook"). He explained this strange behavior: "Das raffinier/te Tier/ tat's um des Reimes willen," translated pretty straightforwardly as "The sopheest/icated beast/ did it just for the rhyme." Here it was obviously not important to have the weasel sit on a pebble in a brook. Max translated therefore: "A weasel/perched on an easel/within a patch of teasel." As he later pointed out in the introduction of his book, it was not important to talk even about a weasel. It could have been a ferret/ nibbling a carrot/ in a garret, or a mink/ sipping a drink/ in a kitchen sink, or a hyena/ playing a concertina/ in an arena.

I participated in the Morgenstern translations only as a nutcracker. Max translated busily, and when he found a hard nut he brought it to me to help him crack it. I tried for possible solutions before falling asleep, when shaving, or at the swimming pool. His volume of about a hundred poems, printed in German and English, was published by the University of California Press, and later also by Piper in Munich.

The success of the Morgenstern poems whetted our appetite for other "untranslatables." We selected three of Johann Nestroy's best-known farces, *Der Zerrissene, Der Talisman,* and *Liebesgeschichten und Heiratssachen* (translated as *A Man Full of Nothing, The Talisman,* and *Love Affairs and Wedding Bells*). Nestroy's idiomatic fireworks were really "untranslatable." We admitted on the title page that we had "translated and fondly tampered with [the comedies]."

We had the most fun with Nestroy's songs he used in a similar way as later Brecht. The actor sings a humorous ditty, with a refrain line at the end of each stanza. Nestroy, who starred in his own farces, made it a custom to sing an additional stanza he wrote as last-minute comments on events of the day. We followed this tradition. In *The Talisman* the leading lady sings a song whose first stanza we translated pretty much literally:

Our extra stanza:
Why a man is neurotic, his inside a void,
was discovered years later in Vienna by Freud.
What Nestroy suspected, the great doctor proved:
your inside is torn 'cause your mother once goofed.
By offering a bottle instead of a nipple
she nipped in the bud, ah, your pleasure principle.
She smashed you to bits in a subconscious wreckup,
so you need a checkup each week from the neck up.
It's a terrible thing if you find
that you don't even know your own mind.

Our hope to make Nestroy well-known to American theater audiences was not fulfilled. The beginning was promising. Our agent phoned excitedly that a producer was interested in *Der Talisman* and would see us. We got a lesson in the workings of the Broadway theater world. The woman was enthusiastic. Only some changes were necessary to make the play acceptable to American audiences. Here a few cuts, there a few new scenes. Later she phoned from New York: she had found a director who planned to engage a famous actress, so the role of the female lead had to be enlarged. The play (about prejudice of nineteenth-century Austrians against redheads) would need to be changed because Americans found redheads attractive. Then a choreographer called who raved about a large ballet scene she planned. This necessitated some cuts in Nestroy's text. Then a set designer wanted to change the setting of the simple Tyrolean village to a gigantic "Tyrol made in Hollywood." Next, a composer suggested that the original music for the songs be replaced by modern music, and a writer wanted to modernize Nestroy's ditties with new lyrics. All these people were enthusiastic about their ideas which moved further and further from the Nestroy we wanted to introduce to America. Max and I decided that we couldn't, in good conscience, agree to these violations, and the project was dropped.

The breakthrough for Nestroy came not in the theater, but in the classroom. Professor Douglas Russell of Stanford University found it wrong that in American schools Austrian literature was part of German, instead of a genre of its own. He published a textbook of Austrian playwrights in English translations, and included our rendering of *Der Talisman*, together with plays by Raimund, Grillparzer, Schnitzler, Hofmannsthal, Werfel, and Hochwälder. The book serves as text of Austrian drama in American universities.

Our translations aroused the interest of Bert Brecht's son and literary executor, Stefan, who asked us to do *Schweyk in the Second*

When a girl is in love with a man who is not –
well, what can she do? Not a heck of a lot.
She can cry, she can moan, she can hang herself, drown . . .
But look what goes on if a *man* is turned down:
he goes to the tavern and orders a beer,
and flirts with the waitress, or whoever is near,
and he may not slow down till the field he has played –
Yes, a man has it made, has it made, has it made.

    Our extra stanza:
The twentieth century brought on a sequel:
the woman has gained her position as equal.
Women vote, run for office, and dress up in trousers,
become independent, divorce their dear spousers,
or go to a school where they pick up some knowledge,
but then take a job, put their husband through college,
run to work, run the house, overworked, underpaid –
Yes, men still have it made, have it made, have it made!

By the time we translated Nestroy's *Der Zerrissene*,]
familiar with the ideas of Viktor Frankl who saw many of to
neuroses caused by a feeling of meaninglessness ("existi
vacuum"). I diagnosed the boredom of the rich *Herr von Lips*
main character of the play, as an existential neurosis, whi
Nestroy's time only the well-to-do could afford but is wides
today. We translated the title *Der Zerrissene* (*The Torn*
with *A Man Full of Nothing*. His entry song:

I'm full of the best kind of food and of likker,
my clothes and my shoes every season get slicker,
and yet, I'm in shreds and I'm falling apart –
I am just a man full of nothing at heart.
My inside is empty, my spirit a hole,
and there isn't a shop where they patch up a soul.
But if someone should ask me why all this should be,
I just couldn't say what's the matter with me:
It's a terrible thing if you find
that you don't even know your own mind.

World War, Brecht's last play *Turandot*, and *The Breadshop*, a fragment, for the Random House Collected Works. What fascinated us in these plays were again the hard-to-translate songs. For the same reason we translated some poems by Heinrich Heine for Random House. A special challenge was Heine's famous rhyme of *Teetisch (tea table)* with *ästhetisch (esthetic)*. Again we resorted to "fondly tampering":

> They sat and sipped from their teacups,
> and love they discussed without end.
> The men had esthetical hiccups,
> the ladies had sentiment.

After all these efforts came the reward. Professor Harry Zohn, chairman of the Department of Germanic and Slavic languages at Brandeis University at Waltham, Massachusetts, asked us to translate *Die Letzten Tage der Menschheit (The Last Days of Mankind)* by Karl Kraus. Tis play, 800 pages long, is considered not only untranslatable but practically unproduceable (although some attempts have been made). The play was written during the first World War, and is full of references to local and timely events and literal quotes from official announcements, edicts, and newspapers not familiar to American readers. It also abounds with wordplays and puns. We carefully selected the scenes, or parts of scenes, which contain the essence of the play, a powerful condemnation of the madness of war, its hypocrisy and nationalism. We tried to make the play performable and cut the text from 800 pages to 98.

We knew we would be criticized for whatever we selected or left out, and rightly so. But a weak representation of Kraus was better than no Kraus at all. In this work, too, the greatest challenge were the satirical songs, an Austrian tradition. Kraus pictures a senile Emperor Francis Joseph, napping at his desk and, in his sleep, singing a ditty that takes seven pages in the original. We reduced it to one page and a half. Its refrain is the line *Mir bleibt doch nichts erspart (I am spared nothing,* rendered by us as *Everything happens to me)* which the Emperor is said to have uttered, after the suicide of his only son and the assassination of his wife.

When I was born to my mother,
the world was a terrible mess.
I looked at all that bother,
 and really couldn't care less.
Wien was a dirndl-and-schnapps burg,
and schnapps was not *my* cup of tea.
Oh, why was I born a Hapsburg?
Everything happens to me.

We crammed all Hollywood cliches about Austria in the six
stanzas we translated. Here is an example:

I gave my life to glory,
 gave smiles to those who cheered,
to girls the Mayerling story,
 to men a style of beard.
Will I become a bigger
concern to history?
Or an operetta figure?
Everything happens to me.

The Karl Kraus book with the title of a famous Kraus saying, *In
These Great Times* (followed by: "I've known them since they were
little") contains also material translated by Professor Zohn and
others. The book was reviewed favorably as a contribution to
building a cultual bridge, my main interest.

At that time I was walking another bridge between Austria and
America, this time in the field of psychology. In 1963 I read Dr. Viktor
Frankl's book *Man's Search for Meaning,* dealing with his survival
in concentration camps during World War II. I found his life
philosophy ("logotherapy", healing through meaning) important for
me and for Americans in general.

I had often asked myself what, if any, meaning there was in
the whole Hitler episode and its tragedies. Frankl had an answer I
had groped for, and even unconsciously found: the meaning of
events lies not in the events but in our attitudes toward them. It's less
important to find out how we got into a difficulty than what we
make of it.

I found comfort in the thought that psychology (and music) are
the only fields where a Viennese accent holds an advantage.

So I became a psychologist through direct contact with Dr.
Frankl. I translated some of his minor works but my main interest
was his message, so important to contemporary Americans. More

and more, in their pursuit of pleasure and material goods, they suffered from a lack of meaning. No book existed summarizing logotherapeutic insights for the intelligent lay reader. Frankl encouraged me to write *The Pursuit of Meaning*, published in 1968.

My new activities led to early retirement from the University of California, in order to found and head the Institute of Logotherapy in Berkeley. And so it happened that my teaching career began only *after* retirement from the university. I taught classes in logotherapy, first at the University of California Extension in Berkeley and San Francisco, then in other colleges, primarily at J. F. Kennedy University in nearby Orinda. I also participate in the Institute's training program and edit its journal, the *International Forum for Logotherapy*.

So you see, my doubts in calling myself an American Germanist are justified but I hope you won't think that the chameleon has changed too many colors or that the duck has laid an egg.

(Symposium, *Life with Austrian Literature*, Vienna, Austrian Society for Literature, 1990. Translated.)

Touching with the Other Hand

When the Nazis threatened to invade England, in 1940, Max and a friend (Kurt) fled to Shanghai, the only place open to refugees. They had only a transit visa across Canada and were not allowed to stay although war between the United States and Japan was threatening and the two, being stateless, faced possible internment in Japanese-controlled Shanghai in case of war.

Kurt and I were in a strange situation: in a luxury cabin, forced upon us by a greedy shipping company, preferred passengers, yet with one-way tickets, emergency travel documents, stateless and unwanted, going toward an uncertain destiny to a country under the control of a Nazi ally. War was imminent. What a relief it would be if that disaster should happen – if it had to happen – just while we were crossing Canada, so our further trip into the jaws of the dragon would become impossible. Our tickets were stamped with big diagonal letters: NO REFUND IN CASE OF WAR. We were traveling first class into war.

Early next morning I was up on deck. I had not slept much and was on the edge of being seasick. There was a shore in the distance. A sailor said: "The Isle of Man." My parents who had been interned on that island as "enemy aliens," might have seen the outlines of the ship. And here I was deserting them. I was so miserable that I slunk back to my cabin, lay down, and skipped all meals. I was fighting both seasickness and guilt feelings.

On the third day the ship's bulletin, reporting the radio news from the BBC, announced matter-of-factly that during the night a 17,000-ton ship in our vicinity had been sunk by German U-boat with the loss of 40 lives.

The next day I felt well enough to pull out my faithful companion, my portable typewriter, and write some letters and draft a short story. I also kept a diary.

The crossing took nine days. On August 19 we first laid eyes on the New World. The brightly lit city of Halifax, the first city lights after weeks of blacked-out London, was as thrilling to us as the Statue of Liberty is to immigrants arriving in New York.

But we were not immigrants, only transmigrants. It took two more nights on board before we were allowed to land. During that time mail was delivered to the waiting passengers. To my great joy, I was among the happy recipients: Letters from Joe, my New York cousin, and, surprisingly, from Gerda (who lived with her husband in Boston). They all said the same: Could we not wait for our quota number in Canada?

Indeed, we thought of nothing else throughout our time in Canada. We boarded a train in Halifax to Montreal, where we were met, unexpectedly, by representatives of refugee organizations who provided inexpensive housing and showed us around town. Paradoxically, we were free and could do anything we wanted in Canada, so long as we met our deadline, September 8, in Vancouver to board the *Heian Maru* of the Nippon Yusen Kaisha (N.Y.K.) Line for Japan. We decided to make the best of these extra days, pretend to be tourists, and see the sights. While in Montreal, we climbed Mount Royal and, looking south, like Moses viewing the Promised Land, we could see the United States.

Through the organizations we were introduced to a number of people who, I hoped, would have enough influence to convince the Canadian authorities to allow me temporary refuge. I also had letters of introduction from England. Harry Freud had given me a request for help addressed to an influential K.C. (King's Counselor) in Ottawa. My days were filled with a weird mixture of elegant sightseeing and desperate efforts – writing, telephoning, meeting people who might be able to help me change my status from transient to resident, all in vain.

Kurt and I kept up a positive front as tourists. Our next sightseeing was Toronto. From there we visited Niagara Falls, directly on the American-Canadian border.

A suspension bridge connects the American and Canadian sides of the river that flows from the falls. At the bottom of the falls the water forms a quiet pool. A small boat, the *Maid of the Mist,* shuttles between the two countries. Passengers on the Canadian side receive Canadian tickets but are not allowed to dis-embark in the U.S. when the *Maid* picks up American tourists with American tickets. Passengers may disembark only on their own side, and must prove place of origin by surrendering their tickets. Tickets are passports and visas, nothing else is needed.

On the boat passengers from the two groups mingle. At least this was the situation on that fateful September day in 1940.

In the next hour we passed through the emotionally most explosive episode of our trip.

It was a hazy day but the weather was good enough for

sightseeing. It happened to be Labor Day in the United States, and thousands of people were milling around on both shores, crowding onto the boat with standing room only, each pressed against the other as in a tightly packed commuter bus at rush hour. Because of the spray from the falls, all passengers were provided with rubber coats covering them completely, even with a hood that made them look like Ku Kluxers.

Kurt and I sat down by the edge of the water, eyes glued on the *Maid of the Mist*, not Niagara Falls. We did not have to talk, we each knew what the other was thinking.

We were not Canadians or Americans, not even Austrians or Germans. We were stateless. We were not tourists, not visitors, just a piece of existence hanging by the thinnest thread – permission to cross the country by a deadline. We were different from every man, woman, or child of any nationality around us, and the feeling of isolation – and opportunity – was crushing. Across that river lay safety and life. And we were on an invisible conveyor belt carrying us into an unknown, threatening world, driven by the Nazis in Europe into the clutches of their allies in Asia. Would we ever get back alive? Would our quota numbers arrive at the American consulate in Shanghai before war between Japan and the United States trapped us in a Japanese camp?

We squatted on the bank of the river, arms around our knees, our mesmerized eyes glued on that little boat as it puff-puffed every few minutes from our side to freedom, then returned. We decided to take the ride.

We bought Canadian tickets. They entitled us to travel to the United States, but not to land there. The boat came over with American tourists who remained on board; the Canadians – and Kurt and I – got on. We slipped into the black raincoats and hoods and squeezed in with the crowd. As the boat returned to the U. S. side, the eyes of the hundreds were on the spectacular falls. Our eyes were on the tickets many of the Americans on holiday held nonchalantly in their hands.

Was there an immigration officer on the U. S. side? Probably not – there was none on the Canadian side. We had carefully watched as the Canadians who had completed the round trip left the ship. They simply surrendered their tickets and stepped back onto Canadian soil. We looked at the tickets Americans were holding with the fascination of a cobra eyeing a mouse (Canadian and American tickets had different colors). Could we persuade two of them to sell us their tickets? They could claim to have lost them, establish their citizenship, and land. But how could we explain why we needed those tickets? Would they denounce us?

We could just lose ourselves in this crowd, unidentified, a hood among hoods, and float along with the rest on the American side. We could jostle someone into dropping his ticket. There was a man in front of me, his back actually pressing against my chest, his hands clasped behind his back, the American ticket casually in his fingers, as he stared at the falls. If I pretended to stumble, sliding the ticket from those fingers, then apologized, no one would be able to find the ticket among the many feet. But what about Kurt? I looked at him and could see from his glassy eyes that the wheels were going round in his head as in mine. Or I could slide the ticket from those loose fingers – no one would ever know who among those sardines had done it. The temptation was so overpowering, our excitement at a fever pitch, we saw and heard nothing of what was going on – everybody else's attention was fixed on those magnificent falls and it seemed criminal to pass up this unique opportunity and not act, NOW.

It seemed equally criminal to act. If we were picked up as illegal immigrants, this could affect naturalization in the U.S., our career, our future. If we *did* get our quota number in China in time, on the other hand, we would be law-abiding immigrants, able to lead normal lives when this nightmare was over.

We reached the U. S. side. The *Maid of the Mist* stopped and the Americans, round trip completed, got off. We saw them surrender their tickets to some officer of the company who carelessly tossed them into a bin. I stood on deck, directly beside a post stuck into the water, painted red-white-and-blue. I touched it, shyly, with one hand – I actually touched America! But I was to travel half way around the world before I could touch it with my other. I did not know whether this would ever become possible.

We sailed back as in a dream. From the high pitch of the first half of the trip we dropped into the nothingness of the second. We arrived on the Canadian side, surrendered our worthless tickets, and sat down again by the dock.

We could not take our eyes off that boat as it turned, again to the American side, back and forth, back and forth, all day. We still had the chance. We still could do it. Perhaps we would have more guts a second time. Another idea: We could telephone our friends in New York, ask them to hurry to Niagara Falls AT ONCE, get on the boat with their American tickets, then exchange them for ours. We would get out on the American side, and they could say they lost their tickets; they would prove they were residents of New York. It was a crazy thought. We looked at our watches – perhaps too late today, maybe tomorrow. But tomorrow would not be Labor Day, the whole tailor-made confusion would be gone, inspection tighter. We would have to try today, now, perhaps simply do some jostling . . .

A voice behind us said: "How do you do."

We turned, and there was a police officer, or rather a man from the Immigration Service. Were we Americans? Canadians? I meant to say, in a belligerent mood, that this was none of his business . . . but, well, it *was* his business. He asked for our papers, said thank you, and disappeared after what seemed to us a penetrating look.

Well, well, well. Somebody *had* been watching us and perhaps read our thoughts. Perhaps it was better, after all, that we had done nothing. The future would tell whether it would have been better to sit in an American or Canadian jail than in a Nazi-Japanese compound dying a slow, disease-ridden, sadistic death .

We returned to Toronto, dazed. Everything that followed, crossing the enormous expanse of Canada, was an anticlimax. We stared from the train window, resenting the endless uninhabited plains that could give refuge and shelter to millions, yet were declared off-limits by an unrelenting Canadian government that would not permit even the trickle of immigrants the U.S. allowed.

On September 8, Kurt and I boarded the N.Y.K. Japanese steamer *Heian Maru* for Yokohama. As the American shore receded we each had a tight feeling in our chests. Would we ever see our friends and families again? In Vancouver we noticed Americans and Canadians returning from the Far East. They did not want to be caught in a possible war zone; that was where *we* were headed.

(*One and One Make Three: Story of a Friendship,* Berkeley, Benmir Books, 1988)

Prelude in Prison

In September 1938 Walt Disney's "Snow White and the Seven Dwarfs" showed in the biggest movie house in Brussels. I bought a ticket and went to see it.

I had arrived from Vienna the day before, with all my earthly possessions: a suitcase full of clothes, a portable typewriter, and ten German marks. The swastika-banded officer had made sure I exited with no more than the allowable amount.

I splurged one-tenth of it on Snow White. I felt insanely happy. I was able to walk on the streets without fear of being arrested. I did not have to scan passers-by for swastikas on their lapels. I could sit on park benches. For two hours I lived in the world of Walt Disney where good triumphs and evil is punished.

There was no reason for my happiness. I had a one-month visa and no hope of finding a country to let me permanently in. My past offered no support, my future only threats. I was a man coming up for air in shark-infested waters. Happiness is the first breath of air.

The Jewish Refugee Committee in Brussels provided survival money for rent and food. We were 27 new arrivals that day. Dr. Siebenschein, a former attorney from Aachen, now an employee of the committee, gave us instructions: no loud German speaking, no large groups, no attention-getting. Most important: no job seeking.

Siebenschein was a role model: mousy, furtive, stooped as if constantly ready to glance over his shoulder.

At least I had my one-month visa. Only Ludwig Sommer, a tailor from Vienna, was more envied. He had an affidavit to America, only had to wait for his quota number. I, too, envied Sommer. Not only did he have an affidavit but he was a tailor. My education in law and writing in German was useless in America, but everyone needs pants.

Every day swarms of new illegals arrived at the Jewish Committee with tales of gloom and doom. Dr. Siebenschein's over-the-shoulder glances became more apprehensive: please, no conspicuous gatherings. We were nonpersons leading nonlives. We met in each other's attic rooms, sharing horror stories which happened to be true.

On October 9 my Belgian visa expired. Three days later a

young policeman stopped me on the street and politely asked for identification. He looked at my passport, then gave me a form to fill out and asked me to bring it to the police station the next day.

My story stirred up a flurry of excitement at the Committee, where refugees met to gossip and warm themselves. We used the Committee like Viennese use their coffee houses. Others had heard similar stories. People were ordered to the police and never seen again.

"They ship them back to Germany."

"Oh no, they wouldn't. It would mean concentration camps."

"What do they care? Antisemitism doesn't stop at the border."

Opinions were divided between optimists and pessimists. "What are you going to do?" they asked me.

I was an optimist. I had a visa, though expired. I was not going into hiding, as the pessimists advised. My background made me believe in law and the world of Snow White. The evil stepmother may have poisoned the apple, but virtue always triumphs.

The next morning a sergeant at the police station leafed through my passport with the big red 'J' for *Jude* and the expired visa. He compared me with my photograph. He had a small button nose and a massive walrus moustache, and spoke French so fast that I barely got the gist of what he said. It was something about formalities – photographs and fingerprinting. Then I was driven by a policeman through the streets of Brussels. We stopped at a fortress of a building and I was led through a gate that said in large letters: *Prison a Forest*. We entered a small room where an officer behind his desk puffed on a fat cigar and squinted at me through the smoke.

"What am I doing here?" I asked, aware that my high-school French teacher, would have clapped his hands in mock desperation at the many mistakes I managed to make in these five words. But the officer understood and he too uttered the magic word, "*formalité.*"

As promised, photograph and fingerprints were taken. My pockets were emptied and their contents placed in a large envelope. To my repeated protests that there must be a mistake, the officer answered benignly, "*Pas erreur,*" and handed me over to a chubby-faced guard. We walked through a steel gate, up a steel staircase, along a steel corridor flanked by steel cell doors. Every step echoed throughout the passageway. I didn't believe this was happening. This was Sing Sing. I had seen the movie last year, about gangsters, murderers, and shootouts, and now here I was, a doctor of law, a writer of short stories, an author of cabaret skits. We stopped at steel door 366, Chubby Face produced a cluster of keys, the door clattered open, and I was in a cell, bare except for an iron cot, a wash stand, and a toilet. The door fell shut and I was gripped by the enormity of what was happening. This was not Snow White. It was Dreyfus.

I had seen the Dreyfus movie, too. I banged at the steel door, shouting, "I am innocent," as Dreyfus had done. The cell reverberated as my screams bounced off the cement walls. Finally, a small peephole opened and an eye peered through, watery gray and impersonal.

"Je suis innocent," I yelled.

The peephole closed. Exhausted, I dropped onto the cot. It was as quiet as in the Vienna Woods at dusk. The stillness cuddled and comforted me. I felt drained and utterly forsaken.

Footsteps outside. They stopped at my door and keys clanked. A uniformed man, topped by a blue, cylindrical police hat, entered.

"Je suis monsieur le directeur," he said.

'Ah', I thought. 'The mistake has been cleared up'.

I raised myself from the cot. He gestured to sit down again, as a host to a guest. He sat down next to me, took off his high cap and placed it at his side on the mattress. A guard stood at the door.

Monsieur le directeur began to speak slowly, considerateley, so I would be able to follow his French. I was not a criminal, he explained. The Belgian government was in a difficult situation. It did not know what to do with the swarm of refugees. He had no choice . *"Mon coeur est brisé,"* he said. "I'm heartbroken." He lifted both arms, palms up, in a gesture of helplessness. "We only have solitary cells, and you must follow prison rules. A *formalité.*" He implored me to understand. The guard would buy me anything I wanted from the prison canteen – cigarettes, chocolate bars, writing paper. The price would be subtracted from the money taken from me. The *directeur* would send me books from the prison library. A barber. Things would straighten out. He looked downhearted. "You are no criminal," he repeated. "Hitler is the criminal. *La canaille!* " He shook my hand, picked up his hat, and left.

Ten minutes later the steel door clanked open again: the barber. He gave me the quickest shave and haircut I ever had, and kept chattering in Flemish, which I couldn't understand. Soon after, the guard handed me three well-thumbed books and asked what I wanted from the canteen. I ordered pencil and paper. He brought me a pencil and stationery. It said in large letters, "*Prison a Forest.*" Why not "*à Forêt*" as I had learned in school? Probably Flemish. The paper listed prison rules, and was lined as for school children.

The stationery presented a problem. I had been writing to my parents twice a week and they would worry if they didn't hear from me. They also would worry at a letter from prison.

I looked at the books. *The Song Birds in West Flanders. The Bantu in the Congo.* The third was a book of prayers with the title,

78

Le Souverain de l'Universe, the Ruler of the Universe.

The absurdity of the book titles helped. I momentarily regained my sense of humor and wrote to my parents. Don't let the stationery scare you, I wrote. It's a formality. I am not treated as a criminal. The director just visited me. He sent me a barber, some books. I'll be here until the Belgian government straightens out my expired visa. I have quiet to write new short stories for sale in England, so I'll have money when I get out. Meanwhile, I have free room and board.

I took inventory of my free room. It was six by five paces, with a cot, a mattress, thin and hard, probably straw. One blanket, folded neatly, no sheet, one small hard pillow, probably straw, too. A wash stand with basin and water pitcher. A cake of soap smelling of disinfectant, pail and mop, a flush toilet with overhead water tank.

Being a compulsive reader, I studied the rules posted on the wall. They were bilingual. A chance to brush up on my French and have a first lesson in Flemish. The rules listed 17 items forbidden, a code of behavior, and a daily schedule. Wake-up bell, 5 A.M., room cleanup 5:15, breakfast 5:30, exercise 9:00, meal at noon, and so on.

My studies were interrupted by a shrill bell. I checked the rules. Right, 5:30 P.M.: feeding time in Zoo a Forest. Clatter on the corridor, approaching cell 366. Doors creaked open and slammed shut. When mine was opened I was ready, as the rules decreed, with tin bowl, cup, and water pitcher. Three guards operated in unison. One ladled out soup from a tank, another splashed black coffee in my cup and slapped a slice of bread on top, the third filled my pitcher by dipping it into a barrel of water. The soup was pale with scraps of potatoes and threads of meat. The coffee was weak and lukewarm. This free room and board left something to be desired.

I picked up *The Ruler of the Universe.* It described a good and just world. My world was shattered. As a guide to living, religion was as useful as Snow White. The happy ending was blocked by immigration barriers. The Snow Whites of the real world were chased and jailed and killed by the witches who were everywhere.

Neither a complainer nor an idler be, the book said in antiquated French. Do not fritter away your precious hours. I thoughts of my parents trapped in Vienna, worrying about their son, without a future, in prison.

A shrill bell and the light went out. The ruler of *Prison a Forest* had decided to end the day at 8:30 P.M. I had no night clothes. I lay down on my cot and had an attack of rage.

The next thing I knew was another shrieking bell. Clanging on the corridor. Breakfast. Black coffee and bread.

I felt strangely refreshed. There was something vital about the chemicals in my body at 5 A.M. which I never experienced. I scribbled in the lined prison notebook a light-hearted short story Max might be able to sell in England, as he had done with our previous stories.

In the middle of writing the bell announced time for morning exercise. I was let out onto the steel corridor. From the rows of doors crept gray figures. We shuffled along the corridor, ten feet apart, single file. On the wall next to the gate that opened into the courtyard flickered a gas flame. As the inmates passed by, they fought for a place to light a cigarette. We could buy cigarettes but smoke only during exercise break. In my short stories, smoking cigarettes was a mark of sophistication. I now saw it as raw, brutal, ravenous craving. It turned humans into jittery animals. I was glad I didn't smoke.

The yard was large, with shaggy patches of grass, surrounded on all sides by cement walls that stared at us with hundreds of barred windows. To the blare of piped-in music we marched briskly and silently in a large circle, ten feet apart. Rule number 14: no talking.

All except six wore prison garb. The six wore suits like myself. This was the only distinction between thieves, robbers, and murderers, and the victims of thieves, robbers, and murderers.

I recognized one man in the circle. We had talked at the Refugee Committee. He was an attorney from Frankfurt, tall, wiry, with tousled hair that looked elegant and slightly disheveled. He was married to Natasha, a flaxen-haired beauty with a childlike voice in a body that was all woman. She had fled from Russia as a child, after the revolution.

"My second time around," she had chirped. "I'm a double refugee."

Benedikt, smoking, seemed purposely to keep out of step with the march music. He was sauntering nonchalantly, for which I admired him. Another suit wearer was gray-haired, balding, heavy rump on spindly legs, eagerly but vainly trying to keep up with the prison-garbed gorilla in front of him. One refugee was a boy, probably still in his teens, looking scared. Behind him walked a slim man with fine features and gold-rimmed glasses which he kept adjusting nervously. On the opposite side of the circle were two more refugees: a frail, red-headed man, hunched over, furiously chain-smoking, and a scholarly looking professor, with a limp. From time to time a guard stepped up to spur him on.

I speculated how we six had been selected out of the hundreds of refugees in Brussels. I counted 83 in the circle. Did our not wearing prison garb mean we would be released soon? How long can you be without a change of clothes? Did the prison canteen sell underwear?

I became aware that Benedikt was trying to get my attention. Whenever we rounded a curve he looked at me and pointed at his cigarette. Did he need money? I rubbed the tips of thumb and forefinger together, a sign in Vienna for "money." He understood and smiled "no." When we passed the gate he pointed at it and moved his lips. For the next few rounds I puzzled over his possible message.

Another bell ended exercise time. We were marched back to our cells. When Benedikt turned into his and I walked by, he again moved his lips. Back in my cubicle, I scribbled in my notebook. School is no preparation for life. It's a preparation for prison: no talking, rules for everything, time regulated by a bell, an hourly time table. The books you read are boring, you can't go home when you want, and you're released with a final report card.

At five the next morning my creative juices flowed again and I finished my story before exercise time. While the smokers crowded around the flame I caught Benedikt's eye. He gestured me closer, and I understood yesterday's message. He wanted to talk to me, and the cigarette lighting offered our only chance. I braved the stampede and maneuvred myself next to him.

"They're sending us back to Germany," he whispered.

I stared at him, unbelieving.

"Natasha told me. She visited me yesterday. You must tell them a hardship story. Being Jewish isn't enough."

That was all the time we had. The guards herded us into the yard. I looked around the circle. Ten suit wearers, but the mousy chain smoker and the limping professor were missing. Was the rumor true? Were two shipped back and six others readied for shipment? I walked in a daze, trying to think of other reasons why the two were missing.

Back in my cell, I asked for the director. He was out of town. Could I see someone else? After a while a young man entered, blond, blue-eyed, with a little blond brush under his nose. A bad omen. Instead of the sympathetic *directeur*, they sent this Hitler type.

I told him about my visa, my selling stories in England. He didn't believe a word. I became exasperated. My brain short-circuited. "Listen," I shouted. "I need underwear."

He looked startled. "I'm not a criminal," I continued. "How do you expect me to wear the same clothes, day and night, for weeks?"

"It won't be weeks," he said.

I was on a one-track path. "I need pajamas, socks, under-wear."

Clearly, he had never faced this problem before. He pointed to the posted rules and said something about visitation rights.

"I've read this," I told him. "I have no spouse or close relatives."

"In your case," he grinned, "the rules can be relaxed. Any friend can bring you underpants."

His irony made me furious. "I have no friends in this whole wide world," I bellowed.

"How about your important newspaper connections?"

This made me even angrier. "Listen," I said. "The man in 358 has a wife. My address and room keys are among the things you took from me. Ask her to bring me a change of clothes. And toothpaste."

"Sure," he said, retreating toward the door. "I'll talk to 358."

I was alone. The bubble of victory burst. I had acted like an idiot. Instead of a permit to stay in Belgium I would, perhaps, get a pair of underwear. I had antagonized the blond Hitler. I would be the first to be shipped off. "It won't be weeks," he had said. That could mean release or deportation. All of a sudden my stay at *Prison a Forest* did not seem so insufferable, even without a change of clothes.

Tell them a hardship story, Benedikt had advised. I did not have to invent one. I had been editor of a satirical weekly that ridiculed the Nazis. Being shipped back meant concentration camp

Gradually, my spirits revived. They would not send me back to certain death. I fantasized a dialogue with the police chief. I cleverly countered all his arguments for returning me to Vienna.

Next morning, at exercise, the number of refugees had increased to 15, but six of the old ones were gone. Deported? I had no chance to get close to Benedikt. He looked downhearted.

Back in my cell I felt utterly forsaken. Then I noticed that I wasn't alone. A column of ants marched down the wall from the barred window, across the wash stand, to a place near the door. I had seen one or two ants before, but now they had discovered a crumb of bread, and the word had spread. They marched, mindlessly, not the shortest route but the path their *führer* led. My frustration vented itself, and I pounced at the orderly column, stamping to death as many ants as I could squash. The floor was strewn with corpses, and survivors scurried in all directions. I went after them, smashing them with passion, singly and in clusters.

Surprisingly, some survived, in cracks of the floor, in the protection of an unevenness, or without any apparent reason. A few emerged from under my shoe where they had been sheltered by some tiny dimple in my sole. Some, seemingly dead, struggled back to life and limped off on their remaining four or five legs.

I sat down on my cot. Was this how the Ruler of the Universe operated? Was our life dependent on whims and flukes, on being sheltered in the random cracks of our existence? On being saved in a dip in the sole of the Ruler? A deep despair overcame me.

The next morning, at the cigarette flame, I managed a brief moment with Benedikt. "Pleienberg can help," he whispered before we were separated by the rampaging smokers. I had no idea who Pleienberg was but drew comfort from the knowledge that there was *someone* who could help. The number of suit wearers was ominously reduced by five, including the scared youngster. There were no new refugees in the exercise circle. But the next morning 15 newcomers appeared and none of the old ones were missing. I spent hours speculating on possible scenarios. Did Pleienberg help?

If so, how?

In my brief moments with Benedikt we exchanged guesses. In the cell, I sat on my cot for hours listening to footsteps. It was as bad as in Vienna when we listened at night for the Gestapo to pick us up.

Familiar footsteps were not threatening, leading to the daily routines. Unexpected footsteps made my heart do somersaults.

On the sixth day unscheduled footsteps stopped at my door and it clanked open. Every muscle in my body tensed. The nails of my clenched fingers dug into my palm. The guard entered and handed me a paper bag. "From 358," he said.

The bag contained pajamas, socks, and underwear. This was not just a set of clothes, it was a message of hope. They would not send me pajamas if they intended to ship me back. Or would they?

Common events became ominous: the expression on a guard's face, a large piece of meat in the soup (the last meal?), a visit of the barber, the waxing and waning of suit wearers in the exercise circle.

On the ninth day, my heart jumped to my throat. Benedikt was missing. Although we had exchanged only a few whispers he had become my anchor. I was certain to be next.

I spent all day and most of the sleepless night arguing with my imaginary judge and executioner. The ants swarmed all over the floor despite my frequent attacks. Some survived, some didn't. If they could talk, what would they say to convince me to let them live?

The next morning, halfway between breakfast and exercise, sinister footsteps stopped at my door. The guard entered.

"Take your things and come with me," he ordered.

"Where are we going?"

"*Monsieur le directeur* wants to see you."

Following him numbly on the nightmare steel corridor, I tried to recapture my arguments, but my mind was empty.

The director again played his role as the superpolite host. He rose from behind his desk and gestured me into a chair.

"*Je suis désolé*," he said, and my throat contracted at this expression of regret. But it turned out that his regret was about his not having visited me again. Important business trips, he said.

His cheerful face brightened even more. "In fact," he continued, "the trips were about you."

The 'you', it turned out, was not me personally but all illegals that posed a headache to the Belgian government. The Bishop of Liège had intervened to find a humanitarian solution. All technicalities were sorted out, and I was to be released into the custody of the Jewish Committee that would arrange our transfer to the camp of Merxplas.

"A camp?" The word sounded ominous.

"A beautiful *établissement. Une colonie de bienfaisance.*"

When I looked puzzled he handed me a dictionary. *Colonie de bienfaisance* translated as 'settlement of charity'.

"Everything is all right," he assured me. "I am happy for you."

"How long will we stay there?"

"Only until a permanent solution is found. Don't worry. Monsieur Pleienberg will explain the details."

We shook hands and a guard handed me the paper bag with the things they had taken from me. He also presented me with a *Certificate de Mise en Liberté.* The graduation report card from *Prison a Forest..*

(*The Next-to-Final Solution,* New York: Peter Lang, 1991)

Features

In Freud's London Home

During my London exile I stayed only a few minutes away from that vine-covered red brick house in Maresfield Gardens, Hampstead, in which Sigmund Freud's architect son Ernst had made room for his father during Freud's last year of his life.

In 1939 we all were Hitler refugees in London. One day, Harry Freud, my old schoolmate, came by unexpectedly. "Hurry up," he said. "Help me in my uncle's home."

Max and I rushed into the bedroom to put on our good suits. Harry stopped us. "Those old pants you're wearing are just right," he said.   Our surprised protest was checked with the curt explanation, "Aunt Martha asked me to unload some furniture that arrived from Vienna. We have to clear the garage to make room for some of Ernst's stuff."

Frau Freud cordially greeted us in the little front garden and led us to the left of the house, where Freud's two sons, Martin, a physician, and Ernst were already at work, with dusty hands and sleeves rolled up. Daughter Anna and another woman stood by, directing operations.

We slipped off our coats and went to work, clearing trunks out of the garage and a shed, and moving others in. A young man I didn't know did some of the heaviest work, lifting cases which two of us could barely budge. "My Dachau training," he explained with a crooked smile.

I was anxious to see Freud again, now that I knew more about his world-famous work than in my high-school days when Harry had taken me to his uncle's home for hot chocolate. About an hour went by, and we had still not even had a good look at the inside of the house.

I picked up a glass plate, about 10 inches wide. On it were the words.

Professor S. Freud
Konsultation 2-4 p. m.

It was the sign that had been affixed for decades at Freud's home in the Berggasse, in Vienna. Here it lay about uselessly, discarded.

We were about to move a trunk when the woman standing next to Anna, cried: "No, you can't move this trunk into the shed. It's too damp there." She placed herself protectively in front of a handsome trunk, on which were inscribed the initials, "P. F." We pointed out to her that all the other trunks were also being taken to the shed, but the woman was adamant. Only later we discovered that the woman was Paula Fichtel, the maid of long standing, and the initials did not stand for Professor Freud, as I imagined (and of course not for Peter Fabrizius) but for "Paula Fichtel." It was her own trunk.

By early afternoon we had emptied the garage, put Ernst's furniture in for storage, and moved the Professor's possessions into the house.

We were perspiring, grimy, with sleeves rolled up. We hastily washed up and began inspecting the house under Harry's guidance. The front door opened into a large hall, with a staircase leading to the first floor. Architect Ernst had put in a small elevator for his father. On the right of the hall was a door to the holy of holies, Freud's study.

"He's in the back yard," Harry said. "In the deck chair, as usually when the weather is good. His study is over here."

In the study his Viennese furniture was already in place. It was separated from the garden by a French window. In front of the window, bathed in light and air, was the Professor's desk.

The chair in front of it had a back shaped like the neck of a violin, constructed especially for the infirm Professor's comfort. I knew that Freud wrote all his manuscripts by hand. Papers with his handwriting lay on the desk. The edges of the desk were covered with Egyptian statuettes, a pantheon of the gods and goddesses of Egyptian mythology. Freud was an enthusiastic collector of such objects, and the desk received his favorite pieces. This was the background against which he concluded his last work, *Moses and Monotheism*.

The study was full of such valuable pieces. In glass cases, on stands, or simply on tables, stood old relics, busts, figures, wooden masks, framed papyri, and portions of Roman frescoes. A separate case displayed small objects, such as gold coins, ear rings and pins, as in a museum. The antiquities, collected during a lifetime, contrasted with the modern simplicity of the room itself.

"Only Paula is allowed to do any dusting here," said Harry.

He told us that it was only through the personal intervention of the Princess of Bonaparte of Greece that the Nazis had been dissuaded from seizing his valuable collection and personal property. Freud turned over millions of Austrian schillings to them, but he was one of the few exiles who left Austria officially with more than the paltry 10 reichsmarks.

The walls of the study were covered with bookcases up to the ceiling. One case four yards wide, with five shelves, contained nothing but his own works. Though a man's life work is not to be judged by the number of books he wrote, it was impressive to see all these books on psychoanalysis in so many languages collected in one place. In the corner were Chinese and Japanese translations in yellow covers. There was no country in the world in which these books were not held in respect, except in the country in which they were written. The Nazis had destroyed these books, as they had destroyed everything of value.

Among this furniture Freud had received his patients in Vienna. In the corner stood the famous couch covered with rich, oriental rugs.

We re-entered the hall and went upstairs. The sidewalls bore evidence of the countless honors the professor had received during his career. Here were illuminated addresses, with pendant seals, written on parchment, presented by leading scientific bodies and universities.

In the living room on the first floor were many family photographs. The room opened out on a terrace, overlooking the lovely garden, which was completely cut off from the gaze of passers-by. Here, on the terrace, Freud could rest in privacy. In the neighboring bedroom hung two portraits of Freud's parents. Two guest rooms and two bathrooms, modernly fitted in red and blue, completed the rooms of this floor.

"Only one guest room is occupied right now," said Harry. "Princess Maria of Greece is staying, an aunt of the Duchess of Kent. She has been one of my uncle's students for many years."

On the second floor was the study of daughter Anna, where she received her patients. It was an airy, sunny room, with a picture of her father hanging on the wall facing the door. Here, too, were many artistic objects, chiefly jade figurines. A silent reminder of the past was a small picture showing Freud's country house at Hochroterd, near Vienna.

"Tea is ready," someone downstairs called out, and we broke off our exploration. We had seen the main sights.

We arrived at the foot of the stairs just as a lady dressed in black, with graying hair, was bidding good-bye to Frau Freud. "It's the Princess," Harry whispered. "She is on her way to visit Queen Mary." It was just after the Queen had a car accident. "Please convey to Her Majesty the deep sympathy we all feel," said Frau Freud, as the Princess left.

"The Princess says that the Queen always asks after my uncle's health when she sees her," said Harry.

A door halfway down the hall led to the dining room, where we had tea. Some of the furniture had been newly shipped from Vienna and the atmosphere already was homelike. The room was on the ground floor and looked out into the garden.

I had expected a Viennese *Jause*, coffee and cake, but was surprised to find tea was being served English style, with triangular sandwiches, jam, and cakes.

Suddenly we heard the barking of Lun, the Professor's shaggy brown chow, and it came bounding into the room from the garden. Then came the Professor himself.

He was at that time so ill that he rarely spoke. Every word was a painful effort. But he walked erect, and smiled in greeting as he entered. "Harry and his friends have been working hard in the garage, and are just being rewarded with tea," said Frau Freud. The Professor, who seemed to be in good humor, expressed his thanks to each of us in turn with a whimsical bow, and signaled to us to remain seated and continue undisturbed with our tea.

I looked at the kindly face, which I had not seen for many years and felt glad that I had been permitted to see him once more. For one could sense that his days were numbered.

(*Delphian Quarterly*, Chicago, April 1941)

There She Goes – *My* Wonderboat!

Our shipfitting crew consists of eight men. Charlie, the leaderman, was a designer of blueprints for 16 years but never had anything to do with ships before coming to Richmond in March, 1942. Bud worked in a garage; Scotty was an insurance agent; Frank used to be a baker; little Chinese Louis, a cook; Everett was a shoe salesman; Harry worked in a filling station; and I had done some editing and writing. None of us have been in the shipyard more than one year. All of us were amateurs. And yet, one day we were told that we were picked to set a new world's record: to assemble a 10,000-ton Liberty freighter in five days.

Next morning, driving to the shipard, I am in high spirits. It's good to belong to that stream of workers. I hum to the tune the motor sings: "I'm going to build a record ship! A Liberty Ship in five days!"

The yard is a strange city of lights. The burners' torches sparkle like Christmas candles; the yard is flash-spangled by the welders' arcs.

Our crew goes to the tool boxes. The spirit of adventure is in the air, the urge to do something important, and do it fast.

"We'll work as if our life depends on it," says Scotty. A deep voice from a dark corner: "If you come to think of it, boys, it does."

The noise of the yard suddenly dies down, as always immediately before the whistle announces the change of shifts.. You can set your watch by that sudden silence.

We climb on the assembly platform. To the left and right are the real workers of the yard, the huge Whirly cranes. Their giraffe necks reach toward the sky, stooping to pick up a heavy unit or a mouthful of smaller parts, rising again, turning around and, sounding a warning bell, carrying their loads overhead.

The sky becomes lighter, and the clouds, pink and fluffy, hover on their blue background. The sun rises over the Berkeley hills and warms up and dries the steel plates which the night had drenched in icy dampness. Every one is working by now, and will continue until the eleven o'clock whistle blows. The sea gulls appear with their usual punctuality to snatch every bit of food they can safely get. They are not the only animal life in this world of steel. There are lots of butterflies and crickets around, lost by the fact that anyone could build a shipyard where only recently an orchard stood. They don't know Henry J. Kaiser.

We sit around Charlie and listen to the lunch-hour music. And learn the disheartening news that many parts of the "record boat" will be assembled all over the yard and that it will take weeks until the keel is laid. We all feel disappointed. Suddenly the record boat has bounced into quotation marks and we feel sorry about that. But a few days later I get to know more from a man who knows the inside story of our record ship.

"It's impossible to start with nothing but plate steel and within five days have a finished ship on your way," he tells me. "This will be the first entirely prefabricated boat in the world. You see, what counts is how long a boat is on the shipway. As long as one is there, we can't build another one. Our yard has 12 shipways, so we can build 12 ships at a time. But the whole yard has lots of space to assemble the units for that boat.

"Formerly, each steel plate was carried up to the boat and put into place. Now we assemble 20 or 30 plates into one single unit, and the cranes carry the whole unit to the boat. Thus we need the crane only once, instead of 20 or 30 times. Most work is aseembled in prefabrication instead of on the precious space of the shipways. So far, we cut down the number of units to 200 per ship. On this boat we'll be cutting them to 90.

"Roughly, 250,000 individual items go into one boat. They will be assembled into 97 mammoth hull sections, to be lifted by Whirlys to the shipway. Some 80 percent of welding and riveting will be done off the shipways Almost all of the ship's six miles of pipe will be fitted on the assemblies, leaving only the joining to be done on the hull. Ordinarily, 25 machinists spend three weeks to assemble the engine room, This time the 135-ton giant pulse will be lifted into the hull 12 hours after keel laying."   From now on things really begin to hum. One morning our sheds are gone and we realize that we are going to build higher than the roofs of the shed allowed. The problem of getting two additional cranes is solved in the usual effective way. One of our original cranes brings a long piece of rail, the ties fixed to it, and puts it down, connecting its own rail with another one about 100 feet away, at a 90° angle. And presently the crane, 100 feet away, travels on this improvised rail to its new destination next to us. Soon we have four cranes at our disposal, able to carry 180 tons each.

Meanwhile, work on the prefabricated units grows to fantastic proportions. The assembly looks like a place where scrap is collected. The cranes bring down bundles of winding pipes that look like a gigantic forkful of spaghetti, and drop them higgledy piggledy.

Valves, brackets, parts of machinery are set in place, watertight covers are fitted, special crews go around drilling, countersinking, inserting screws and bolts. The place is tangled with the hoses of welders, burners, chippers, grinders, a labyrinth of hopelessly entangled snakes that threaten to grab your foot .

Welders work in manholes just big enough for them to squeeze through. You sometimes don't see more than their feet; their body is hidden in little compartments below the steelplates you walk on and make the ground hot under your feet. Sparks break out from the most unexpected spots, and although you often need something to hold on, you must be careful not to grab anything that might turn out to be several hundred degrees hot. There are many little round holes for pipes and it might happen that smoke pours out just as you bend over them. In short, it feels like working on top of a volcano, wading ankle-deep in lava.

And yet, everybody loves this madhouse; we are pioneers. Workers who never saw each other before look at one another and pause a second to shake their heads in amazement. They don't say a word, and if they would they would not be heard over the din, but the look says: "Can you beat that? Crazy, but that's the stuff!"

I'll never understand how everything went right. Surely, mistakes were made, but always someone spots a flaw and corrects it. We figure things out ourselves and if we get stuck, we go to one of the other half-completed boats and study "what makes the wheels go round."

First we complete the inner bottoms, the lower part of the boat. Imagine you are building a three-story house and are assembling the first floor a few hundred feet from the place where the house is eventually going up. You have a dining room and a living room in one piece, two bedrooms in another, the kitchen, bathroom and toilets in a third piece. The electricians, cabinet makers, plumbers and other craftsmen work on your preassembled first floor. They put in the wiring, the pipes and valves, lay down carpets, put up curtains, build in all the furniture, paint and varnish the doors, paper the walls, place the refrigerator and stove into your kitchen, and the telephone next to your bed. That will give you an idea of how our ship was built.

Atop the inner bottoms the bulkheads are set, like the walls of a house, until the boat looks like the inner partition of an eggbox.

More and more the whole yard swings into the spirit of the "wonderboat." Everywhere you can see units saying in big letters: "For Hull 440 – don't touch," or "Redhot, Hull 440." The number 440 can be seen and heard everywhere.

We had no rain since last April, but on November 8th, the

morning of the keel laying, a slight drizzle begins, When I arrive in the yard, it is raining. But nobody pays attention. When swing shift starts, the boat is seven hours old. The keel was laid at 12:01 A.M, but already weighs about 500 tons. A big sign announces: RICHMOND NO. 2 PREFABRICATED SHIP. Two clocks are underneath. One showing the days from the start, the other the hours. We are in a race against time.

Speed, however, does not mean that safety is neglected. Dozens of safety men are watching anything that might cause an accident. About every 20 minutes a warning shout goes up: "Heads up!" The cranes bring another 100-ton unit. All step aside, but as soon as the crane has set its load in place, the wave of workers flows back to work. When our day ends at 3 :30 P. M., 1,008 tons have been erected in 15 hours. This is 10 times as much as a good average daily performance. The swing shift comes in and finds a third of a boat where there was nothing when they left work the day before, 16 hours ago.

The rain stops in the afternoon but a thick fog envelops the yard. Ship and cranes are in a haze, but the work goes on. It's cold, but we are wet with perspiration. Every man and woman works with clocklike precision. "Anthill with cranes," someone remarks.

When the fog clears, we are five hours behind schedule. But now we show what we really can do. As we leave work, another 1,000 tons have been added. Two-thirds of the boat are now up.

The third day brings, among other heavy stuff, the deckhouse, weighing 190 tons. It comes in four parts on a trailer with 24 tires, and is lifted by the crane to the hull. It contains a completely equipped wheelhouse with a confusing number of switch boards; the galley with cooking range, heater, several sinks, hot-water heater, and cabinet for the dishes; the messroom, including tables and chairs; toilets and showers; equipment for the officers' and the captain's rooms, a leather-covered couch with built-in cupboard, closets, table, chairs, washstand with soap dishes, a bathroom glass, rack for towels, medicine chest with mirror, four electric lamps, radiator and ventilator.

At the end of our shift of the third day, 2,684 tons are erected and we are actually ahead of schedule. Masts and smokestack go on board early the fourth day and from now on the welders, electricians, and carpenters are in command. It is fascinating to see how a collection of plates, brackets, stiffeners, all ordinary steel, become rooms, compartments, outfitted and equipped for their eventual use. It's particularly fascinating if you have put on some of these plates and brackets yourself.

The fifth day begins. It's a bright day. In spite of the rain and fog of the first two days, the ship will be launched today, in less than five days. After a hectic 100 hours, the spirit of work gives way to celebration. While hundreds of workers still are busy, others clean the boat, hoses are rolled up, scaffolding is knocked down. A sign on the deckhouse says:

"Compliments of the workers at prefab plant. Lots of luck!"

A string of flags is hoisted from stem to stern. A large board on the bow of the ship announces:

"Robert E. Peary, keel laid November 8, 12:01 A.M., launched 3:30 P.M.: 4 days, 15 hours, 29 minutes."

A group of boys and girls in lavender graduation gowns appears: the choir of the San Francisco Junior College. The number of police increases, photographers and newsreel reporters prepare for the big event. An artist sketches the boat in its festive dress. Microphones are ready, so is the crew for the broadcast.

The guests flock in: men, women, children, many babies. 25,000 workers get half an hour off to watch the launching. Our leaderman Charlie is right up there, next to the microphones. He did his part. And we helped him. Something deep inside that huge ship is a bracket that Harry welded, a girder that Frank set, a manhole that Louis burned. Four thousand workers have had their hands on that ship.

Here she was, the "Robert E. Peary," a wonder in more than one respect. A wonder of coordination, of free collaboration, a triumph of the democratic system.

The choir sings the Star Spangled Banner, and the flag is raised in front of the speaker's platform. Henry Kaiser, unable to attend, sent a phonograph message from New York City. Then a thousandfold cry: "There she goes!" That's more than the routine shout of every launching, for while the ship slips down the way, the red-white-and-blue streamer with the broken champagne bottle waving behind her, something in each of those thousand voices says:

"There she goes – MY Wonderboat!"

(*Delphian Quarterly*, Chicago, April 1943)

Wiedersehen mit dem Wiener Telephonbook

Heute (1949) fand ich in der Universitätsbibliothek von Berkeley ein Wiener Telephonbuch. Es hat zwar schon leicht ergraute Schläfen (Jahrgang 1946) aber für mich war es eine Sensation, wie eine an Robinson's Insel geschwemmte, drei Jahre alte Zeitung aus der Heimat.

Seit 10 Jahren habe ich kein Wiener Telephonbuch gesehen. Der letzte Anruf, den ich in Wien machte, war am Tage meiner Ausreise, an jenem unvergesslichen 11. März, als ich nach dem nächsten Zug fragte.

Da ist es also. "Amtliches Telephonbuch" steht darauf. Etwas dünn ist es geworden, in der Zwischenzeit, 192 Seiten, dafür hat es aber einen mehr als 50 Seiten starken Anhang, "Änderungen während des Druckes".

So um 1946 herum hat's halt viel Änderungen gegeben. Das alte Wiener Wappen ist wieder auf dem Deckel, als ob's nie andere Symbole gegeben hätte: der alte Adler mit der Mauerkrone, der Sichel und dem Hammer. Neu ist nur eine gesprengte Kette, die halb und halb von je einem Haxl herunterhängt. Alte Symbole, neue Inhalte.

Etwas scheu fange ich an, herumzublättern. Eine Reklame für Ankerbrot. Zu meiner Zeit gab es die sprichwörtlich gewordene Reklame: "Worauf freut sich der Wiener, wenn er vom Urlaub zurückkommt? Aufs Hochquellwasser und Ankerbrot." Der Urlaub war lang, diesmal . . .

Schnell schau ich ein paar bekannte Namen nach. Nichts. Keiner mehr da. Weder der Friseur, noch die Trafikantin, noch der Bäcker. Die Vindobona Apotheke am Bauernfeldplatz steht da, aber ein Magister Billeg hat sie übernommen; den kenn' ich nicht. Was sie wohl mit unserem Magister Silber gemacht haben?

Mir fällt ein, ich könnt' mich selber nachschlagen. Ich heisse nicht mehr Kühnel, wie einst. Also: da gibt es sieben Kühnels. Hier zwischen der Josefine Kühnel und dem Ingenieur Robert Kühnel, da würde ich jetzt stehen, wenn . . . Ich starre zwischen die Zeilen, als ob's da eine leere Stelle gäbe. Was für ein fremdes Buch das doch ist!

"Entstörungsstelle". "Fernschreibverkehr". Was das für Wörter sind; wie Fussspuren von einem längst vergangenen SS Mann. Ob diese Wörter zum Aufgabenkreis des "Liquidators der Einrichtungen des Deutschen Reiches in der Republik Österreich" gehören? Er ist als "Nachgeordnete Dienststelle" des Bundes-kanzleramtes angeführt. (Nachgeordnete Dienststelle, du lieber Kaiser Franz Josef!). Na ja, da ist noch eine andere Erinnerung an die Zeit, bevor der Adler auf den Umschlag zurückkehrte: "K.Z.-Verband, I. Renngasse 12." Ein Büro. Man kann "Mitglied" werden, wenn man gewisse Qualifikationen hat, zum Beispiel ein jährlichcr Beitrag, Überleben von Auschwitz u. dgl.

Das erinnert mich: Sehen wir einmal nach, wie viele Kohns es gibt. Drei. Einen Hugo, ein Möbelhändler in der Blindengasse; einen Dr. Josef, der ist Rechtsanwalt in der Porzellangass; und einen Zahntechniker Robert in der Rotenlöwengasse. Fünf weitere im Anhang. Da ich nun schon dabei bin: Es gibt immerhin 6 Rosenbergs, 4 Rosenthals, 3 Rosenbergers, 2 Rosenfelds und je einen Rosenblatt und Rosenbusch. Und 19 Vertreter der Löwen Familie, einschliesslich -steins und -thals.

Beim Blättern stosse ich auf vier Spalten von Nummern, die dem gleichen Abonnenten gehören: der Kommunistische Partei. Wie schau'n denn die anderen Parteien aus? Die Sozialistische Partei hat eine halbe Spalte. Die Österreichische Volkspartei (das sind die Christlichsozialen "unserer" Zeit) eineinhalb. Sitzverteilung im Telephonbuchparlament.

Also so was! Das Zentralkomitee der KP ist in der Wasagasse 10 – das ist "mein" Gymnasium! Was wohl unser Direktor Valentin Pollak dazu sagen würde? Ob er noch lebt? Nach der Matura ging ich an die Universität und landete, wie Tausende, im juristischen Einpaukerkurs von Diwald, geleitet vom unermüdlichen dicken Dr. Rischanek. Sie sind noch am gleichen Platz auf der Freyung, sogar der Rischanek steht da, und ein Hofrat ist er geworden!

Nun bin ich so ziemlich mit dem Durchblättern fertig. Ich sehe, dass es nur 11 öffentliche Telephonsprechstellen in der Inneren Stadt gibt, eine einzige im zweiten Bezirk, sechs im dritten, zwei im vierten, und so weiter, keine 200 in der ganzen Stadt. Wenn ich an die zahllosen Drugstores in Amerika denke. . .

Ein Schwarm von Verhaltungsmassregeln, wie man's Telephon benützen soll. Punkt 9: "Nicht gleich ungeduldig werden"! Alles Österreichertum ham die Nazis doch nicht ausrotten können. Was schon aus den drei Spalten von Kaffeehäusern hervorgeht.

Trotz allem - dieses Buch ist eine Mumie. Eine Mumie, die gelegentlich mit den Augen zwinkert. Der Rückenumschlag hat das einzige ganzseitige Inserat: Gemeinde Wien, Leichenbestattung.

(*Aufbau*, New York, Feb. 25, 1949)

Die fliegenden Fische der Sierra Nevada

In der Sierra Nevada regnet es jetzt Forellen. Tausende werden vom Flugzeug aus in den hochgelegenen Gebirgseen ausgesetzt, um den Fischbestand zu erhalten.

Wir beobachteten den Vorgang von einer Hochgebirgswiese aus, umgeben von steilen Gipfeln, darunter dem höchsten Gipfel des nordamerikanischen Festlandes, dem 4,425 Meter hohen Mount Whitney. Ein kleines, zweimotoriges Flugzeug kreiste in immer enger werdenden Schrauben über dem See. Als es etwa 100 Meter über der Oberfläche war, öffnete sich eine Tür an der Unterseite des Flugzeugs, ein Gischt von Wasser zischte heraus und plantschte in den See. Das Flugzeug schraubte sich wieder in die Höhe. Jeden Augenblick schien es an den nahen Bergen anzuprallen, gewann aber schliesslich den freien Himmel.

Eine Stunde später sass es friedlich neben uns am Rande des Sees. Der Pilot Al Reese und sein Begleiter tranken Kaffee mit uns, den wir auf unserem improvisierten Steinherd gebraut hatten. Die beiden waren gelandet, um den Erfolg ihrer Mission besser beobachten zu können.

Reese ist Beamter des kalifornischen Fischkonservierungsbüros. Das Aussetzen von Fischen durch die Luft ist seine Idee.

"Im Sommer ist die Sierra voll von Anglern," sagt er. "Für die meisten Touristen hier sind Forellen die einzige frische Nahrung. Also müssen wir jedes Jahr neue Fische aussetzen."

Wir fragten, ob denn die Fische den Fall ins Wasser aushielten. "Ich hab mich heiser geredet, das zu beweisen," sagte Reese. "Jeder behauptete, man müsse die Fingerlinge ins Wasser *legen*, nicht werfen." Er machte eine wegwerfende Handbewegung. "Darüber sind wir jetzt hinaus. Ich hab einen kleinen Wassertank mit Fingerlingen auf eine Wiese abgeworfen, nicht ins Wasser. Alle sind nachher im Tank herumgeschwommen. Jetzt glaubt man mir endlich." Er wurde lebhaft. "Und wissen Sie was? Nach der alten Methode sind halb die Fische umgekommen." Die alte Methode war, die Fische auf Mauleseln heraufzuschleppen. Stundenlang. in Wassertanks, die immer heisser wurden. "Die meisten Fische haben das nicht ausgehalten. Ihnen ist mein Zwillings-Beechcraft lieber."

Im Innern des Flugzeugs standen Reihen von grossen Behälter, die aussahen wie Milchkannen. Darin schwammen winzige Fischlein. Sie hatte Reese "Fingerlinge" genannt, denn sie waren nicht länger als die Breite des kleinen Fingers. Da sie so eng gedrängt waren, brauchten sie extra Zufuhr von Sauerstoff, der in Schläuchen zu jedem Behälter geführt wurde. In der Ecke war ein Wassertank, der sich wie ein Trichter nach unten verengte. Sie war durch eine kleine Tür verschlossen, die an die Aussenseite des Flugzeugs führte. Durch den Druck eines Knopfs konnte sie geöffnet werden. In diesen Tank wurden die "Milchkannen" geleert, wenn man die Fische in die Seen fliegen lassen wollte.

"Ich bin der Pilot, und mein Begleiter bedient den Tank", sagte Reese. "Er beobachtet, ob die Fische wirklich im Wasser landen. Diese Seen sind manchmal sehr klein, und wir fliegen mit 200 Kilometer Geschwindigkeit und können oft nicht tiefer als 300 Meter herunterkommen, wegen der umliegenden Berge."

Die Landkarte vor dem Führersitz war besät mit kleinen blauen Flecken, den Seen. "Es gibt 632 kleine Seen hier," sagte Reese. "Und wir müssen wissen, wieviele Fingerlinge wir in jeden fliegen lassen sollen, je nach der Grösse des Sees."

Das normale alljährliche Fischprogramm des staatlichen Fischbüros dauerte drei Monat. Seit Einführung des Flugzeugs dauert es eine Woche. Dieses Jahr wurde es erstmals in vollem Umfang verwendet, eineinhalb Millionen Fingerlinge im Jahr, meist Steinforellen; aber auch die vielbegehrten Goldforellen.

Die Flieger nahmen auf ihren Sitzen Platz. "Wir haben heute noch 12 Seen vor uns. Dann zurück in die Fischzüchterei, eine halbe Flugstunder. Ein Fussweg von 30 Stunden."

"Aber billiger," sagte einer von uns unvorsichtigerweise.

Reese wandte sich ihm zu. "Wissen Sie, was das Fischaussetzen die Steuerzahler gekostet hat, bis voriges Jahr? Im Durchschnitt $16 für je 1,000 Fingerlinge. Und wissen Sie, wieviel es jetzt, mit dem "teuren" Flugzeug kostet? Einen Dollar und 62 Cents, ein Zehntel. Na sehen Sie."

Das kleine, weissgestrichene Flugzeug begann zu brummen, lief an, schwang sich in die Höhe. Eine Minute später sah es aus, als ob es am Mount Whitney zerschellen würde. Aber eine weitere Minute später sahen wir es als einen kleinen Punkt über dem Gipfel verschwinden.

(*Aufbau*, New York, June 13, 1952)

Fred Hickenlooper's seltsame Sammlung

Am letzten Märztag, kurz nach Mitternacht, konnte Polizeisergeant Mortimer J. Leavenworth im "Prominentenviertel" von Beverly Hills einen interessanten Fang tun. Vor dem Bungalow der bekannten Filmdiva Jean Peters verhaftete er einen jungen Menschen, der sich offenbar beim Herabspringen vom Fensterbret den Fuss verstaucht hatte.

So schonungsvoll wie es unter den Umständen möglich war weckte der Polizeibeamte die Filmschauspielerin. Sie hatte nicht von einem Einschleicher bemerkt. Weder Geld noch Schmuck fehlten Der Mann gestand, im Zimmer gewesen zu sein, hatte es offenba aber weder auf Raub abgesehen, noch auf Jean Peters selbst. Sie wa nicht einmal erwacht, während er in ihrem Schlafzimmer war.

Die Beamten auf der Polizeistation nahmen an dem Mann ein Routine-Untersuchung vor. In seinen Taschen fanden sie Schlüsse Kleingeld, eine Brieftasche mit verschiedenen Papieren auf de Namen Fred Hickenlooper, Chemiestudent der Universität vo Kalifornien, und einen mit Spitzen besetzten, aus rosa Sati geschneiderten Büstenhalter. Mit einem halb ärgerlichen, hal verlegenen Griff nahm Jean Peters den Büstenhalter an sich. "De gehört mir," sagte sie. "Wieso hat ihn dieser Kerl nu mitgenommen?"

Mit dieser Verhaftung begann eines der merkwürdigste Kapitel in der an amüsanten Fällen gewiss nicht arme Polizeichronik Hollywoods. Die Lokalzeitungen hielten da Geschichtchen für einen Reklametrick und schrieben ironisch Überschriften, wie etwa: "Sucht Jean eine Stütze für ihren nächste Film?" Aber in einem Kreuzverhör stellte sich heraus, da Hickenlooper ein Rädelsführer in den sogenannten "Panty Raid gewesen war, jener Epidemie von halb-narrischen Studente raubzügen auf weibliche Unterwäsche, die im Vorjahr d amerikanischen Hochschulen heimgesucht hatte.

Die Polizei nahm eine Hausdurchsuchung bei Hickenloop vor, die ein Resultat zeitigte, wie es keiner der Beamten je erle hatte. Im Zimmer des Studenten befand sich eine grosse, a mehreren Fächern bestehende Kommode. Jedes Fach war in klei Abteilungen zerlegt, wie etwa eine Mineraliensammlung. Und dar

gab es tatsächlich eine Sammlung – von Büstenhaltern! Jede Abteilung war mit einer Vignette versehen, die den Namen einer berühmten Frau, das Datum der "Erwerbung", und den Namen eines Parfüms trugen.

Obwohl sich Lokalreporter von Hollywood solche Leckerbissen nur ungern entgehen lassen, erschienen nur am Tage der Entdeckung selbst Artikel über die Affäre, die aber "öffentlich" nicht weiter verfolgt wurde. Zwei bekannte Filmdivas ersuchten die Polizei, ihren Einfluss geltend zu machen und die Einzelheiten, zumindest in Amerika selbst, nicht weiter bekannt zu machen. Wohl gibt es keine Zensur in Amerika, aber die Wünsche von Prominenten werden oft berücksichtigt.

Wir fragten den Deliquenten nach der Herkunft einiger der vorgefundenen weiblichen Kleidungsstücke. Derselbe erklärte, er hätte sie im Laufe mehrerer Jahre gesammelt – offenbar ein Beschönigungswort für "gestohlen", denn der Mann machte folgende Angaben über die Art, wie er in den Besitz einiger der Objekte gekommen war:

Objekt Nr. 1 (weisser Nylon, Grösse 36, beschriftet "Esther Williams") stammte aus einer Badekabine der bekannten amerikanischen Schwimmerin und Filmschauspielerin. "Ich habe es bei einer öffentlichen Schwimmkonkurrenz im August 1952 in Santa Monica gesammelt," erklärte er. "Ich schlich vor der Veranstaltung in die Damenabteilung und versteckte mich in einer Kabine."

Objekt Nr. 2 (schwarze Spitze, Grösse 34, beschriftet "Rita Hayworth" mit einer gezeichneten Krone versehen, die die Worte "Mein Glanzstück" trägt): Dieses Objekt stammte von der indischen Köchin Ali Khans, der eine zeitlang in Beverly Hills ein Haus für Rita gemietet hatte.

Objekt Nr. 3 (ein aus Kork bestehender Gürtel, der nicht in die Sammlung zu passen schien): "Diese 'Mae West' sammelte ich nur aus Gefühlsgründen," sagte er. ('Mae West' ist ein Rettungsgürtel, benannt nach der für ihren Busenumfang bekannten Schauspielerin).

Objekt Nr. 4 (Drahtgestell mit Satin überzogen, stark verbogen, beschriftet: "Jaqueline Tunne") stammte aus der Bühnengarderobe der jungen Künstlerin, die er betrat, ohne zu wissen, dass sie sich gerade umkleidete. "Es gelang mir, das Objekt mitzunehmen, obwohl die Schauspielerin es mir beinahe entriss und bei dieser Gelegenheit verbog."

Objekt Nr. 5 (Fischbeinmodell zum Schnüren. Grösse 33, fleischfarben, beschriftet "Gloria Swanson"), erworben von der Reinigungsanstalt, in der die Künstlerin waschen liess. "Ihr Dienstmädchen brachte die Wäsche jeden Freitag Ich brachte meine Wäsche im gleichen Augenblick, stiess mit dem Mädchen zusammen

und erwarb das Objekt." Der Polizeiakt zählt 28 derartige detailierte Fälle auf. Er enthält auch Schreiben von bekannten Filmgrössen, die erklären, sie fühlten sich nicht geschädigt und wünschten keine weitere strafrechtliche Verfolgung. Den Papieren angefügt ist ein Gutachten des bekannten Psychiaters, Professor Rufus Thornton, der erklärt, Hickenlooper sei ein sexual-pathologischer Fall, aber nicht gemeingefährlich. Er habe eine fixe Idee, die sich nicht nur auf die entwendeten "Objekte", sondern auch auf die von den Trägerinnen verwendeten Parfüms bezieht. Dem Professor war der starke Duft der Wäschestücke aufgefallen, der sich, nach den "Erwerbungsdaten" zu schliessen, schon längst verflüchtigt haben hätte müssen. Es stellte sich heraus, dass der Chemiestudent ein Spezialist in der Identifizierung der verschie-denen Parfüms war und die Beutestücke von Zeit zu Zeit nachpar-fümierte, wie etwa ein Museumskurator seine Bronzen aufputzt.

Der Berichterstatter sprach mit Hickenlooper, als er nach seiner Verhaftung mit einer strengen Verwarnung entlassen wurde. Er ist ein sportlich trainierter junger Mann, der hofft, in einer bekannten Seifenfabrik angestellt zu werden. Nun fürchtet er, dass seine "Liebhaberei" ihm in seiner Karriere schaden würde.

"Ehrlich gesagt", erklärt Hickenlooper, "kann ich den ganzen Rummel nicht verstehen, den sie auf der Polizei machten. Gewiss, ich hätte nicht durch ein offenes Fenster steigen sollen – Hausfriedensbruch undsoweiter. Aber sonst? Ist schon je ein Gymnasiast bestraft worden, weil er in einer Badeanstalt durch ein Astloch guckte? Der "Wert" dieser Dinge spielt doch keine Rolle bei diesen wohlhabenden Frauen! Manche Leute sammeln Autogramme – trockene, leblose Buchstaben. Ich sammle etwas, das gewissermassen atmet, ein Ausdruck der Persönlichkeit, das nur mit Courage oder List erworben werden kann."

Der Leser mag sich zu dieser Erklärung seine eigenen Gedanken machen. Der Wäschedieb Hickenlooper ist ein armer Teufel, der seine Überspanntheit hinter einer "logischen Begründung" verbergen möchte. Dennoch entbehrt seine kleine Tragödie nicht der Komik. Um ihretwillen haben wir sie nicht vorenthalten wollen. *Honi soit, qui mal y pense.*

This story is a spoof perpetrated on a Swiss weekly, which printed it as fact (the result of a bet, reminiscent of the Grubenhund spoof by Karl Kraus, which older generations of Austrians will remember). Not one word of the Hickenlooper story is true.

(*Wochenzeitung*, Zürich, July 29. 1954)

Return to the Alps

I had not seen the Alps for 15 years.

When I was four, my father rolled my jacket, my windbreaker, and my lunch in a bundle and stuffed them into a tiny rucksack which I was to carry myself when we hiked in the Vienna Woods. When I was five, I got my first Lederhosen to take the place of my short linen pants. When I was six, my father mailed me postcards which showed a snow-covered peak and meadows with Alpenrosen, gentians, and Edelweiss.

When I was 17, I stood on that same Tirolean mountain with a heavy rucksack, a pair of Lederhosen greasy from years of hiking in the Alps, a sprig of Alpenrosen pinned to my jacket. A dirndl-skirted girl sat beside, barefoot, her hands clasped around her knees. The grass of the mountain meadow was short and mossy and had the feel of a bearskin. With sun-flushed faces we looked toward the surrounding peaks, breathing the cold, fresh air.

When I was 18, I hitchhiked to Switzerland heading for the Matterhorn, which for years I had longed to see. On the way a motorist offered me a ride to the Dolomites, a temptation I could not resist. So I allowed myself to get sidetracked, trusting I would get to the Matterhorn another time. I did – twenty-five years later.

When I had made my home in California and the years passed, the memory of Austria faded, except for the Alps. I traveled and visited many peaks, Canada's proud Rockies, Japan's venerable Fujiyama, California's magnificent Sierra. But my Lederhosen were locked in a basement trunk, and the memory of the Alps lived on.

Occasionally, when I admitted I was thinking of the Alps – the Vienna Woods, Tirol, the Matterhorn – friends would tell me that I was just yearning for bygone youth. Many a Sunday I drove in search of a small green patch for a family picnic – a patch with grass grown naturally, not coaxed into existence by sprinklers in a public park. I longed for the lush Almen, the pastures of the Alps. They became a never-land of green.

In this summer of 1953, I was looking straight at them. For three hours the Arlberg Express was speeding along in this blessed land as I stood by the window drinking in the changing scene.

As I stood by the train window I realized that although I had remembered the grass, I had forgotten the flowers. The train followed a green lane dotted with millions of buttercups and foxgloves and larkspurs and snapdragons and wild pansies and bellflowers and cornflowers and red poppies and daisies and many others whose English names I didn't know. Hour after hour these welcoming flowers would be with us in a never-ending stream, and I affectionately watched them as we rode along. Later, when I was up in those mountains that were now visible in the distance, I would come across people who asked me why I had picked weeds along with my flowers. I did not explain that these were not weeds to me, but friends whom I had not seen for a long time.

The mountains narrowly squeezed the flowery lane between them. We rode in a valley between the peaks. They had snowy caps, and from them wild foaming brooks tumbled down. You thought you could almost feel, just by sight, how cold they were.

The green lane was paralleled by a country road. We passed some horse-drawn wagons with racks. Hay was stacked high, and kerchiefed peasant women sitting on top waved to the train. Gabled wooden houses with begonia-decorated carved balconies appeared and disapeared. No billboard spoiled the scenery.

As we approached Vienna, I greeted every familiar hill of the Vienna Woods. On this one we had our boy-scout headquarters in the quarry; on that one you could find shell fossils; here we bandaged Lotte's leg when she got caught on a rusty barbed wire. I could not going to visit these hills; they were in the Soviet zone.

Eight hours I stood by the open window with wind and sun beating down on my face. When we arrived in Vienna I had as much of a tan as if I had already spent a week in the mountains.

Before I had my suitcase unpacked in the morning, I was on my way to the Kahlenberg. The 760-mile range of the Alps begins in Vienna; here are the foothills that rise to those heights in Tirol and Switzerland. The Kahlenberg is the first rung of the ladder that makes up the Alps. It is only 1,400 feet high and still within the metropolitan limits of Vienna, hence within that internationalized island that is surrounded by the Soviets. Beneath us lay the city of Vienna. To the left, the Danube with the bridges restored except one, still gaping, a reminder of the violent days of 1945; to the right, the soft rolling hills of the Kobenzl; in front of us, slightly below, the vineyards of Sievering and Grinzing, with a sweep and sweetness that made you understand the inspiration of Schubert and Mozart; in the distance, the hazy outlines of the Hungarian hills.

As the shadows grew longer I slowly walked up to the Sofienalpe, a neighboring hill. A playground for Vienna's Sunday hikers, it was today quiet and peaceful and infinitely lovely. The

beeches were tall and slender, their nodding crowns forming arches
through which you could walk. No one was around. The parting sun
shot horizontal beams of light through the trees, outlining them as
dark silhouettes. This place was a symbol of my childhood; it had
determined much of my standards of beauty. I had been here many
times – when I was happy and when I thought I was not, when I felt
on top of the world and when my boyish heart was broken. I walked
among the trees. The fallen leaves formed a soft cover on the
ground. Never had I noticed the delicate fragrance of this place; I
had always taken it for granted.

I picked a couple of beech leaves to be taken to America. As I
walked down twisting trails in the darkness, I did not realize until I
reached the bottom an hour later that not once had I lost my way.

From the Vienna Woods I followed the Alps westward into the
lake world of the Salzkammergut. A bumpety toy train took me from
Ischl to Salzburg, a two-hour ride. An old bearded peasant got on
and was greeted by a young woman in the car.

"Where d'you come from?" asked the man.

"From Ischl."

"Ah, Ischl! Aren't you enterprising! I won't get there any more. I
was there once, when the old Kaiser still lived."

The mountains of the Salzkammergut were rich with
memories: Dachstein, Traunstein, Totes Gebirge. They averaged no
more than 5,000 feet, and I had caught the fever for the higher peaks.
The glaciers and the Almen of Tirol were beckoning.

I followed the chain of the Alps to Innsbruck, Tirol's capital.
The train was full of youthful mountaineers. Many had to stand up,
and I was among them. But I didn't mind. I wore my old Lederhosen
which I had exhumed from their California basement grave and
taken along; I felt young, forgetting the years that had passed, as my
eyes rested with pleasure upon a young dirndl of 18 or so who sat
next to where I was standing. She returned my glance, got up and
offered me her seat. That took me down a peg.

The Stubai Valley and the Ötz Valley are two of several
parallel Tirolean mountain valleys that run each at a right angle to
the Inn River, the main tributary of the Danube. These Tirolean
valleys are not connected with each other; if you want to cross from
one to the other you have to follow the first down to the Inn, then
follow the Inn until you reach the mouth of the second one, then go
up. Otherwise you can cross from one valley to the other only by
climbing the intervening mountains up one side and down the other.

I did that. Joining a small group of tourists, I took several days
to cross from the Stubai Valley over a 10,000-foot peak into the Ötz
Valley. It took us one day to ascend leisurely to a mountain hut which

was built at the edge of a glacier. We had decided to stay in that hut overnight, then cross the ice-bound top on the second day. We planned to spend the following night in hut number two, built at the opposite side of the glacier, beyond the top, on the way down to the Ötz Valley.

Perhaps it is absurd to acknowledge that there were few hours I have ever enjoyed as much as the ascent to the first hut while rain was falling. It wasn't a downpour, but a refreshing spray which bothered none of the company in their watertight boots and Loden cloaks. I had brought a poncho, which had rendered good service many times in the Sierra and was duly admired as something rare in the Alps.

The fine rain added to the feeling of freshness from dozens of cold brooks that came down from the glacier we would be crossing tomorrow. Everything around was green and rich and growing abundantly. I found the first gentian, that deep blue single bell that has become the symbol of the Alps, sharing the affection of mountain climbers only with Edelweiss and Alpenrosen. There are several varieties of gentian. The one we found was stemless and had a metallic luster inside. We didn't pick it.

When we arrived in the Alpine Club hut we found Schorsch and Willy, two German students, talking with the hostess. These huts are usually owned by tourist clubs and leased to hostesses.

The woman was cooking noodles. "How much a helping?" asked Schorsch. The hostess looked him over. "I'll let you eat your fill for 4 schillings." That's about 17 cents. He pointed to a pot in which rice was boiling. "We've some rice left in our knapsack, uncooked. May we trade a plateful of your rice here for some of our own?" The woman nodded, and the two helped themselves.

We sat down, sharing a table with the students. The hostess was busy with the noodles, the rice, and the *Kaiserschmarrn* — scrambled pancakes which we had ordered. We heard her husband chopping wood outside. A flock of well-behaved children played in one corner of the room. Its center was taken up by the huge wood stove; it had a rail all around on which the woolen socks of the students were hanging to dry; several pairs of hobnailed boots were close against the stove for the same reason. It was dark outside. A bowl of Alpenrosen stood in the middle of the table which was illuminated by a kerosene lamp.

Our guide, a Stubai Valley native, roused us from our bunks at 4 A.M. We poured a little cold water from the china pitcher in the basin and dipped our fingertips into it, going through the motions of a morning wash. It was very cold, and we didn't thaw out until we got to the warm kitchen and filled up for the trip.

As we started across the glacier just beyond the hut, the snow was crisp. We took our time, patiently putting one foot in front of the other. After a couple of hours we had left every bit of soil behind us. This was the zone of eternal snow. It was an unreal world, with the reflection of light from the snow hitting our eyes despite our dark glasses and despite the fact that the sun was hiding. We walked in single file, the guide ahead carrying rope and ice axe. All around, snow-covered mountains loomed high above us, as we slowly crawled to the top like black beetles.

We reached the summit at noon. It gave us a superb view back into the Stubai Valley whence we had come, and ahead into the Ötz Valley where we were bound. The glacier on which we stood reached quite a way down into the second valley. Where the ice ended we could see hut number two, our goal for the day.

There was a snow-free spot on top, swept clean by the wind that was blowing over the crest. When we arrived, the sun came out and we took our shirts and shoes off. Fine small flowers, like strawberry blossoms, grew here. "Gamskresse," said the guide, plants eaten by chamois.

We spent half the afternoon at the top. We were in no hurry. As we lay there, at peace with a tranquil world, we were flanked by two chains, the Stubai Alps on one side, the Ötz-Valley Alps on the other, summit after summit as far as the eye could see. The endless row of peaks accompanied us into a nap.

A short descent in the late afternoon took us to the second hut, where we stayed for the night. We were a third of the way down into the Ötz Valley. The next morning we continued under our own power. The guide had us taken safely across the glacier.

We were now in the lovely country of the Almen, the classical pasture land of the Alps. Soon after leaving the second hut we discovered a bright red spot in the near distance. It was the first shrub of Alpenrosen, an exciting, moving sight. As we descended further, more Alpenrosen appeared, at first in little islands, then in large patches, until finally the whole mountainside was covered with them, cascading down for miles.

After two hours the steep trail flattened out, allowing a small unbridled brook, which had issued from the glacier and had followed us all the way down to overflow its shallow banks, irrigate the surrounding meadow, turning this mountain valley into a flower garden. Below us lay the valley with millions of colored dots strewn in the pasture; left and right, the mountain-sides enclosing the valley were covered with Alpenrosen in full bloom; at the foot of the valley, a white foaming stream wound its way; above us, the tops of the snow-covered Stubai Alps looked over one end of the valley, those of the Ötz-Valley Alps over the other; in the center cuddled hut number three.

We were halfway down the Ötz Valley. Two of us decided to stay in the hut for a few days. The rest went on.

If the Lord is black for Negroes, paradise is green for Austrians. I closed my eyes and tried to remember how I had dreamed about some mountain Shangri-la as I had known it in my childhood. On my way to Europe I had prepared myself for some rough awakening when I should actually see the places I had probably glorified in memory. Reality, I had thought, can never catch up with dreams. Now I remembered how I had anticipated this moment: a velvet-thick meadow, a blue sky, sparkling air, a light cool breeze in the sunshine . . .

When I opened my eyes I saw that I had been all wrong. This place was much more beautiful than I had dreamed. It was not just a bucolic painting; it lived, breathed, overflowing with the moisture of life. The sounds of the grass moving in the wind, of the insects, of the brook, were sweet and familiar. I moved to the brook that came bounding over the rocks, stooped down, and took a long draft of cold water. I sat down on a boulder, dipped my toes in the spray, felt the soil with my hands. The impact of being a visitor in my native land hit me with full force.

I returned to the meadow. Its grass, as I lay down, half buried me. The flowers were at a level with my eyes, some looking down on me. It grew dark as I still lay there, conscious of the moment, conscious and grateful and happy in this hour of fulfillment and pause and unity with the world. I truly felt that, like Faust, I could "tell time to linger."

Time did linger, forgotten for three timeless days. Then I returned to the world, descended to Sölden, mostly walking barefoot across the Almen. A few days later I was on my way to the Matterhorn.

I followed the Alps from Austria, across the incomparable Arlberg Pass, to Zürich and Lucerne. Like sentinels the mountains looked down as I crossed the Four-Canton Lake to Fluelen; they closed in on the cogwheel train to Göschenen; and they opened up in a wide view from the top of Furka Pass. Farther along the road I stopped at the Belvedere Hotel, 7,600 feet, built on a crag directly alongside the incredibly bright blue Rhone Glacier where you can see the melted ice trickling down into the valley to become the Rhone River.

I arrived in Zermatt, the Matterhorn town, at midnight and went directly to the hotel without seeing The Mountain. Zermatt offers a peculiar mixture of a fashionable tourist resort with palatial hotels, and the original unsophisticated mountain village with ramshackle barns on the main street from which the goats are driven to pasture (through the center of town) every morning.

I was aroused by their bells the morning after my arrival and went to the balcony to see what this jingling was all about. As I looked out I stared the Matterhorn directly in the face. I hadn't thought of it just this moment and the surprise was overwhelming. There is no mountain on earth like the Matterhorn. Its celebrated pyramid towered over the picturesque town with its picture-book church steeple. The white edges of the snow-covered mountain were set off sharply against the deep blue sky. I could understand instantly the sphinx-like fascination that peak had for the early mountaineers. It has it still for me.

A puffing cogwheel train took me with a party of international tourists from Zermatt up to the Gornergrat from which one has a panoramic view of the Matterhorn and its surrounding giants. I shall not try to describe my feelings as I faced the spectacle from the Gornergrat.

There are people who see the Mona Lisa, listen to Bach, look at Michelangelo's David and still feel no more than respect. Up at the Gornergrat I found it hard to imagine that anybody, young or old, man or woman, American or Chinese, would not be stirred. Surely there cannot be many sights in the world that match it. This had been the way I felt when I first came upon the Grand Canyon; and like this, I suppose, one feels at first seeing the Himalayas from the south.

The physical setting is this: You stand on top of a high mountain – 10,300 feet (3,130 meters) – on a platform which affords an unobstructed view all around. You are surrounded by a wreath of more than 20 *Viertausender*, mountains higher than 4,000 meters (13,000 feet) . Every one of them has, like a symbol of its majesty, an ermine train, a glacier that flows down in a powerful yet graceful sweep. Many of the glaciers come together at the base of two or three of these mountains, forming medial moraines between them. The mountains carry names glittering in the history of mountaineering. Assembled here in a ring around you is Monte Rosa, the highest of all, 15,300 feet, half Swiss and half Italian; the mighty Lyskamm, 15,000 feet, the regal Breithorn, 13,800 feet, and many more. The Matterhorn, 14,870 feet, is not the highest, but it is by all odds the most arresting, the *primus inter pares* in this illustrious company. It presents to the eye a main pyramid on which a small second pyramid, with a slightly tilted peak, seems superimposed; and it is this little extra twist that to me is the most telling characteristic of this peak.

As I hiked down during the afternoon, not taking the cogwheel train back to Zermatt, the Matterhorn variously seemed to me like a sphinx, a rearing giant seal balancing an invisible ball on its nose, or a watchdog. The last impression was especially strong, for the mountain seems to watch you all along the way as you descend; it peeks over the tops of the trees as you enter a forest, and it peers between the clouds when evening overtakes you. Sometimes the watchdog will growl when the storm blows the snow away from its nose in long horizontal streaks.

It was late when I got back to Zermatt. I had seen the Matterhorn, 25 years after I had been diverted by that hitchhiked ride to the Dolomites.

If Austria has the loveliest part of the Alps, and Switzerland the most dramatic, France has the highest. It is only a short ride from Zermatt to Chamonix. And what the Gornergrat is to Zermatt, Le Brevent is to Chamonix. A daring two-section suspended cable car lifts you from the town to the dizzy heights of a mountainous viewing platform. The first section goes up from Chamonix along the side of that mountain to one of its peaks. From there, a second section will take you from this peak to a neighboring one, called Le Brevent, from which you get a magnificent view of Mont Blanc. In this peak-to-peak trip the cables are hanging free in the air, like a tightrope, and you sail along 300 feet above the highest crag beneath you.

This, then, was Mont Blanc, Zeus of the Alps, 15,800 feet high (4,800 meters), higher than any other mountain in Europe. When I saw the gentle pure-white dome I realized why it was called the White Mountain. Unlike the Matterhorn, Mount Blanc does not stand by itself, but is part of a massif which it dominates. If the Matterhorn is a king among princes, Mont Blanc is a chairman in a directors' meeting. Grotesque needlelike crags form the neighboring spires: L'Aiguille du Midi, L'Aiguille du Plan, L'Aiguille Verte. Angry banners of fog and clouds whipped the tops. Like a huge white gnarled index finger squeezed into a narrow vertical furrow between dark green forests, the Mont Blanc glacier reached deep into the valley where were clearly to be seen the tiny dots of Chamonix houses.

With my eyes I followed the glacier back up again from where it came, to the top of venerable Mont Blanc. This was the end of my trail. If the Alps had started with Schubert in the Vienna Woods, here they ended with Beethoven. A dream only a few weeks ago, they had become reality, a real chain of mountains rather than a memory. These mountains were no longer a second world of the past, but had become a living experience, part of a unified world of the present.

The rest of the trip was long in miles, short in time. A few days in Basel, Geneva, and Paris, a brief stopover in New York. A week after I said good-bye to the Alps I said hello to the Sierra as I flew over it.

I am back again in California with the family, and the *Lederhosen* are again in that trunk in the basement.

(*Sierra Club Bulletin*, San Francisco, June 1954)

Der Vater der Österreichischen Verfassung

In den Supermarkets von Berkeley kann man häufig einen kleinen freundlichen Mann mit einem hier recht ungewöhnlichen dunkelblauen Baskenkäppchen sehen, der mit Kennerblick sowohl die einladenden Aufschriften der Konservenbüchsen wie die Kurven der Verkäuferinnen studiert. Niemand würde in dem jugendlich aussehenden, bescheidenen Mann einen Menschen vermuten, der eben seinen 75. Geburtstag gefeiert hat, oder einen, der "der führende Rechtsgelehrte unseres Zeitalters" genannt wurde. So hat Roscoe Pound, Amerikas grösster Rechtsphilosoph, Hans Kelsen bezeichnet, den Schöpfer der österreichischen Bundesverfassung, Architekten seiner Weltruf geniessenden Rechtslehre, Autor von mehr als 40, in alle Kultursprachen übersetzten wissenschaftlichen Werken, Ehrendoktor, Mitglied der hervorragendsten wissenschaftlichen Akademien (einschliesslich der von Galilei gegründeten *Academia Nazionale dei Lincei* in Rom), und trotz allem ein erstaunlich einfacher, zugänglicher, warmherziger Mensch.

Kelsens Rechtslehre, wie die Lehren Freuds und Einsteins, hat Anhänger und Gegner gefunden, aber keine juristische Fakultät der Welt kann sie ignorieren. Zu seinem 75. Geburtstag bekam Kelsen aus aller Welt Glückwünsche von Regierungschefs und Universitäten , die ihn als Begründer der österreichischen Rechtsschule und Schöpfer der österreichischen Bundesverfassung von 1920 begrüssten.

Er hat es weit gebracht, der Sohn eines ungebildeten Juden, der als Laufbursche in einer Meerschaumpfeifenfabrik in Wien angefangen hatte, wohin er als Vierzehnjähriger aus Brody gekommen war.

Kelsens grösste Leistung ist die Begründung einer in der Welt als "österreichisch" bezeichneten Schule der Rechtswissenschaft, die *Reine Rechtslehre*, die die Rechtswissenschaft streng von Ethik und Soziologie scheidet. Sie ist, wie alles Fundamentale, von trügerischer Einfachheit, das Einmaleins der Rechtswissenschaft.

Ein Student, der zum erstenmal Kelsen vortragen hörte, sagte erstaunt: "Er hat gesagt, dass zwei mal zwei vier ist." Ein Student in einem höheren Jahrgang antwortete: "Allerdings. Nur wissen das leider die wenigsten ."

110

Der für den Laien faszinierendste Teil in Kelsens Leben ist die Geschichte seiner Verfassungsschöpfung, die gleichzeitig ein Teil von Österreichs Nationalgeschichte aus der dramatischen Zeit des Zusammenbruchs der Monarchie ist. Während des ersten Weltkrieges war Kelsen (damals Privatdozent für Staatsrecht an der Wiener Universität) Auditor in der Justizabteilung des Kriegsministeriums. Eines Tages hörte er von einer neuen, vom Armee-Oberkommando herausgegebenen militärrechtlichen Zeitschrift, die Beiträge suchte. Damals war viel von Verfassungsänderungen die Rede, die nach dem Krieg durchgeführt werden sollten, besonders auch die von den Ungarn geforderte Trennung der österreichisch-ungarischen Armee in zwei nationale Armeen. Kelsen schickte einen Artikel über eine solche Trennung, die ohne Änderung der damaligen Verfassung nicht möglich war, an das Magazin und kümmerte sich weiter nicht mehr darum.

Einige Zeit später erschien sein Vorgesetzter, der Generalauditor, in Kelsens Büro. "Herr Oberleutnant," sagte er ernst zu dem aus allen Wolken gefallenen Kelsen, "Sie sind von Seiner Exzellenz, dem Herrn Kriegsminister, zum Rapport befohlen worden. Was haben Sie nur angestellt?"

Der Chef der Chefs, Generaloberst Rudolf Freiherr von Stöger-Steiner, empfing den kleinen Oberleutnant mit den Worten: "Wie können Sie ohne meine Bewilligung Artikel über militärrechtliche Fragen fürs Oberkommando schreiben?" sagte er. "Sie sind hier im Kriegsministerium!"

Kelsen begriff nun. Die Armeereform war eine hochwichtige Angelegenheit, an der der Kaiser selbst interessiert war, denn er hatte bei seinem Thronantritt unter ungarischem Druck Versprechungen bezüglich einer Trennung machen müssen. Der Minister, der in dieser Sache Kaiser Karl bisher beraten hatte, hatte keine Lust, das rivalisierende Armee-Oberkommando seine Nase in diese Sache stecken zu lassen, die er als rechtmässige Domäne des Kriegsministeriums ansah.

Kelsen sah, dass er einen Protokollfehler gemacht hatte, aber er sah auch seine Chance. Er war ein Spezialist in dieser Sache und er hatte die Aufmerksamkeit des Ministers auf sich gelenkt. Der Artikel selbst war äusserst interessant, aber Kelsen, der ihn aus einer grösseren Arbeit herausgeschnitten hatte, hatte bei weitem mehr zu sagen, als darin stand. Er erklärte sein Bedauern über seinen Fehler und sprach weiter über die Armeereform. Er würde sich glücklich schätzen, dem Herrn Minister weiter seine Dienste in dieser Sache zur Verfügung zu stellen. . .

Die Aussprache dauerte länger als vorausgesehen. Sie endete mit einem Befehl des Ministers an seinen Adjutanten Fürst

Starhemberg, dem Vater des nachmaligen Heimwehrlers, dem Herrn Oberleutnant ein Büro direkt neben den Amtsräumen des Ministers anzuweisen. Kurz darauf sass der eben noch unbekannte Beamte, an der Seite des Ministers, dem Kaiser gegenüber und referierte über die Armeetrennung.

Während der zweiten Hälfte des Krieges arbeitete Kelsen als Rechtsberater Stöger-Steiners an verfassungsrechtlichen Fragen. Im Zuge seiner Studien hatte er auch mit den kommenden Männern der Republik zu tun, unter andern mit Karl Renner, dem späteren Staatskanzler der ôsterreichischen Regierung.

Kelsen war es, der in den letzten Tagen der Monarchie einen verfassungsrechtlichen Plan entwarf, der die Ungarn, Tschechen, und die anderen Minoritäten doch noch, wenn auch in einem loseren Staatengefüge, zusammenhalten sollte. Der Minister trug den Plan zum Kaiser und dieser akzeptierte ihn. Kelsen hatte vorgeschlagen, dass eine Kommission einen solchen Bund vorbereiten sollte und nannte als Chef den Rechtsprofessor Heinrich Lammasch. Der Plan scheiterte am Widerstand der Tschechen. Lammasch wurde kurz nachher zum letzten Ministerpräsidenten Österreich-Ungarns ernannt und verlangte bei der Kabinettsbildung die Einbeziehung eines politisch unbekannten Theologen als Sozialminister – Ignaz Seipel, den späteren Staatskanzler.

An einem der letzten Oktobertage 1918 erhielt Kelsen um Mitternacht einen Telephonanruf, zum Kriegsminister zu kommen. Dieser empfing ihn im Schlafrock und überreichte ihm ein Telegramm, das eben von Präsident Wilson gekommen war. Es war die Antwort auf den Vorschlag Österreich-Ungarns, der Kaiser würde den Nationalitäten Autonomie gewähren, **falls** die Vereinigten Staaten auf dieser Basis Frieden schlössen Wilson lehnte den Vorschlag ab: man müsse die Durchführung der Autonomie den Nationen selbst überlassen, sie dürfe nicht von Österreich "gewährt" werden.

Als Kelsen das Telegramm gelesen hatte, war seine Mission erfüllt. Aber der Minister ersuchte ihn noch etwas zu bleiben und von der Privatwohnung hinüber in die Amtswohnung zu gehen, die im selben Gebäude war. Auf dem Weg zum Büro kamen sie durch einen enormen, reich dekorierten Empfangssalon.

"Was für eine Ironie," bemerkte der Minister. "Diese Prunkräume, in so ernsten Zeiten."

"Besonders wenn man weiss," setzte Kelsen unerbittlich fort, "dass Sie, Exzellenz, der letzte Kriegsminister der österreichisch-ungarischen Monarchie sind."

Er hatte ausgesprochen, was der Minister nicht zu denken gewagt hatte.

"Sie sind ja wahnsinnig", sagte er. "Die Monarchie hat Jahrhunderte bestanden. . ."

Kelsen deutete bloss stumm auf das Telegramm in seiner Hand.

Am 11. November dankte Kaiser Karl ab. Die Abdankungsurkunde war die einzigc Leistung des im ganzen 15 Tage amtierenden Lammasch-kabinetts gewesen und Ignaz Seipel hatte den Text formuliert.

Kelsen wurde sofort von Renner mit der Ausarbeitung einer neuen republikanischen Staatsverfassung beauftragt. Er machte mehrere Entwürfe. Einer davon wurde fast unverändert von der konstituierenden Nationalversammlung angenommen und trat 1920 in Kraft. Sie erfuhr einige Novellen und wurde im Jahre 1933 durch die faschistische Ender-Verfassung und schliesslich 1938 durch die Nazigesetze abgelöst. Aber die zweite Republik griff im Jahre 1945 wieder auf die alte Verfassung zurück, ein glänzender Beweis für die Wertschätzung, deren sich Kelsens Werk erfreute. Österrcich lebt heute wieder unter dem Grundgesetz, das Hans Kelsen, einer seiner grossen Söhne, geschaffen hat.

(*Aufbau*, New York, February 1, 1957)

Atomic Birthday Party

To nine-year-old Tony Knight, Nobel prize winner Glenn Seaborg was Superman, Roy Rogers, and Davy Crockett all wrapped in one. From his bedroom in Berkeley, Tony could see the "Hill," containing the atom-smashing bevatron and Seaborg's radiation lab, but access to all this was impossible because of the uranium curtain of security regulations.

Tony's chance came one morning when his mother read a newspaper article quoting Seaborg as having expressed concern about the critical shortage of American scientists. "Enthusiasm for science," the chemist had said, "must he kindled in the very young."

With a smile in her eye, Tony's mother picked up the phone and called Dr. Seaborg. "I just read what you said about young scientists," she told him. "We have one right here at home. He's blown up our basement twice. His greatest wish is to see your lab. He'll be 10 next week, wouldn't that be a chance to kindle his enthusiasm?"

Seaborg agreed without hesitation. "Bring him up on his birthday and let him bring a couple of friends along. We'll make it a party."

For a week Tony Knight was the happiest and most important fourth-grader in his school. Even the mighty sixth-graders wooed him for the chance to be taken 'up to the Hill.'

But Tony was loyal to his friends. He picked Peter, the co-blaster of the basement and, interpreting Seaborg's "couple of friends" generously, also Larry, his butterfly-chasing buddy, and Jeffery, the sharer of a junior-set microscope. The principal gave the boys the day off. "No school on Tony's birthday for you four," he said. "Just like Washington's birthday."

When 'the day' arrived, Mrs. Knight drove the boys up the Hill. Their first thrill came when the policeman at the gate checked the list of expected visitors and stuck a permit under their windshield wiper. The boys, noses flattened against the car windows, pointed out the various buildings as they popped into view.

"The old cyclotron," Tony said. "The first atom splitter. It's out-of-date."

"They have one that's a million times bigger," Peter volunteered. "And it has a magnet so strong it pulls the bobby pins out of ladies' hair when they go by. A girl who works here told me."

"And it wrecks watches. Mommy, better leave yours in the car."

Seaborg sat by a wall-filling chart that gave the room its character. The room was airy, sunny, with a large view over the San Francisco Bay. The scientist was a towering man, slightly stooped, with dark hair and deep-set eyes which looked as though they had been especially made for searching into the unknown.

He extended a hand. "Happy birthday, Tony. Glad you came." He shook hands with the other boys, then introduced his associate. "This is Dr. Choppin who will help me show you around."

"What did *he* discover?" Peter wanted to know.

"One of the new elements," said Seaborg. "Mendelevium."

"Let's see it," demanded Tony.

Choppin, regretfully, explained that it couldn't he done. A single gram would cost trillions of dollars and would vanish in three hours.

"Shucks," said Tony, "what good is it then?"

"You got a little brother?" Seaborg asked. Tony nodded, surprised.

"Remember when he was born? What good was he then ?"

Tony's expression indicated that he had doubts about that himself.

"Well," Seaborg went on, "he might become a great scientist. You never know what will become of babies – or discoveries."

The boys mulled that one over. Then Peter asked, "Where is your Nobel prize ? "

"Sorry, boys. Can't show you that either. It's in the bank."

"Well," Tony challenged. "What *can* you show us?"

Seaborg and Choppin led the boys to the chemistry lab. A sign on the door announced that only holders of Pass Q were allowed inside.

"What does this sign mean?" Peter inquired.

"It means that only very special people may enter," said Seaborg without the trace of a smile. He opened the door, slid open a glass-paneled cabinet, and took out a jar, much as a mother would reach for the cookie jar in the kitchen. This jar, however, held a two-inch-long sealed glass vial, containing a dark-gray square of thin metal, about a half inch across.

"Plutonium. Enough to blow up every person in Berkeley. "

Four pairs of widening eyes attested that Seaborg had been restored as Superman plus. He replaced the vial in the cabinet.

"Isn't that sort of d-d-dangerous?" asked Jeffery.

"Not in the vial," Seaborg assured him. "But we do have to

handle dangerous materials, of course, and we must be careful of those that give off poisonous fumes. See those upside-down funnels over our experiment tables? They suck radioactive air from the room. Watch."

He picked up a piece of tissue paper and let it flutter in the airstream. He motioned to Tony. "Pass me that brick, will you?" Eagerly Tony grabbed for the gray brick on a table but found he couldn't lift it.

"Magnetized or something?" Larry asked.

"No, just heavy. It's pure lead. Some elements are heavier than that. Try lifting these two cubes. '

Tony grinned as he managed to hold up a one-inch gray cube of uranium. Then he weighed the silvery one in his palm: beryllium.

"Jeepers ! It's so light it almost flies away. Try this." He passed the cubes to his friends who all acknowledged that they were indeed – jeepers! – very different in weight.

"What makes uranium so heavy?" asked Larry.

"More protons and neutrons in the nucleus. "An atom of beryllium has nine protons and neutrons together, an atom of uranium has 238."

You could almost hear the wheels going around in the boys' heads. "But . . . an atom is so small you can't even see it in a microscope," Jeffery said. "It can't make much difference what it weighs."

"Oh, but it does. Most of the atom is empty space, but the tiny bit of matter in the center, the nucleus, is unbelievably heavy. If you could pile up the nuclei from a billion uranium atoms, they still wouldn't cover a pin head but would weigh as much as 8,000 battleships."

"Aren't we all made of atoms ? " asked Tony.

"Right."

"Then – are we mostly empty spaces ?"

"Right again. If you could take away all the empty space from the atoms in your body, what's left would be no bigger than a spot of dust."

"How does all this happen: big things get tiny, and tiny things get big? What makes them change?"

Seaborg raised his palms and shrugged his shoulders.

"Don't you know ? " Tony's eyes took in the shelves reaching to the ceiling. "Can't you find out, with all these books around ?"

Seaborg tousled the boy's reddish hair, saying nothing. Choppin gave each boy a test tube and let them fill the tubes with water, adding a few drops of iron chloride and hydroxide. "Now shake." Spectacular red grains developed from nowhere: iron hydroxide. Here was the miracle of chemistry in a nut shell, or rather in a test tube. The boys held on to the tubes for the rest of the trip and were later allowed to take them home.

Jeffery sniffed at his tube. "Is that radioactive ?"

"Oh. no. Radioactive material we handle in The Cave."

The word "cave" alone made the boys practically trip over each other as they pushed behind the scientists in entering another room. Here was a large lead box in which radioactive chemicals could be grasped with steel claws operated from the outside. A glass window, six inches thick, allowed the boys to watch as Seaborg used the claws to pour a radioactive liquid from a test tube into a beaker.

"Oh, boy," whispered Larry. "Like one of those machines in which you drop a penny and try to make a little crane inside pick up prizes buried in candy beans. I bet I could work this one."

"Go ahead," said Seaborg.

Before long the boys were working the claws, trying to catch each other's steel fingers. Choppin caught Mrs. Knight's apprehensive glance.

"Don't worry," he assured her. "We prepared everything so they can't get hurt."

Back in Seaborg's office Tony spotted a small cylinder of clear plastic, with fine vein-like cracks in it like the roots of a dainty plant.

"That's what happens when an electron hits plastic," Seaborg said. "Isn't it beautiful ? "

"Is that what they are doing in the bevatron?"

"Something like it. Would you like to see it?"

They stepped outside. The bluish roof of the huge circular bevatron gleamed in the sunshine. The inside was like a circus arena into which the boys could peer through glass windows. A bewildering maze of gadgets surrounded a gigantic ring-shaped magnet in the center.

"Boy! What a big thing to smash tiny atoms," murmured Tony.

"Where are the bombs?" Larry wanted to know.

"We don't make bombs here. We just try to find out what the atom is and what it can do, such as running a power house or driving ships."

"Or shooting space ships to the moon ?"

"Perhaps, some time."

"Gee, and I thought atoms were just for making bombs!"

"Well, the energy locked up in the atom can be used for all the things I've said. Just as you can use the energy that's locked in gasoline for all sorts of things. If you throw a burning match into a gasoline tank, it'll blow up. Use the same gasoline in an engine, and it'll drive a car."

"And how does the bevatron work ?"

"Look at this model here. I use it on my TV program."

"You have your own TV program ?" Larry asked, eagerly.

Tony nudged him in desperation. "Of course . . . 'Know Your Atom' on KQED."

"The more people know about the atom the better for all of us," Seaborg said. "This model shows the principle of the bevatron. The electron is driven around this magnetic field, in a circle. Every time it whirls by here . . . and here . . . it gets a kick, like a ball hit by a bat, until it finally travels almost as fast as light."

"Wow! Why do you want it to zoom around like that?"

"By then that little electron has as much power as a rocket. So when it smashes the atoms in the target, it releases energy."

Jeffery asked, "Are we radio-active?"

"We'll see about that," Seaborg promised. He led the boys to what looked like a cross between a coke machine and a clock.

"You stick your hand in here," Seaborg said, pointing at an opening. "If you picked up radioactivity, this needle will show it."

The boys had fun sticking in their hands, watching the needle.

"You're all right," Seaborg said, leading the way back to his office.

Here Choppin gave each boy a folder he had prepared just for them. In it were pamphlets explaining nuclear research, some simple drawings, and a chart of the elements, from the lightest to the heaviest, with their chemical symbols, weight, date of discovery, and name of the discoverer.

"Where is the one you found?" asked Peter.

"Oh, we've discovered several, and not all are on the chart ."

"You find 'em quicker than they print charts, huh ? Which ones are missing?"

Seaborg took out a fountain pen and filled in the missing elements. "Berkeleyum goes here, Californium here, and here Einsteinium; then come Fermium, and our latest, Mendelevium."

He autographed the charts, wrote some extra birthday wishes on Tony's, and shook hands with the boys.

"Good-bye," said Tony. "I'll be back."

"I guess you will." Seaborg rested his hand on Tony's shoulder. "Especially if you will keep on asking those questions. Anyone can teach people to give answers. But cooking up questions, that's a gift."

Tony's face glowed. A new element had been added. Seaborg was not only Tony's Superman, Roy Rogers, and Davy Crockett, but a real-life human who had given him a rare birthday present.

(*West Magazine*, Las Vegas, November, 1957)

Fritzi

My visits to the Alps mostly started in the Vienna Woods. These woodlands have been overadvertised, sugarized, and strausswaltzed, and inevitably fall short of expectations for visitors. Not for our son Anthony, then ten, who had his day in one of the frillier episodes of my Alpine wanderings.

Anthony was impressed by the green, grassy expanse spread before him from one of the hills. "Wall-to-wall meadow," he said. But later his attention was arrested by something else: he spotted a snake, three feet long. When he grabbed it, it whipped around and bit him. Anthony screamed, not from pain but because he had let go. "Grab him, Daddy, quickly, before he escapes."

If I had only known what I was getting myself into when, induced by the urgency of his request, I chased the snake. I managed to pin it down in the middle, but its head shot out like a jet plane, and it bit me too. I seized it behind the head, while the rest wound itself around my arm. Anthony heaved a sigh of relief. The snake was ours.

Two small drops of blood seeped from his finger and mine. We did not know what kind of snake we had caught. We decided to take it to the Hameau inn, hoping that someone there would identify it. "If it's poisonous," Anthony said, "at least we'll know what we died of."

The Hameau inn was full of snake experts, but they disagreed with each other. Still, they all said that the snake was not poisonous. As one of them summed up: Rattlesnakes do not exist in the Alps, and if it were a Kreuzotter (the only poisonous Alpine snake), I would not have been so foolish as to have myself bitten without rushing to see a doctor.

On our way to the trolley that was to take us back to the city I tried to persuade Anthony to let the snake go; our hostess, Frau Minna Donner, would not appreciate it.

Have you ever tried to persuade a ten-year-old to give up a pet snake? Exactly.

Did Frau Donner scream when she opened the door and saw the snake? She has two boys herself and cut short Anthony's prepared speech. "There's a shoebox in the bathroom," she said with a wry smile.

Days went by, and weeks. Anthony found a picture of Fritzi in the encyclopedia: it was a harmless aesculap, symbol of the peaceful medical profession. Our wounds had healed, Fritzi had eaten a mouse Anthony had purchased in a pet store, and now was satisfied for an indefinite period. Fritzi, by now, lived in a luxurious terrarium, unconcerned with the future.

But Anthony pondered the future and our pending return to the distant shores of America. Waiting for a psychologically felicitous moment, he aired the question of the snake's immigration to the United States.

"You're crazy, Tony," I said with conviction. "There are undoubtedly a dozen regulations against this – a veterinarian's certificate, quarantine, inoculation, what do I know. We won't even discuss it. The snake, of course, stays here."

Why "of course"? Couldn't I inquire at the Customs Department of the U.S. Consulate in Vienna?

"Sorry," said the Customs man, "we don't know about snakes. If you really want to pursue this, you'd have to get in touch with the Consulate at Frankfurt am Main." I gritted my teeth and wrote to Frankfurt.

The answer came promptly, with Yankee efficiency: "Sir, concerning your inquiry we wish to inform you that the importation of a live snake is not against any federal law, provided you can produce a certificate of the U.S. Consulate in Vienna confirming that the export of the reptile does not violate Austrian law.

"So far so good," said Anthony. "Now the ceritificate."

Shortly after, I received a letter on official stationery ("The Foreign Office of the United States of America") informing us that, after consultation with the Office of the Veterinary of the City of Vienna, it had been determined: no objection to the export of aesculaps; this letter to be presented to the customs official at the port of arrival in the United States.

Armed with the letter and with a wooden box made for the occasion with air holes, we were ready for landing at New York airport . Anthony had given fresh water to Fritzi at short stops in Shannon and Gander and had determined that she was not airsick and was evidently content curled up among her leaves.

But just before landing, Anthony felt uneasy. Would the customs people pay any attention to the certificate? Perhaps there were some local regulations after all – you cannot carry even an apple over the California border, for example. Did the officials in Vienna know everything? He took his Alpine import from the box and slipped the snake inside his shirt. But Fritzi, instead of obligingly straightening out, rolled herself into a ball that clearly protruded above Anthony's belt; a customs man would have to be blind not to see it.

The plane rolled to a halt, and we had no more time. I grabbed Fritzi, stuffed him into a plastic bag with a pull string, which previously had housed my shaving cream, and stuffed the bag plus contents in the pocket of my Alpine loden coat.

Anybody who has gone through the New York customs in summer knows how long it takes and how chokingly hot it is. I was sorry for Fritzi, and afraid she would suffocate. Charitably I slipped my hand in my pocket and loosened the string . . .

The customs man noticed nothing. The ordeal over, I slumped down on a suitcase ten feet away, breathing relief. It was at this moment that, like Venus from the waves, Fritzi rose from my coat collar, standing up vertically as if she wanted to give the customs man an especially good view of herself.

Laocoon never wrestled as fiercely with his snakes as I did when I grabbed the refugee, pulled her out and pushed her into a hurriedly unzipped suitcase.

Customs men in New York are busy people. No one had observed the incident. Fritzi and we arrived safely in California. I had done my fatherly duty and brought home our guest from the Vienna Woods. I did not wish to break a boy's heart.

Immediately after arrival at home, Anthony disappeared next door to see his pal Victor. When he returned, five minutes later, he sported a new wrist watch. "Where did this come from?" I asked.

"From Victor. Swapped it for Fritzi. It has a red dial."

(*Return to the Alps*, San Francisco: Friends of the Earth, 1970)

A Master Cobbler

The story of Joe Wurnitsch begins with a big crimson boot, cut out of steel like a guild sign of the Alpine countries, and fastened above the door of a cobbler's shop at Rose and Grove in Berkeley. On a hunch, I walked into the shop. A woman customer was talking with a gaunt, white-haired man who critically looked at one of her shoes in his hand.

"Wouldn't last, if I repaired it the way you want it," he said.

"But I want it that way," she said. "It's my shoe."

"Then do it yerself." He gave her the shoe and, without another look, sat at his bench and resumed work on another shoe.

The woman left, shaking her head, and I started a conversation with Joe, one-way for a while. He was a Tirolean from a remote valley at the foot of the Grossglockner. He was 70, and had come to this country at 16. At first he had worked for a chain shoe-repair store. But not for long. "My boss always said to me not to fuss so much, and to polish and push."

"What's polish and push?"

"Means to shine up the shoe quick after the work is done, and push it on the shelf for the customer to pick up Then do the next job in a hurry. No one cared whether the shoe would hold together another week."

Joe had learned his craft in the mountains where you need shoes that will hold together. He did careful work, and that took too long for his employer. After three days of polish and push he'd had it. When his boss hurried him again, he took off his green apron – Joe showed, as we talked, how he had lifted the strap over his head – and hung it on the hook.

"I got my own hole in the wall and been here ever since."

He was a free man, a master craftsman. The trickiest jobs interested him most. He knew the human foot as any orthopedist, and merely needed to look at a shoe to tell where it hurt and how to fix it. In his independence and appearance he was like the minnesinger Hans Sachs."Have you been back to your village in those 54 years?" I asked him.

"No," Joe said, leaning against the cash register which would be the envy of the Smithsonian Institution.

"Any relatives there?"

"A brother in Hinterlingen. He doesn't write to me."

"Do you write to him?"

"No. We had a quarrel."

A quarrel (something about an inheritance) half a century old. I thought I detected a trace of regret in his voice but I couldn't tell. I asked him if I should visit his brother next time I got to the Alps.

"Hinterlingen is out of the way. In the Lenzinger valley."

On my next trip I could see what Joe had meant. The Lenzinger valley, a dead end, was a forgotten pocket of the Alpine world. The mountain road, just wide enough for a minicar, followed a lustily tumbling brook between narrow mountain walls. There were few villages and scarcely any people on the road. Finally I reached a road sign: HINTERLINGEN.

I stopped to take a picture . Three old bearded men happened by and posed beside the sign, providing "human interest." I asked them if they knew a man by the name of Wurnitsch.

"Yup. Up the road, the wooden farmhouse on the right."

I walked on. There was a stone wall on the right; I walked through an opening in it; behind it were a farmyard and a Tyrolean-style gabled house. I knocked on a rough wooden door and a man opened it a crack. He wore coarse but good peasant clothing, and was the unmistakable younger edition of Joe Wurnitsch, cobbler in Berkeley.

"What do you want?" he said without greeting.

"I'm a friend of your brother. I bring you greetings from him."

He stayed behind the crack. "Brother? I have no brother."

"You have a brother Josef in America. I live in the same town, and he asked me to look you up."

"America? Anybody could say that." The crack narrowed.

"But I am! I'll show you some papers if you don't believe me, and tell you things about your brother no one else would know."

He asked me what I really wanted and I said I wanted the two brothers, half a world and half a century apart, to write to each other again. And to take a picture of him to show to Joe.

It was the wrong thing to say. "A picture, eh? I know that trick. There was a fellow here five years ago, taking pictures of everybody. Later he came back with the pictures and wanted money for them! "

"No, damn it! I want no money. They're for free."

The crack widened. "They better be. And it won't do you any good if they aren't. I won't buy any."

I did not gain the man's complete confidence, but he softened up enough to come outside and allow me to sit beside him on the wooden bench before the door. He never asked me in, but I had a chance to explain and to take a picture. He remained cautious as I tried to make my point. Wasn't it a shame to have a brother in America and remain completely cut off? Did he know that his brother had been married for 50 years, had a daughter? Would he write to his brother now and let bygones be bygones?

No, he wouldn't.

Would he answer, if his brother were to write to him?

He stared into the air. I said good-bye, and he did not shake hands, as would have been customary. But he saw me down the steps. Did he have a message for Joe?

"Tell him I'm all right."

"That's almost a letter, " I said. "I'll tell him. And I'll send you a picture, then you'll believe me."

"I believe you. But don't charge me for it."

A month later, the cobbler in Berkeley passed his hand over his eyes to hide his emotions as he looked at my photos. So this was his valley. This was the sign with the name of the village. And this was his brother! Did he, by any chance, happen to know any of these bearded three men?

"This one," he said, "is my brother-in-law. And this one is my other brother-in-law. And this one is my cousin."

Was he kidding? How could he tell? He had not seen them in 54 years. They must have been youngsters then.

"I can tell," he just said. "I recognize 'em." He took the photographs, the picture postcards, the map I had brought home, and some pressed leaves from a tree in his brother's farmyard, and stowed them all away under the counter. He gave me a look that was reward enough for a much greater effort than making a detour into the out-of-the-way valley.

The next day he wrote a postcard to his brother.

If you need a job that calls for a master cobbler, see him at Rose and Grove, where the crimson boot hangs out. If you can win his favor he will do anything for you.

(*Return to the Alps*, San Francisco: Friends of the Earth, 1970)

Raising Ostriches in California

During the winter of 1882, Billie Frantz, a successful chicken farmer near Anaheim, California, received a strange visitor.

"I'm proposing to you the most profitable poultry venture in the world," he said. "Raising ostriches for their plumes."

Frantz was unimpressed. "I'm doing fine with my chickens."

"One ostrich," said the stranger," produces $500 worth of feathers. Your farm is perfect for ostriches – sand, sun, and just about as far north of the equator as the best ostrich ranches in Africa are south."

Frantz discovered that ostrich feathers were part of the English court dress and ladies all over the world were willing to pay $10 to $15 apiece. South Africa was the only place where ostriches were raised for their feathers. Half the crop went to American ladies and brought the grower five million dollars a year. The birds had modest needs, thriving on a diet of grass, grain, weeds, broken bones, and gravel. Each hen laid 50 to 60 eggs annually, and they outlived chickens by some 100 years.

Frantz went to San Francisco, where the importer was exhibiting his flock until he could find a suitable ranch. The birds were nine feet tall balancing tiny bald flat heads on the end of long, plush-covered necks attached to bodies of beautiful white, black, or drab feathers. The birds stalked with jerky, spasmodic movements as if bowing in welcome. Occasionally, they broke into a comical waltzlike trot. Often, without apparent reason, they angrily inflated their necks in cobralike fashion, then let out the air in violent bellows.

Frantz decided to start what soon became known as "the craziest chicken ranch in California." He raised $30,000, founded the California Ostrich Company, and remodeled his place to accommodate poultry weighing 300 pounds apiece.

Fencing was important. With a single kick an ostrich could break most ordinary fence posts and escape. Since the big birds could easily outrun a horse, catching them was a problem. Barbed wire fences were not advisable since ostriches were extremely stupid and frequently cut their throats on barbs. Frantz made a nine-foot-high fence of inch-thick, 12-inch-wide redwood boards and hoped for the best.

Next, he sold all his fine fox hounds. Dogs made ostriches

nervous, and they might panic and kick each other to death. Nothing must be done to excite the birds, for their legs were as brittle as porcelain, and once they broke a leg they had to be killed. While ostriches could reach an age of more than 100 years, few did because they killed themselves long before by their own stupidity.

This was only a taste of the troubles to come.

When the 22 ostriches arrived, they were nervous. Their 23,000-mile trip from South Africa, via Buenos Aires and New York, and their exhibition in San Francisco had worsened their tempers. Visitors came to see the "crazy farm" by the hundreds, trampled crops, pulled down fences, and plagued the birds, which either fled in fright or ferociously attacked. As Frantz soon found out, the birds' taste was far more extravagant than claimed. During the first week they snatched and swallowed six earrings, a dozen pins, and several hatpins (sometimes with hats attached) from terrified tourists. Even a lighted pipe and a rolled-up newspaper proved edible. One fascinated gentleman watched his watch and chain slide like an oyster down a bird's long neck.

Ostriches like things that glitter, and eat jewelry "as a sort of tonic." They use it in their gizzards, with broken bones and gravel, to grind up food. One bird snatched a diamond pin from a gentleman's tie. Frantz held a one-man court-martial. The diamond was worth $600, the ostrich $1,000. The bird was acquitted. Frantz paid up, and the ostrich was allowed to use the diamond as an elegant millstone.

When visitors kept coming, Frantz charged 50 cents for a look through the fence. In spite of large signs that dogs would be shot at sight, people kept bringing them. Frantz posted guards around his grounds, and tourists were shocked to learn that the signs meant what they said. After a dozen dogs were shot and trespassers prosecuted in court, the visitors' enthusiasm waned. Just to be sure, Frantz raised the visitor's fee to $25. Things became quiet, and the ostriches settled down to their business of breeding.

Ten pairs were separated in paddocks. They began to dig nests in the sandy ground. Working with their sharp claws and bills, each set of honeymooners made a hole about three feet long and one foot deep. The first eggs were laid.

This called for celebration. Stockholders were invited to a party. Tiptoeing quietly through the maternity poultry ranch they tried to spy eggs in the nest holes. But the hens were sitting and the cocks were standing guard, erect and serious. When one visitor ventured too close, the cock crouched on the ground, extended his wings outward and forward and drove back the trespasser with a lion-like roar and a swaying motion of his body.

Frantz took his guests to the ranch house for lunch. One egg would feed everybody. Armed with a thistle, Frantz bravely approached a nest. The feathered sentinel challenged him but Frantz coldly thrust the thistle in his face.

"This forces the ostrich to close his eyes," he explained to his guests, "and as soon as he sees nothing he imagines the threat is gone. That is perhaps the source of the fairy tale about his hiding the head in the sand." He returned with an egg, six inches long, creamy white, and pitted all over. It weighed four pounds, and contained as much yolk as 28 chicken eggs. Its shell is used in Africa to carry water, Frantz told his guests.

While waiting for the egg to hard-boil (which took an hour and a half), the group inspected the nests. An ostrich hen lays one egg every two days until her pit is filled, about 15 in all. But if you take the eggs away from her, she will keep on laying up to 30. The guests feasted on their egg, which tasted just like duck egg.

The first California ostrich egg crop was disappointingly small. All 12 hens produced less than 50 eggs. The excitement of immigration to a new country apparently had taken its toll. The hens and cocks took turns sitting and standing guard, the hen putting in 16 hours sitting and eight in guarding, and the cock doing the baby-sitting at night. While the birds were trying to keep away imaginary enemies, they trampled and broke some 20 eggs.

On July 4, 1883, the first American-born domestic ostrich chick poked its flat bill through the shell. It had pink eyes, a swelled neck, rubber legs that didn't support it for days, and a body full of short quills that made it look like a porcupine. To Frantz, it was a lovely sight; he described it poetically as "wild, shy, and active as an antelope fawn." For 24 hours it refused to eat, then settled down to a meal of small gravel and crushed sea shells.

Sixteen chicks hatched. When their soft gray fuzz began to lengthen into little downy sproutings, the time had come to harvest the first crop of feathers from their parents,

The farmhands, who had been roared at, hissed at, chased away, and kicked by furious ostriches when doing nothing more hostile than bringing them their food, refused to go and pluck the nine-footers which they knew could outkick any mule. Anyone who has been kicked by a mule will stay away from its back; anyone kicked by an ostrich will stay away from its front. Ostriches cannot kick back; as long as you get behind the bird and pivot faster, you are safe. If you lie flat on the ground you are protected from a kick even in front because the bird cannot kick anything below three feet (which is probably the reason why they are afraid of dogs). The worst that can happen to you then is that the ostrich will step on you. The plucker has to bring along a supply of women's stockings, put some food for the birds on the ground, and when they stoop to eat, sneak up from behind and pull a stocking over their heads. As soon as they can't see, their courage is gone and they will let you pluck them.

The first clip was poor. Too many feathers had been damaged on the trip and during those confusing first months on the ranch. Even so, the quills brought a profit of $500.

By fall, the hens were ready to lay again. The total egg crop was 305, mostly infertile. By Christmas the adult birds yielded a second crop of feathers, worth $2,500. Other poultry farmers pricked up their ears and went to South Africa to buy ostriches. But the Cape Town government, its monopoly on ostrich feathers threatened, imposed an export duty of $500 per ostrich.

This was good news for Frantz, who started to sell his chicks to prospective ostrich ranchers at $450 a piece. Within a few years there were two dozen ostrich ranches in California. They spread to Arizona and Texas where cattlemen talked about using the swift-footed birds for rounding up cattle and carrying couriers across the wide spaces. Ostrich farmers also dreamed about the time when the ostrich would be the Easter bird as the turkey is for Thanksgiving.

But it never got to that. Profits were not bad, but Frantz's neighbors made more from conventional crops like oranges. While his hens laid eagerly, most eggs remained unfertile; it was small comfort that he could sell them, blown out and cleaned, for three dollars as souvenirs. The ostriches got used to visitors and the public was again invited to see them (without dogs) at 50 cents apiece. One pair of birds became so tame that Frantz used them to pull a little cart. But they continued to kill themselves out of sheer stupidity. Often when in a good mood the birds began to waltz, became dizzy, fell, and broke their legs. Occasionally they flew into rages and kicked each other to death. They refused to sleep under protection but lay down wherever dark overtook them; many caught colds during the rainy season. Sometimes they simply refused to eat and died out of what seemed to be spite.

An unexpected drawback was their strong feeling for monogamy. Many would not take a new mate even after their old one had died. New husbands were not only henpecked but hen-kicked to death. It was little comfort to Frantz that young ostrich meat tasted like beef and made good soup; that the fat could be used for guns, saddles, and boots; and that stuffed ostriches and skeletons fetched good prices from museums. Neither did he derive much comfort from the thought that many of the by now 6,000 ostriches on California and Arizona ranches came from chicks raised by him. Looking around his prospering neighborhood, he quietly planted some acres in oranges.

Then came the day when a dog sneaked into the Frantz ranch and started a stampede. Within minutes the stronglegged birds had kicked a hole in the redwood fence, and Frantz watched helplessly as his entire fortune in poultry took off with the speed of greyhounds, flinging their clumsy legs and twisting their bodies as they raced all over the countryside. Some cowboys gave chase, and succeeded in lassoing half a dozen. Others were found crushed against houses and fences, stuck in wells, or electrocuted by torn wires. The survivors were found slumbering peacefully where they had happened to be at nightfall.

Frantz had 11 birds left, their plumes soiled and broken by the flight. He decided to keep one pair as pets, sold the rest to zoos, and planted orange seedlings. Orange juice became fashionable about the time that ostrich plumes on women's hats ceased to be.

The last two ostriches were allowed to wander around in a small enclosure within the orange grove, a garden of Eden story in reverse. Whether Eve once more persuaded Adam to taste the forbidden fruit never will be known, but one day Frantz found his ostriches dead below a tree with bumps all down their long necks. They had died of an overdose of oranges.

(*The American West*, Tucson, Arizona, 1970)

Bertolt Brecht, as Seen in the East

Entering East Berlin is like a piece of epic theatre written and directed by Bertolt Brecht. It doesn't seem real. It's a scene played by actors who want to make sure they don't behave like officials but like actors playing officials. They are replaying something from another time and another place, maybe Russia in the twenties, or Germany in the thirties, or China in the sixties. The standing in lines, the filling out of forms, the forced exchange of piddling sums of currency, the surrendering of your passport for an interminable wait, all this makes no sense from a Western point of view. But in East Berlin the two opposing "theses"– letting you in and keeping you out – lead to a "higher truth": that the German Democratic Republic has the power to do either. This is your education in dialectical materialism.

This was also Brecht's purpose, as explained to me by those who carry on his dramatic heritage: his widow and executrix of his literary estate, Helene Weigel; the directors and actors at the Brecht theatre. Brecht's plays have been performed in 57 countries, from Ghana to Iceland and from Monaco to China. West Germany has produced more Brecht than East Germany, and the United States more than the Soviet Union. The West considers Brecht one of the most important playwrights of the twentieth century. The East sees him as a pioneer of the twenty-first, a Marxist century in politics and economics, but also in art.   To the East, Brecht is using the theatre to teach, make the social laws visible, and arouse the audience to action. The West considers the Marxist drama mere propaganda. The East sees it as a new type of theatre, replacing the expressionism. Brecht's admirers see him do to the stage what Sergje Eisenstein did to the movies: create a revolutionary drama, to pick up where young Georg Büchner had left off in his *Woyzeck*. Brecht expressed his goals in a poem (1938):

> The regulation of a river,
> the improvement of a fruit tree,
> the education of a person,
> the rebuilding of a state -
> these are examples of a productive critic.
> And they also are
> examples of art.

How does one educate a person and rebuild a state by showing a play? Three of Brecht's disciples, directors handpicked and trained by the master during his last, East Berlin, period – Manfred Wekwerth, Manfred Karge, and Matthias Langhoff – answered my questions by discussing Brecht's *The Mother,* a drama based on Maxim Gorki's novel about the women's part in the October Revolution of 1917, written in 1930 - 1932.

Brecht first directed *The Mother* in Berlin in 1932, in the style of Agitprop, as propaganda of the Communist Party. "The purpose of the play," Brecht said at that time, "was to teach the audience, especially the women, certain forms of political struggle." The performance, at the eve of Hitler's advent to power, was an open agitation to political battle. When Brecht staged the play again, in Berlin 1951, the Hitler nightmare had passed and he presented it no longer as agitation but as a historical play "of an epoch that had become a classic." The German audience, after 12 years of Hitler, didn't know much about the Russian Revolution, and *The Mother* was to teach them historical facts.

In 1952, the German Democratic Republic began a systematic reconstruction of communism, and Brecht again strengthened the Agitprop elements of *The Mother,* adding direct addresses to the audience, and scenes of agitation, political training, and indoctrination. Wekwerth directs the current East Berlin production. Following Brecht's intentions, Wekwerth tries to synthesize the Agitprop and the historical approaches. In East Berlin, having had its own revolutionary history, "we need to show the historical connections between the new revolutionary German history and the Soviet October Revolution, and to mobilize all the means of Agitprop to master the tasks of present-day socialism."

The three Brechtian directors emphasize that Brecht should be judged not only by his plays but by his staging. Wekwerth rejects the Western idea that Brecht is a "classic" who "perfected" himself in his late works. He maintains that Brecht never perfected himself, nor did he want to. He kept his plays open until he produced them, and even afterwards. Such openness to change, Wekwerth insists, allows director and actors to become co-authors with Brecht in every new production. Only in this way can one bring out the "permanent contradictions" in Brecht's method.

Brecht's method, Wekwerth explains, can be worked out in his fragments. In them, plot, characterization, and dialogue can and *must* be manipulated because scenes are put in sequence, duplications and contradictions eliminated. The production of a Brecht fragment shows that his literary output is "a process, in which individual plays attack historical events from many sides, to find a lever through which one can come to grips with them."

Karge and Langhoff had just shaped a full-length play, *The Bakery*, from fragments, and Helene Weigel had approved its production at the Berlin Ensemble, a precondition for any play Brecht himself had not staged. "The play contains not a single word not written by Brecht," she said with obvious satisfaction.

Karge and Langhoff had selected material from 600 loose pages at the archives, about five times the manuscript needed for a full-length play. Available were several complete scenes in various versions, pieces of dialogue, notes, songs, sketched-out situations, drafts of characters, and different versions of story line. Karge: "What we present is *one* possibility offered by the material, a suggestion." Langhoff: "You have to see in the material a product of history, not a piece of work left unfinished. The eminence of the subject matter, the complexity of the problems, the wealth of observations and facts do not permit finality. Such a view enabled us to produce a fragment because it communicates insights about society."

The Bakery, written in 1929-30 at the height of the German depression, deals with the social battles between the exploiters and the exploited for food, shelter, and work, and, by stressing the victims' passive acceptance of their fate, provokes the audience to do something about the situation. The literary circles of East Berlin, at the premiere, were arguing about its form. Brecht often uses parables laid in other countries (*The Caucasian Chalk Circle, The Good Woman of Setzuan*) or other times (*Mother Courage, Galileo*) to comment on local and topical situations. *The Bakery*, however, describes the misery of German unemployment at the time and place it happened. It's the story of a complicated economic situation in a deceptively simple tale about a woman, Niobe Queck, who loses everything – job, apartment, belongings, even her children – because she doesn't know the economic laws ruling her life. The chorus of the unemployed, like a Greek chorus, points out the irrevocable laws of fate:

> Meals and work/follow unchangeable laws,/unknowable laws.
> But all this time/people drop out of sight,
> through manholes in the asphalt,all kinds of people
> without marks or brands.
> Out of sight,suddenly, silently, quickly sink from sight,
> from the midst of the crowd,at random, six out of seven,
> but the seventh/goes to the dining hall.
> Who of us will it be?/Which one is destined to be saved?
> Which one is marked? Where is the next manhole? Unknowable.

132

"*The Bakery* ." said Karge, "is a call to the unemployed to find out about their condition." Under his direction, the almost childishly simple story pushes the audience toward protest like a pile driver.

The Bakery, " explained Helmut Baierl, an East German writer, "is a fable in which Brecht manages to give a general picture of a situation and also a very specific story. Every sentence refers to hundred thousands of examples, and at the same time is unique." When Brecht's disciples talk about the "fables" in his plays, they talk about dialectical materialism on the stage: the fables refer to Hegelian contradictions synthesized into a higher truth. Brecht's fables are full of contradictions, full of breaks in the action; the play moves in epɪsodic leaps, and actions need not be motivated: contradictory means are synthesized into a higher end. If the play itself does not contain such contradictions, Karge argues, the director must supply them. *The Bakery*, being a fragment, is a case in point. The "fable" in *The Bakery* results from the contradiction between the way the characters act (in ignorance of the economic laws that allow their being exploited) and the way they face the results (being crushed by the economic conditions). Karge: "Every exaggeration, improbability, slant, propaganda, and grotesquerie becomes reality." The higher truth that emerges differs with time and circumstances of the production. For the Berlin Ensemble, *The Bakery* states that economic justice is impossible under capitalism; no need to stress here that communism is the answer. Emphasis on communism as the solution may be the truth for a production in, say, Czechoslovakia. In the United States, the truth may be the reminder that a depression happened and could happen again.

This Eastern picture of Brecht as the creator of a new dramatic art developed from Marxist dialectical materialism, differs substantially from that of Bertolt Brecht as seen in the West. Here he is considered one of the great dramatic geniuses of the twentieth century, with a gift to entertain, arouse, fascinate, and provoke the public with interesting, contemporary drama. To Western audiences, he is a playwright of wide variety, from the amusing satire of *The Three-Penny Opera*, through modern dramas such as *The Caucasian Chalk Circle*. Eastern audiences see an underlying pattern in his varied output. To Helene Weigel, *The Three Penny Opera* is just as much a part of Brecht's new dialectic drama as his popular dramas. "If you'd study the total work of Brecht," she said a bit testily, "you would see how *The Threepenny Opera* fits in." The total output consists of 36 volumes, plus stacks of manuscripts still in the archives. It includes such oddities as *The Baden-Baden Didactic Play of Consent*, with music by Paul Hindemith, presenting the doctrines of humility and salvation in Marxian terms; the *Joe Fleischhacker* fragment, explaining capitalism in a story about speculations at the Chicago grain market; and an attempt to render the *Communist Manifesto* in hexameters.

How does *The Threepenny Opera* fit in here? Brecht himself supplies the answer. After the unprecedented success of the *Three Penny Opera* in 1928, his friends took him to task because the play was not socialistic. His Marxist biographer, Ernst Schumacher reproached Brecht for not treating the material dialectically, and for not making the sharks and bandits of the eighteenth century into capitalists of the twentieth. Brecht promptly changed his interpretation: When a movie was made of *The Threepenny Opera*, he insisted on having Mackie Messer identified as a bank president, and even went to court over the issue. When he failed, he wrote his *Threepenny Novel*, making the bandits capitalists.

Brecht kept insisting on dialectic interpretations of his plays, even when he lived in exile in the United States, and his insistence cost him his only chance of success in Hollywood. When Charles Laughton translated Brecht's *Galileo* and starred in the title role, Brecht insisted on an epic production. He did not want the audience to identify with this seventeenth-century scientist fighting dogma and prejudice; he wanted to arouse the audience to action to help the atomic scientists in their conflict of conscience after Hiroshima. The play flopped, and Brecht soon afterwards returned to Europe where he could stage his plays dialectically. "American producers and audiences do not know what Brecht is all about," Helene Weigel stated flatly. "They have made good beginnings, but they will have to realize that modern theatre, including Brecht, is more than gimmicks and gadgets." She believes that the American theatre would gain much by a visit from the Berlin Ensemble.

But the West has its own appreciation of Brecht. His success here is based on the dramatic genius of *The Caucasian Chalk Circle*, *Mother Courage*, *The Good Woman of Setzuan*, *Galileo*, and *Herr Puntila and his Man Matti*, all written during his years in exile. There he was able to free himself from the doctrines of the Party and his natural gift broke through, enabling him to write good, almost "classical," drama instead of Marxistic experimentation. His Western biographer, Willy Haas, calls him "the most grotesque, misled, doctrinaire rebel who half of his life stubbornly worked against himself, his dramatic genius, and his genuine, natural appeal to the public."

Haas believes that Brecht turned away from the public after several failures (such as *Mahagonny* and *Happy End*) that followed the triumph of *The Threepenny Opera*. He then turned to propaganda, teaching, information, the didactic play, the Agitprop play. He became the teacher with the threatening cane, pedantic, merciless, and direct. The West is inclined to disregard this part of his work.

The East, however, sees in him the dramatist of the future. To the East, Brecht's contribution is a new way to educate the public and improve the world. "It is true," Brecht wrote, "that we imitate incidents from life, but that is not all. It depends why we imitate them. [We do so] in order to fill men with passion and emotion, to pull them away from every-day incidents. The incidents are only a scaffold on which we build up our art, the jumping-off point." What is important in the dialectic drama is the effect on the audience. "We must develop two arts," Brecht wrote. "The art of the actors, and the art of the audience." Both are developed powerfully by the disciples of Bertolt Brecht at the Berlin Ensemble.

(*Michigan Quarterly*, Ann Arbour, Spring, 1970)

A Birthday Present

When the Austrian Empire collapsed, three priceless cultural treasures survived the catastrophe: the venerable name of Austria itself, applied to a smaller area after the independence of Hungary, Czechoslovakia, and other parts of the realm; the imperial palaces, galleries, museums, collections, and gardens which were nationalized; and my mother's handwritten cookbook. Had it been published earlier, World War I would undoubtedly never have been fought because the powerful statesmen would have been distracted from politics, satisfied with a world made palatable to them by their wives using *Blue Danube* recipes.

There are Austrian, Hungarian, Bohemian, Serbian, and Polish cookbooks, so why one more?

First, because this cookbook presents "imperial" dishes, the finest developed in Austria proper, and also by the individual nationalities that made up the former Austrian Empire and were commonly served in Vienna: Hungarian goulash, Bohemian dumplings, Polish hot fish sauce, and many others. The title of this book was chosen to indicate the multinationality of these Empire dishes: Johann Strauss's beloved Danube connected the two capitals of the former Dual Monarchy, Vienna and Budapest.

Secondly, because every dish here described has gone through my mother's testing process. Her dinner parties used to be the talk among our friends; many of her recipes, especially the desserts, are never-published family treats created by her or handed down by family tradition; the principal virtue of her cooking was not this or that sensational dish, but her own little touches, the result of a sensitive taste.

Her emphasis was on quality not cosmetics. When she made a birthday cake for me, what was *under* the frosting was important, not gaudily colored sugar roses on top. Expert though she was, she regarded herself as a student all her life, reading, clipping, and collecting recipes printed in newspapers. Every morning in my native Vienna, even before my mother arose, my Aunt Alice would show up, sit by her bed, and they would hold a war council on the meals to be cooked that day. Aunt Alice was mother's peer in the art of the taste buds, and the two women were forever experimenting with new nuances. As a youngster I often mocked Aunt Alice for her

ungrammatical stock phrase: "Und dann gibbich hinein. . ."
inadequately translated as : "And then I put in . . . " There would be a
pinch of this and a drop of that and, particularly, a specific method to
improve a dish.

The happy results of these discussions and try-outs all went
into a much-thumbed handwritten cookbook whose marbleized
cover is, in my memory, a symbol of my childhood. Long after I was a
grown man, my mother still wrote in that same book, several pages
in it covered with my crayon drawings – the beautiful white sheets
having been too tempting for the young artist to resist.

My mother prepared her formal dinner parties carefully. The
day after those dinners the telephone rang constantly. The ladies
wanted the recipes. My mother, generous with her discoveries and
methods, discussed the procedures at length on the wall telephone.
When the ladies tried out the recipes and were not satisfied with the
results, there were more telephone follow-ups. What had gone
wrong? Like a doctor my mother would diagnose the situation. Had
the lady done this or that correctly? The cooking time and the amount
of ingredients were checked. Sometimes, to bring out the finer
points, my mother would demonstrate her cooking. She was patient
in answering questions, but never stopped marveling why people
were disappointed when they had not followed her recipe. I
remember a young lady complaining that her vanilla "Kipferln,"
prepared from my mother's recipe – or so she claimed – did not turn
out. "Yours were so much better, Mrs. Kühnel," the lady said. "Why?"
When my mother was through checking, it turned out that the lady
had used margarine instead of butter, vanilla extract instead of
vanilla beans, and peanuts instead of almonds.

The cookbook with the marbleized cover survived the second
World War as well as the first. It traveled to the United States, but
still was not finished. Aunt Alice was long gone, but new refinements
were added to the book nevertheless, and even a few American
recipes were included. The Blue Danube had reached the Pacific
Ocean when Mother Kühnel settled in her little house in Albany,
California.

The time for elegant dinner parties had passed now, and her
art could be appreciated only when she invited a small circle of
friends to a Vienna *Jause,* or her grandchildren, my wife, and me to a
birthday party. But, much as we appreciated her treats on those
special occasions, the value of her art was to make the every-day
meals more enjoyable, to give them the full dimension of one of life's
pleasures. Enjoying a carefully prepared meal was entirely
comparable to listening to good music or reading a good book.

As my mother's eightieth birthday approached I decided, as a tribute to her, to preserve the results of decades of "Und dann gibbich hinein." The book was transcribed, typed, translated from its original German into English, edited and, finally, printed. I needed all my training as an editor of the University of California Press to get the manuscript through its many stages, to interview my mother many times to supplement the instructions, and to clarify points that seemed "perfectly clear" to her as she had put them down in that book.

Thus, the result is not a professional-scientific book on the culinary arts, it's a "mother's cookbook" rooted in the kitchen. When I asked my mother for some advice on cooking that could apply to the preparation of all dishes, she said: "Cook with love; your family will taste it."

(Foreword to *The Original Blue Danube Cookbook*, Berkeley: Lancaster-Miller, 1979)

Sigmund Freud Remembered

On June 12, 1900, Sigmund Freud sent a photograph of his summer home "Bellevue" near Vienna to his friend Wilhelm Fliess, with a note saying: "Do you think that one day there will be a memorial tablet on this house saying, "Here, on July 24, 1895, the secret of dreams was revealed to Dr. Sigmund Freud? So far the chances seem rather slight." Freud's skepticism proved justified. That particular tablet was never presented, and it took the city of Vienna until 1954 to place a tablet at the entrance of the apartment house, Berggasse 19, where Freud lived and worked from 1891 until his exile in 1938. And in 1971 Freud's former consulting room and study were converted into a museum.

The letter to Fliess is one of the exhibited items.

I happened to be in Vienna at the time. Dr. Frederick Hacker, president of the Sigmund Freud Society, arranged 152 documents, photographs, mementos, letters, and first printings collected from Freud's relatives, friends, archives, and libraries.

The exhibit allowed personal glimpses at Freud, ranging from the family chronicle in which his father Jacob in 1856 had recorded the birth of his son "Sigismund"– a spelling Freud did not change until 1878 – to his last photograph in his London exile, before his death in 1939.

To me, the most memorable piece of the collection is an entirely unremarkable photo of Freud in his study with his dog Jofi. As a high-school pal of his nephew Harry, I knew "Uncle Sigmund" long before I was aware of his significance. To me he was a quiet, jovial old man who was remarkable only as a superb teller of Jewish jokes. Little did I know that he was researching the psychology of humor on which he had published his book, *Der Witz.*. Usually, Uncle Sigmund would politely excuse himself and retire to some rooms that were off limit to us children.

Of course, we were curious about those rooms, and it was because of the chow-chow Jofi that we eventually got to see them. Freud took daily walks in Vienna's huge natural park, the Prater, accompanied by Jofi. He always took a *fiaker*, the two-horse carriage of Old Vienna, had his walk, and took a *fiaker* back. One Sunday, Jofi had disappeared during the walk chasing a rabbit. Freud spent some time looking for him, and finally returned home, only to be greeted by Jofi at the door. The dog had gone to the place where the coaches waited for hire, and one of the coachmen, knowing the dog, had taken him home.

In the confusion Jofi, followed by us children, ran through the apartment, including the consultation room with its plush-covered couch whose significance was lost on me. Afterwards Jofi was known in the Freud family as "the dog that isn't walked – he takes a *fiaker.*"

In the exhibit, Jofi was exhibit number 119.

Not shown in the collection of letters is a brief exchange of notes which had amused the Freud family in the early twenties.

Freud had received a letter from the Austrian income-tax office, expressing doubt that Freud's income was as low as he had declared: "A man whose fame has spread beyond Austria's borders must be making more." Freud sent back a sarcastic little note: he was happy to receive the first official recognition of his work from an Austrian government office, adding: "You are mistaken in only one point: My fame is not spreading beyond Austria's borders; it begins there."

In the exhibit, only the waiting room contained some of the original furniture, supplied from his London home by daughter Anna. The consulting room and study were bare except for the display of photographs, documents, letters, and mementos. "Here," Dr. Hacker declared," originated psychoanalysis; here also originated most of the important works of Freud which go far beyond medical significance. They revolutionized our under-standing of ourselves, with implications in all fields, from education to prison reforms, from family relations to political propaganda, from commercial advertising to religion."

To me, wandering about the exhibit, the museum was a bit of my childhood revisited. I did remember the mass of books that filled the shelves to the ceiling, and the antique figurines that crowded glass cases and spilled over to all available spaces on the desk, the doily-covered little tables, and window ledges, now bare.

On the place where the couch had stood, Freud's first scientific work was displayed in a vitrine. Written in 1877, it had nothing to do with the unconscious but with organs of the eel. Freud's drawings to this work were also shown. Along the wall were photos of the house where Freud was born in Freiberg, Moravia, and a series of photographs showing Freud as a child, with members of his family, with colleagues and friends, and his visit to the United States in 1909. The vitrine in the center of the room contained a number of awards, including the scroll of Freud's honorary degree from Clark University, Worcester, Massachusetts. In a footnote to history, a page from the audience list of Emperor Francis Joseph, Monday, October 13, 1902, was exhibited. "Name: Freud S. Dr. Purpose of audience: to express thanks for receiving the title of associate professor at the University of Vienna." Other exhibit items gave mute evidence that he never received the title of full professor from his *alma mater* although scientific triumph after triumph was shown. The last photograph showed his house Berggasse 19 draped in swastika flags, pictures of Princess Marie Bonaparte of Greece who helped Freud to leave Austria, his arrival in London. There Freud lived the last year of his life and saw his book on Moses published, in which Freud argued that Moses was Egyptian rather than Jewish. Harry told me that his uncle felt sad and had said: "Now that they take everything from the Jews, I even take their best man!"

I kept wandering about the rooms in search for something that had remained unchanged. The walls had been repainted and the floors, without carpets, looked bare and strange. I finally discovered a familiar sight in an unexpected place: the toilet with its old-fashioned water tank up the wall, and the flushing chain hanging down from it.

Anna Freud did not come to the opening of the museum, but had "lent" Paula Fichtel to supervise the physical arrangement of the museum. Paula had been a maid in the Freud household for more than 40 years and had served us our hot chocolate and *Guglhupf* cake. Among all the documents and photographs, she was the only living link with past as I had known it. Harry died in New York. A phrase from his last letter stuck in my mind as I looked at the mementos of a famous life. I had sent Harry my book, *The Pursuit of Meaning*.. "I hope,' I had written, " you will not see the book as an attack on your uncle." I treasure his reply: "Only an orthodox Freudian would consider it an attack, and if my uncle, were alive today, he would not be an orthodox Freudian."

("Personal Glimpses of Freud," *San Francisco Chronicle,* Jan. 28, 1972, supplemented by personal notes)

The Father of the Comic Strip
(Review of Walter Arndt, *The Genius of Wilhelm Busch*)

It took three quarters of a century after his death in 1908 until Wilhelm Busch, the double German humorist – poet and artist – was adequately translated into English. Busch, if known at all in America, is acknowledged as the unwitting father of the comic strip. On W. R. Hearst's suggestion, Rudoph Dirks began in 1897 to draw on the brilliance of Busch's pair of mischievous lads, Max and Moritz, for inspiration of the primitive Katzenjammer Kids.

Busch is unique as a cultural phenomenon. The translator-editor of the first English Busch anthology, Walter Arndt, says in his introduction: "As a lyric, satiric, aphoristic, and comic poet, and simultaneously a graphic genius in motion, gesture, and physiognomy, Busch attained a Shakespeare-Webster-and-the-Bible sort of household stature in German-speaking countries. and renowned wherever his verse was well translated elsewhere.

"That he remained untranslated into English is the more curious as his amalgam of two unique talents is not only unrivaled in his own country – which has produced perhaps only one other outstanding humorist of light verse, Christian Morgenstern – but unmatched even in the homelands of his kind of humor, the English-speaking world."

Translators in many languages – including Latin – have tried their hands at some of Busch's picture tales. The main target was *Max and Moritz* which Arndt defines as "a rustic tale in verse of evil gusto, sardonic bathos, and ultimate grotesque." He calls it "quite possibly the most universally quoted work in the German language." Indeed, when one hears a quotation in a German conversation, it is likely either from Goethe's *Faust* or from Wilhelm Busch (Arndt translated both). Busch's lapidary verses by themselves would fill a thesaurus of quotations.

But translation efforts into English have failed pathetically; also annoyingly, because they all use, and trade on, Busch's illustrations. To translate an inspired genius, a translator has to be inspired himself, an alter ego of the author.

Busch aimed his darts at pseudo-scholarly bombast, the hollowness of authority, the facile self-righteousness of the burgher, the moral squalor of yokeldom, also at the malice of inanimate things. To make his points, he used verbal acrobatics, slapstick rhymes, shocking surrealism, cold-blooded grotesquerie reminiscent, as Arndt says, of "Ogden Nash and Thurber rolled in one, and Lewis Carroll and his younger contemporary, the inspired fantasist-parodist, Christian Morgenstern."

All these facets must be reflected in the translation. Busch's verses flow deceptively easy, read "natural,"and have a beautiful, quotable click. Arndt splendidly succeeds in recreating them, with sovereign use of emendations, where the spirit of the original calls for them. In the words of poet-critic Babette Deutsch (in a *New York Times* review of a Morgenstern translation): "The English lines dance to the metrics of the German."

Here are some of the celebrated lines, which have become proverbs in German: "Being father is a thing/harder far than fathering," "From ancient times it has been true:/he who takes licks, takes liquor, too," "Much talking never wearies us,/ unless it's someone else who does."

Arndt wisely omits a complete translation of Busch's work, but does not gloss over his anti-Semitic passages and anti-Catholic picture tales. Arndt treats the "genteel" anti-Semitism leniently as "a streak of homegrown prejudice in the young Busch," but Busch was 50 when he wrote the lines and drew the scurrilous caricatures that served as a "model for the Nazi gutter press." Arndt argues that they are "deliberately and farcically overdone," and, as it were, not to be taken seriously, a delicate point in view of later history. But Arndt acknowledges Busch's "virulent anti-clericalism."

In addition to the judiciously chosen picture tales, the anthology includes graphics and vignettes, poetry and prose, an autobiographical piece, a biographical chronicle, and a critical bibliography. An appendix contains the German originals of the translated tales.

The publication of this volume is a major literary event and a feather in the cap of the University of California press. *The Genius of Wilhelm Busch* will undoubtedly become the definite English version of the work of this immortal classic of humor.

(*San Francisco Chronicle Review*, February 28, 1982)

The Meaning of a Cemetery

One afternoon, while walking in our neighborhood cemetery, I heard fast footsteps behind me. A man of about 50 was holding a small piece of paper toward me.

"Could you please help me find my mother's grave?" he asked in a broad Australian accent.

I looked at the slip the cemetery office had given him and directed him toward a hill near the entrance. But there was something so helplessly pleading about him that I led the way. I looked again at his paper. "Your mother died in 1925?" I asked.

Somehow he read a reproach into my question. "It's my first chance to visit her grave," he said. "She died when I was born and my father took me and my brother to Australia when I was six months old." The words were tumbling from his lips. He was with the postal service in Sydney, had never married, his brother drowned as a teenager, his father died six months ago. They had saved money for the trip and now he felt he could afford it. He had landed yesterday, and his first way was to his mother's grave.

To locate it, however, did not prove easy. He knew that her grave had no stone, and in the row indicated on his slip were several stretches of grass with no markers. I felt I should leave him alone with his thoughts of his mother who had left life when his began. But he looked so forlorn that I suggested he find out from the office who was buried next to her so he might orient himself by the gravestones of others. He mumbled something about not wanting to trouble the office a second time. I was about to say that a man who had come all the way from Australia was certainly entitled to this information, when I was struck by the serenity that had spread over his face.

"It doesn't matter," he said. "Mother knows I'm here."

This episode is one of the treasures my memory has collected on my frequent walks in that cemetery which faces our home, offering a view not always appreciated by our visitors. The word "cemetery," with its grisly connotations, prevents them from seeing the beauty of this sanctuary of nature in a suburb of concrete and neon lights. Whenever visitors accompany me on a walk to the top of the cemetery, they admit it was a highlight of their sightseeing in the

San Francisco area. It doesn't take long for the cemetery to work its magic. The silhouette of palm trees against the clear-washed sky; orange sunsets over the Bay; the fata morgana of San Francisco and the Golden Gate Bridge; the drama of the fog rolling in from the Pacific; the pungency of the eucalyptus trees; the owl-like lament of the mourning doves; the unexpected appearance of a family of deer watching humans with unafraid eyes – they all refresh the soul and delight the senses. All visitor find their special spellbinders. Mine is a group of weeping willows, gnome-like trunks with graceful cascades of branches, equally enchanting in their light-green spring foliage, the lush braids of summer, their fall brilliance, and their Japanese-painting-like bare twigs against the winter sky. To me, these trees make a dramatic statement what life, death, and rebirth are all about.

I remember a woman I met on the path near the trees. I was a stranger to her, but she wanted to talk about her daughter who was buried nearby. "Why?" she asked. "She was only 24. She had hardly begun living. Why?" Perhaps the weeping willows inspired my answer which seemed to comfort her. "No one knows why," I said. "But some questions do have answers. What has it meant to you that she was with you for 24 years? What did it mean to her that she had you as a mother?"

Wandering about the gravestones above the Bay alive with sailboats, touches my center and releases memories and sets fantasies adrift. The first cemetery I remember was in the tiny village in which my father had grown up. It was in newly established Czechoslovakia. This Jewish cemetery had been closed for years and we had to get a key to open the creaky iron-wrought gate. The gravestones were bedecked with moss and overgrown with brambles. We found my great-grandfather's grave, and I was delighted to see some wild strawberries growing on it. I was about nine then, and I still remember the joy of eating them. I shall never cease to be grateful to my parents for not interfering. They might have reacted in horror: here I was eating what might have been part of my ancestor. To me, it was an lesson about the continuation of life. Somehow we believe that cemeteries are the property of the dead. My childhood incident and my parents' reaction showed me that they are an invitation for enjoying life.

They are an invitation to live and to think about what it means to be alive. Gravestones contain little information: a name, a date, a family relationship. Yet, what rich sources for fantasizing! A couple buried together, the wife surviving her husband for 51 years: how much loneliness, courage, and resilience are contained in those chiseled dates! A grandfather buried with two grandsons: did the children's parents die and he had to bring them up? Both grandsons died within a few weeks from each other, in their thirties; were they victims of an epidemic? An accident? How fortunate for their grandfather to have passed on a year before! A mother, 93, departed one year before her daughter who was still bearing her maiden name at 68 – did the daughter devote her entire life to her mother and died when her task was fulfilled?

In the cemetery, a life is reduced to two dates and a dash in between. How much is contained in that dash – all the hopes, joys, fears, disappointments, achievements, and failures! All the meanings of a person's life are captured in that short line between the two dates of mystery, birth and death. Sometimes the space behind the dash is still open: the pledge of the survivor to join the partner when the time comes. We all walk through life with an open space behind our dash: what a challenge to live and pack that dash with meanings while we can!

Nothing puts living in perspective as much as wandering among the dead. When I visited the grave of a friend, I was shaken by the smallness of the freshly replaced turf that covered her urn. Barely one square foot covered all that was left of a human being who had loved, gathered possessions, fed a family, comforted pain, smoothed over quarrels, and inspired by example. A square foot of grass on a grassy slope, a marker among markers.

One of my most moving memories is a bouquet of fresh forget-me-nots on the grave of an infant that had lived for only six weeks in 1919. I marveled about the richness of the human spirit still lovingly relating to a dead baby after more than 60 years.

The magic of the cemetery turns every-day events into symbols. A thrush sitting on top of a pine tree singing its heart out becomes a challenge to do my very best even if no one is watching. The carmine disk of the setting sun staring through the flaming haze is a reminder that clouds are needed to create beauty.

Returning from my walk among the dead I know what it is to live.

(*West County Times*, April 20, 1985)

Look Ma, I'm a Grandpa!

Both my parents' families came from Sudentenland and moved to Vienna in the 1880s, as did many Jews from the Austrian provinces, after an edict by Emperor Francis Joseph gave them equal rights. Father did not finish high school. In Vienna, he took a handyman's job in a warehouse and eventually became director of the municipal warehouses. He was an utterly common-sensical man who found solutions for problems as they cropped up. Family members came to him for advice and help. Father always knew best. His judgment failed tragically in his own case when he decided the Nazis would let them live in peace because he had done nothing wrong. When he realized the values of his world had drastically changed, it was too late.

Mother completed high school which was rare for women. She played the piano and was interested in music and the arts. She believed in the intrinsic goodness of people. She was frugal and never wasted anything. She saved things like pins, thumbtacks, buttons, and wrapping paper. Two built-in cabinets were filled with remnants. Other family members came to her for trimmings, ribbons, lace, or pieces of fabrics. She was considerate to the point of self-denial. She lived her life for me, her husband, her mother, and anyone who needed help. She seemed to understand others from *their* points of view and found excuses for their behavior. She was honest to a fault and would not take advantage of others.

Both had an instinctive understanding for my needs without ever talking about them. Love was a given.

In 1938, reason, unselfishness, and honesty were not qualities for survival. My parents recognized too late that having broken no law was no protection against shipment to concen-tration camp Theresienstadt.

In 1990, on a bus trip from Berlin to Prague, I was idly watching the ribbon of the road being gobbled up. Suddenly the sign of the next town flitted by: Terezin. The name hit me with the force of a body blow. Terezin was the Czech name of Theresienstadt! The little town in the distance was the nightmare place where my parents died.

A burst of rage exploded in me. The enormity of the crime leaped into consciousness. I seized my wife's hand and told her. Tears flowed. The old wound had broken open.

*

I visualized dialogues with my parents on many occasions.

I drive along the Berkeley hills, overlooking San Francisco Bay with its sailboats, bridges, islands, and the spectacular skyline. The orange globe of the sun dips into gold-rimmed clouds, throwing a dazzling ribbon across the water. After many years, the sunsets on the Golden Gate still take my breath.

Father sits next to me, mother in back. They have not aged since I saw them last. They are as old as I am now.

"San Francisco Bay," I point out proudly, as if I had created it.

"Fantastic." Father looks out. "Like Venice. Remember Venice, Irma? Our honeymoon. We thought it was paradise."

Mother, from the back: 'You have done well for yourself, Bubi. I knew you would. And you have a car! You can drive!"

I glory in her marveling. She puts a hand on my shoulder. "Don't drive so fast, Bubi. Be careful."

I feel in control. "Yes, Mama, I am careful. I'm a good driver. I am no longer a child. People call me Joe. I'm no Bubi."

"Yes, Bubi," she says."I mean Joe. But please drive carefully."

Father adjusts his pincenez, and peers at the dashboard. I explain the gadgets. When I come to the radio, father is amazed. "A radio in a car! What will they think of next?" And with a daring flight of imagination he adds, "Pretty soon they will have phones in the car!"

"They already do. People transact business from their cars. Some even have small televisions."

"Tele-what?"

I explain, pleased to enlighten father: "It's like radio with pictures. Like movies. We have one at home."

"A movie at home?" I love mother's tone of disbelief.

"Oh yes." I try to be matter-of-fact. "We can also rent movies on tapes we can put into our pockets and show at home."

"A whole movie in a pocket!" father marvels. "In color, of course, and talking. Do you have movies that smell and taste?"

"Not yet," I smile.

"We'll leave that," father suggests, "for future inventors."

The sky darkens and lights go on all over the Bay. I enjoy sharing my awe with my parents.

We drive silently, then mother says: "Remember, Ernstl, when we got married, we changed our gas lighting to electricity? We thought it was a miracle. We had three bulbs. Now this! And you are part of it. Your house is one dot among the thousands." After a pause. "You have done well, Bubi." I don't correct her. For her I remain Bubi for eternity.

*

1972. My first grandchild is born. Heidi, a pretty name. My first glimpse through the hospital window. One infant among many, but by far the prettiest. The nurse picks her up for me to see.

Mother joins me."Look, Ma," I greet her, "I'm a grandpa!"

"You made me a great-grandma," she says. "And I haven't met my grandchildren. You are starting a new family in America."

"I'm the only one left to do it," I remind her.

But she is in no mood for sadness. She knocks at the glass window . "Hello, Heidi. Things are different. The family is gone. We were about 30, meeting on birthdays . Where are they all?"

"Maybe they are all gathered, somewhere," I say, not really believing it. "Maybe they see her."

"Yes," she agrees. " Somewhere and somehow. Maybe just in your head. Maybe in Heidi's head,"

"Or in her genes," I add, knowing she doesn't know about genes.

But she knows in her own way. "Heidi," she says. "I come from the 19th century. Your father lives in the 20th. You are reaching into the 21st. You're the future, baby, keep it going!"

*

1966. Claire's wedding. Arm in arm we marched down the aisle, she and I, father of the bride. We moved slowly, step by step, organ music playing. Friends, flowers everywhere, Claire in a white gown, with lace and a train trailing . She walked on my left.

Father walks on my right. "My younger daughter," I introduce her. "Isn't she beautiful?"

Father nods gravely. "She looks like Elsa. The same white teeth, that silvery laugh. Elsa was very choosy. She was 38 when she married Rudi. He escaped to Poland and disappeared. She was taken to Dachau. All this is past. Here is the future."

"Claire is only 19. She's very choosy, too. When she decided to marry Rich, she said, 'I know, Dad, I'm young to get married, but I cannot find anything wrong with Rich.'" I point to the chancel. "Rich is the tall one, waiting for us. He's only 21."

"My grandson-in-law. I can't find anything wrong with him either." He flicks one of his ironic smiles. "Not at this distance."

"He's going to be an engineer. I don't know much about him. It's scary. I give my daughter to a stranger. My precious Claire. She's always been my joy, even though she wasn't the easiest to bring up.

"That's the way it is," father says, "We had to let you go under much worse circumstances. But we knew you'd make it."

Back to reality. I let go of Claire's arm, stepping back to join Judith. My thoughts flew back to our own wedding, in New York,

1940, in a Rabbi's home, a fellow refugee from Vienna. We had no money for a wedding with guests, white bridal gown, and flowers. We marched into the little room, under a canopy, a *chuppe*, as Jewish law requires. The *chuppe* was carried by four people, almost the only ones we knew in the United States: Judith's cousin Fred, her employer Dr. Eliasberg, my schoolmate Harry, and Blanche, the daughter of my sponsor. Unbeknown to all but me, my parents were also part of my wedding party.

"How will it all end?" mother says fearfully. "Bubi earns 12 dollars a week as a factory worker."

"Judith earns another 12 dollars as a secretary." father comforts her.

"How will it all come out?" mother sighs. "Bubi cannot make a living by writing because he doesn't know the language. His law degree is no good here. He can't work in a factory forever."

"Judith is an American," father says. "She'll help him. America is the land of opportunities. He'll make his way."

"I know he will," mother agrees. "But I can't help worrying. Maybe we spoiled him too much."

"We gave him our love. Now Judith will ccarry on. She's a good woman, believes in him. Just as we did. Trust me."

"I always did. But things are different. Times have changed."

"But he hasn't," father says firmly. "There's something that remains in us, regardless of what happens."

I listen to them while we walk under the chuppe. *I don't know what that something is that is so firm and unchangeable, but I know father is right, against all the evidence. We come to the rabbi and for a moment I have that unreal feeling that I've melted with father and Judith with mother. And, as from a distance, I hear myself say, "I do."*

*

1971, at Montmartre in Paris. We visited Heinrich Heine's grave and wandered around, looking at the paintings displayed by the artists. It was June 23, the one-hundredth birthday of my mother. We settled down in one of the open-air restaurants and ordered dinner. In a spurt of sentimentality I asked for a bottle of champagne and filled our glasses.

Mother joins us, more wrinkled and bent than I remember .

I lift my glass. "To 120!" I toast her, in the Jewish tradition.

She smiles. "Not long to go." She loooks at me with affection. "I'm glad you could afford to visit Paris. I was worried you would have a struggle. Three children!"

"We are doing well, Mama," I assure her.

"And you have taken in Cousin Irma."

"A substitute grandma."

"Her name is Irma, just as mine," mother says.

"That's a bit of trouble," I confess. *"Sometimes I resent her. She's alive, and you aren't."*

"Don't look at it that way. I wouldn't be alive now, anyway. A hundred years! She's only 74. Make her feel part of the family."

"But she is, she is!" I assure her.*"The kids love her. She spoils them just as you would. She lost all her possessions in the London Blitz. Including her photos. She needs a family."*

"We all do." Mother sighs, bobbing her head as old people do. *"Irma had tough luck. Her husband and daughter both died of TB. Terrible."*

"She talks of them often. And how glad she is to have a family again. Only I wish it were you. That we could spend birthdays together, the way we did in Vienna. Including this one."

"I' m here," she said.

A flower vendor approached with a basket of red roses. She was as wrinkled and bent over as the image of mother. Only, she was real.

"I'll take all the six bunches in the basket." I handed the old woman some francs. "One I keep, the others are for you." She peered at me over the rim of her glasses, smiled, and shuffled on. I handed the bouquet to Judith. She understood.

*

November 4, 1987, the first anniversary of Wendy's death. Wendy is buried on a hill overlooking San Francisco Bay.

"She was born a few months after you died," I tell mother standing next to me. *"When we learned we would have her, you still were alive. We sent you a Red Cross message to Vienna that we were expecting, but I guess you did not receive it."*

"My first grandchild," she muses. *"It would have made dying easier had we known."*

"Our first child." My thoughts race back through 43 years. *"She made me a father. I remember when I first saw her, a helpless bundle wholly dependent on us. I felt responsibility clearly for the first time. Little Wendy did it. She did many things for me without knowing it. Just by being there. She gave content to my life. And now she is dead. She cannot do anything more for me, and I cannot do anything for her. It was a terrible moment, holding that small cardboard box in my hands, with her ashes. A whole life, hopes, love, joy, reduced to a boxful of ashes!"*

"Poor Bubi," mother laments. *"Your parents murdered, your aunts and uncles murdered, and now your daughter murdered, too,"* Mother repeats, so mournfully I want to comfort her. *"I know how it is to lose a child. When we said goodbye to you at the railroad station*

in Vienna, I knew we'd never see you again."

"Wendy was so happy," I tell her. "She had found a man who was both physically attractive and spiritually in tune with her. She told us she had looked for this combination all her life. And she finally met him."

"A whole life ahead of her," mother sighs.

"Yes, Mama, hard to take. Wendy was only 43."

"We had you only for 28. But if Wendy made you as happy in the 43 years, as you did in the 28. We all can be satisfied."

We sit quietly , looking at the view Wendy loved so much. Then mother says. "Don't you wonder what really happened?"

"Of course I do. But he killed himself, too."

"Do you speak with Wendy the way you speak with me?"

"Many times," I confess, "Here at her grave. But you can't get information from the dead. They only tell you what you want them to tell you. They only say what's in your heart."

*

Thanksgiving 1990. We sat around a long table in our son Richard's living room. He carved the turkey. A 12-foot embroidered tablecloth covered the table, hundreds of red cross-stitches on white. I thought of the story of that cloth. Another tale of Thanksgiving.

Sophie Beck, my father's cousin, had rescued me by sending the life-saving affidavit. She had five children and a dozen grandchildren, whom I met at a Seder at her home in New Jersey after my arrival in America, in 1940. When Sophie died and we moved to California, I lost contact with her children. When I wrote my autobiography, I wondered if some of them were still alive so I could send them my book. Looking up the Becks in the Newark telephone directory, I discovered that the widow of Sophie's youngest son was still alive, Jennie Beck. We corresponded. She was 83. Her daughter, the eight-year old with whom I had played at that long-ago Seder evening, was a grandmother.

On the next trip east we visited Jennie in her home. She brought out the tablecloth, hand-embroidered by my mother. Now Jennie wanted me to have it for my family. It had served the Becks on many Seders and other festive occasions, and now it was to continue to serve for my new California family. This Thanks-giving was the first time it was so used.

I touched the cross-stitches. Mother had touched them, too.

"A lot of work," mother says "I'm glad you make use of it."

"You were always embroidering and knitting," father reminisces. "This is the only piece that survived." He looks around the table. then turning to me. "You can use a big table cloth. Our American family is growing."

152

"Bubi is the only one that can keep it going," mother says sadly..

"Judith's brother Dick was a big help." I admit. "He had four children. Two of them are here, Katherine with husband and baby, and David, his wife and the two boys. Carol is in Hawaii and Lindy inTexas. Americans spread all over the country."

"You got quite a collection here," father observes.

"California attracts people," I say, and mother adds: "I bet you attracted them, too. It's good to have the family together."

I continue the introduction. "Over there is the widow of Judith's older brother Ralph, and her new husband. We remain very close. Her daughter, our niece, is married in Washington, expecting a baby." A tinge of pride creeps into my voice. "And to the left are our own children. And grandchildren."

Father looks around – the impressive living room, the spacious deck, the eucalyptus trees outside, the staircase leading up to the balustraded hallway.. "This is Richard's house? Is he a millionaire?"

"Oh no," I laugh. "He's paying a hefty mortgage. But he's doing all right. He publishes a magazine. Our 'baby', 40 years old! I It took him a while to find his way. He's very gifted, creative."

"He got it from you," mother interjects.

"He does things I couldn't do," I say with a mixture of modesty and pride. "I supported him with whatever he tried – photography, film making, astrology. . ."

"Astrology?" Father's eyebrows go up.

"I always trusted Richard, even with that, although I don't believe in it. But I believed in him. I learned that from you. You believed in me. I wanted to become a writer, you didn't think that was much of a way to make a living. You wanted me to become an attorney. But when my short stories were published in news-papers, you even typed my manuscripts."

"I was retired and didn't have anything else to do."

"You backed me. I backed Richard. His magazine comes out every two months. 9,000 copies."

I hear father's appreciative click of the tongue and see mother's approving glance at Richard across the table. I feel good.

"Claire's husband is doing well, too," I report. "Imagine their having their silver anniversary next June! And look at their two beautiful daughters over there. Shala is15, Heidi 18. Heidi graduated from high school with honors."

"You can be proud of your family," mother says, and father squeezes my shoulder, as he did on rare occasions. I dig into my turkey. What a Thanksgiving!

(Happy Endings, Berkeley: Self-publication, 1990)

Translating German Humorous Verses

Der Lattenzaun
Es war einmal ein Lattenzaun,
mit Zwischenraum, hindurchzuschaun.
Ein Architect, der dieses sah,
stand eines Abends plötzlich da –
und nahm den Zwischenraum heraus
und baute draus ein grosses Haus.
Der Zaun indessen stand ganz dumm,
mit Latten ohne was herum.
Ein Anblick hässlich und gemein.
Drum zog ihn der Senat auch ein.
Der Architekt jedoch entfloh
nach Afri- od- Ameriko.

The Picket Fence
There used to be a picket fence
with space to gaze from hence to thence.
An architect who saw this sight
approached it suddenly one night.
removed the spaces from the fence,
and built of them a residence.
The picket fence stood there dumbfounded
with pickets wholly unsurrounded,
a view so naked and obscene,
the sheriff had to intervene.
The architect absconded, though,
to Afri- or Americo.

In German-speaking countries these verses by Christian Morgenstern are as familiar as Mother Goose here. But in the English-speaking orbit they were not until recently, when they were published in translation. I have been fond of them since I grew up in Austria, but when I came to this country and wanted to share this poems from his volume *Galgenlieder*, with my American friends, I found no translation in the library. Cassell's *Encyclopedia of World Literature* (1954 edition) declared Morgenstern as untranslatable.

It was a challenge.

154

What's so difficult about translating the "Picket Fence"? Translating this poem is no more difficult than translating any rhymed poetry. It permits an almost mirror-like word-for-word rendering of the original. The unit of translation is the individual word:

> Er nahm den Zwischenraum heraus
> und baute draus ein grosses Haus.
> . . . removed the spaces from the fence,
> and built of them a residence.

But the unit of translation is not always the word. Every language has idioms that would be meaningless if translated literally, hence the unit has to be the entire idiom. There is a German idiom for somebody giving up in disappointment.Translated literally, he is said "to toss a rifle into the wheat field," whatever the origin of that phrase might be. Now Morgenstern, taking the idiom literally, tells of a man who walks in a wheat field, finds a rifle, and mournfully reflects on the hopeless poor devil who cast away the rifle. If the poem were translated word for word into English, it would make no sense. Here the translator has to find an idiom that could convey the same idea. If you translate the German word for rifle by "towel," the meaning clicks: Somebody finds a towel and is sorry for the discouraged loser who has thrown it in.

Related to the idiom, from the translator's standpoint, are plays on words, the puns that are accidents of language. Puns have a bad reputation, but a pun can be as subtle as it can be crude, depending on the punster. Here is an example of translating a pun:

Das Gebet
Die Rehlein beten zur Nacht,
hab acht!
Halb neun!
Halb zehn!
Halb elf!
Halb zwölf!
Zwölf!
Die Rehlein beten zur Nacht.
hab acht!
Sie falten die kleinen Zehlein,
die Rehlein.

The task was to find a substitute or at least an approach for the daring jump from *hab acht* to *halb neun*. The solution chosen was to use the syllable "-ate" (as in navigate, speculate, congregate) as if it were spelled like the figure 8.

The Does' Prayer
The does, as the hour grows late,
med-it-ate;
med-it-nine;
med-i-ten;
med-eleven;
med-twelve;
mednight!
The does, as the hour grows late,
meditate .
They fold their little toesies,
the doesies.

Karl Kraus, the Austrian essayist, satirist, and critic, was a master in using plays on words. Here is a tender poem in which he uses a multiple pun, based on the German word *Fehler*. In the first stanza he says that his beloved has some physical imperfection, but it is this very flaw that endears her to him. And then, in the last stanza:

Doch träte selbst die Schönste vor mich hin,
und fehlerlos,
ich wäre meines Drangs zu dir kein Hehler.
Ihr, die so vieles hat, fehlt eines bloss
und alles drum – ach wie vermiss' ich ihn –
ihr fehlt doch, Liebste, was mir fehlt: dein Fehler!

The three German words in the last line have the same sound but three different meanings: *ihr fehlt* : she lacks;*was mir fehlt:* what I miss; *dein Fehler:* your shortcoming, flaw, imperfection. Still, they can be reconciled in translation:

Yet if there came the fairest of the fair,
and flawless she,
my thoughts of you would linger and keep haunting.
No matter what her charms and virtues be,
her fault would be the flaw that wasn't there –
I would not want her if your want were wanting.

The translation unit, then, can be larger than the word. It can be an idiom (throw in the towel) or it can be a pun (meditate, Fehler) that requires adjustments going beyond translation of one word.

But the translation unit can be larger still. It may be the entire poem, the idea. In translating the songs of the Austrian comedy writer Johann Nestroy, I felt free to write entirely new stanzas retaining only the refrain line. For example, one such new stanza begins, in anachronistic translation (Nestroy died in 1860), with the words:

They now have a bomb that more damage can do
than all bombs together in World War Two.

Such treatment goes beyond translation; nevertheless, it is part of the translator's work. This kind of updating has been done by the producers of all stage productions since Nestroy's death, and was done by Nestroy himself who wrote last-minute encore stanzas for his productions alluding to current events. The translator's task is to create a reaction in the audience similar to that produced by the original, even if the words are different.

There is yet another dimension, going beyond the one-word unit, the multiword unit, and the entire piece to be translated: the problem of slang or dialect. How can one translate this? Nestroy wrote his comedies in Viennese dialect. They were deeply rooted in the Vienna scene of the second half of the nineteenth century. Nestroy remained untranslated, although, to this day, he is the most-played comedy writer in the German tongue if, indeed, you accept Viennese as German. Nestroy was not even translated into standard German until after World War II. The slang could not be translated. Thornton Wilder adapted one of Nestroy's plays into *The Merchant of Yonkers*, which became *The Matchmaker*, which was transformed into the world success of *Hello Dolly*. Joseph Fabry and I, inspired by Wilder, tried our hands, translated three plays, and sent the manuscript to him for criticism. Here, in part, is his handwritten answer:

Many thanks for translating the Nestroy plays and letting me see them. But, God in Heaven, how can you be both such good and such bad translators?. . . The element I thought you'd be worst, you do best: the couplets. Where you fall flat on your faces is in your use of contemporary American slang . . . [Slang expressions transferred to] another country, another epoch, stick out like sore thumbs, they loudly call attention to themselves. . . "But, Mr.Wilder," you will say, "Nestroy's low-life characters do talk constant and vivid slang. How can we translate that truth and that force?"

By art. By skill. By invention. By substitution. That's your job. Give all the feeling of working-class character anywhere without planting their talk in England or America. You are very good translators, except for this blind spot. . ."

So what is he saying'? If a character is, for example, a lowly cobbler, Let him use words that are germane to a lowly cobbler, let him use language that characterizes his social position without placing him in any particular country. Mr.Wilder, in the same letter, cited examples from our manuscript of words *not* to use because of its typical American cast: "pooped", "vinegar puss", "my doll."

We combed our translation carefully for Americanisms, and Mr. Wilder was pacified enough to write the foreword for the book.

The translations of Nestroy, then, were not "faithful", yet Wilder approved. Few translators escape the challenge of being unfaithful, but the choice between translating freely or faithfully usually does not depend on the translator but on the nature of the original. The "Picket Fence" could be translated faithfully, the "Does' Prayer" could not. The pleasure of translating, however, inheres in both approaches. See how beautifully the rhymes and meter click in this more or less literal translation of lines by Wilhelm Busch done by Walter Arndt of Dartmouth College, describing the arrival of a newly born:

> Früh zeigt er seine Energie,
> indem er ausdermassen schrie;
> denn früh belehrt ihn die Erfahrung:
> Sobald er schrie, bekam er Nahrung.
> He is robust, as one can tell
> by his all-penetrating yell;
> Experience led him to conclude:
> Persistent yells result in food.

There is not a word too much or to little, and nothing is twisted to fit the meter or rhyme. The pleasure, the satisfaction, comes from the naturalness of the lines, from the unforced pitter-patter. The danger of artificial twisting is strong in translating German verse. German word order invites inversions, which are usually unacceptable in English.

The successful literal translation, then, is a pleasure to the translator and the reader, but the free translation has its own rewards. It allows the translator creativeness. Although bound by the words and ideas of the original, the translator's work is highly personal. He can choose from alternatives and interpretations, making his version as revealing as a Rorschach test. A translation, like handwriting, shows the character of the translator.

When it comes to the charge of unfaithfulness, the translator of verse is in double jeopardy. In addition to translating the words, he has to recreate the meter and rhyme, and it is there where his creativeness has an opportunity. A business letter can be translated by a businessman. A poem has to be translated by a poet.

Over the centuries, keen observations have been made about the art of translating, applying to both prose and verse.

A Hebrew teacher of the first century, Jehuda ben Ilai, talking about translating the Bible, said that literal translating means lying, and free translating means blaspheming. A much-quoted French saying claims that translations are like women: "If they are beautiful, they are not faithful, and if they are faithful, they are not beautiful," matched by the equally well-known Spanish saying (credited to Cervantes) that "translating from one language to another is like gazing at a Flemish tapestry with the wrong side out."And there is the classic Italian verdict, unbearable in its succinctness: "Traduttore, traditore" – translator, traitor, a pun in itself untranslatable with equal pungency. And to include with one American quotation in this United Nations of condemnations: John Ciardi in the *Saturday Review of Literature* has called translation flatly "the art of failure."

Yes, yes, they all are right. But even John Ciardi gives us a chance. He says: "What a translator tries for is no more than the best possible failure." We have at least the challenge of aiming at a good failure.

But the worm can turn. Sometimes a good translation, far from being inferior to the original, may be superior to it. A provocative statement. But a good translator works in a double capacity: as translator and as editor. He looks at the original with more searching eyes than most readers. He has to plumb the depth of the meaning of every word.

Karl Kraus wrote a poem about a park surrounding a Czech castle. It seemed a rather formal park, with a pond and swan, with flowerbeds, and possibly statuary. One line says: "*Wie lange steht er schon auf diesem Stein, der Admiral,*" Literally: How long has the admiral been standing on this stone." Apparently there was a statue of a navy warrior in that park. I translated accordingly, but it didn't seem quite right. There is a butterfly called admiral. I wrote to Czechoslovakia, and learned that there is no statuary in that park and never was. So Kraus must indeed have meant the butterfly. (The preceding line in Kraus's poem actually speaks about flowers.) I changed my translation from "admiral" to "butterfly" and from "standing" (which Kraus evidently used in poetic license to indicate the folded vertical wings) to "sitting": "Upon the rock is sitting the butterfly." Such interpretive translating I hoped would make the poem more understandable to foreign readers not familiar with the park.

Because of this "posthumous," as it were, cleaning up of over-looked flaws, Roda Roda, the Austro-Hungarian writer of the First World War, in opposition to John Ciardi, said: "A translation is good only when it is better than the original."

Ordinarily, though, the chick will not try to he wiser than the hen. The translator will make the best effort, and aim at excellence. The aim is two-pronged. One is devoted identification with the original: the trans-lator is the alter ego of the author. The other prong is the creativeness that is the translator's own, highly individual expression. The synthesis of these two divergent aims makes for the finest translation.

In my own work, I thought that at least once I was close to that synthesis, when I felt the author was smiling down from the heavens seeing what was being done to his work, as I was sailing precariously between Ciardi and Roda Roda. Trans-lating literally means "carrying across": carrying the text from one side of the linguistic border to the other, visually expressed perhaps by turning over the palm of your hand.

Morgenstern's most celebrated, indeed most eloquent poem permits that synthesis. Here is the original of *Fish's Nightsong* (left) and the translation at the right.

Fisches Nachtgesang   **Fish's Night Song**

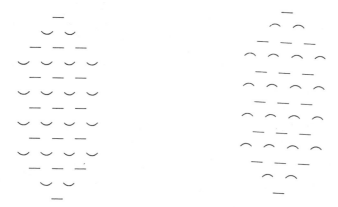

(*META, Translators' Journal*, University of Montreal Press, September. 1992)

Autumn Leaves

Verses
Essays

Verses

Additional verse translations can be found in the articles Building Language Bridges (p. 63), Brecht as Seen in the East (p. 129), *and* Translating Humorous Verses (p. 153).

Christian Morgenstern

Die unmögliche Tatsache

Palmstrom, etwas schon an Jahren,
wird an einer Strassenbeuge
und von einem Kraftfahrzeuge
überfahren.
"Wie war" (spricht er, sich erhebend
und entschlossen weiterlebend)
"möglich, wie dies Unglück, ja –:
dass es überhaupt geschah?
"Ist die Staatskunst anzuklagen
in Bezug auf Kraftfahrwagen?
Gab die Polizeivorschrift
hier dem Fahrer freie Trift?"
Oder war vielmehr verboten,
hier Lebendige zu Toten
umzuwandeln, – kurz und schlicht:
Durfte hier der Kutscher nicht – ?"
Eingehüllt in feuchte Tücher,
prüft er die Gesetzesbücher
und ist alsobald im Klaren:
Wagen durften dort nicht fahren!
Und er kommt zu dem Ergebnis:
Nur ein Traum war das Erlebnis.
Weil, so schliesst er messerscharf,
nicht sein *kann*, was nicht sein *darf.*

The Impossible Fact

Palmström, old, an aimless rover,
walking while in deep reflection
at a busy intersection
is run over.
   "How, now," he announces, rising
and with firmness death despising,
"can an accident like this
ever happen? What's amiss?
   "Did the state administration
fail in motor transportation?
Under the police chief's sway
had the driver right of way?
   "Isn't there a prohibition,
barring motorized transmission
of the living to the dead?
Did the driver lose his head?"
   Tightly swathed in dampened tissues
he explores the legal issues,
and it soon is clear as air:
Cars were not permitted there!
   And he comes to the conclusion:
His mishap was an illusion,
for, he reasons pointedly,
that which *must* not, *can* not be.

Auf dem Fliegenplaneten

Auf dem Fliegenplaneten,
da geht es dem Menschen nicht gut:
Denn was er hier der Fliege,
die Fliege dort ihm tut.
An Bändern voll Honig kleben
die Menschen dort allesamt
und andre sind zum Verleben
in süsslichem Bier verdammt.
In einem nur scheinen die Fliegen
dem Menschen vorauszustehn:
Man backt uns nicht in Semmeln
noch trinkt man uns aus Versehn.

At the Housefly Planet

Upon the housefly planet
the fate of the human is grim:
for what he does here to the housefly,
the fly does there unto him.
To paper with honey cover
the humans there adhere,
while others are doomed to hover
near death in vapid beer.
However, one practice of humans
the flies will not undertake:
they will not bake us in muffins
nor swallow us by mistake.

Die Trichter

Zwei Trichter wandeln durch die Nacht.
Durch ihres Rumpfs verengten Schacht
fliesst weisses Mondlicht
still und heiter
auf ihren
Waldweg
u. s.
w.

The Funnels
[Two versions]

Two funnels travel through the night;
a sylvan moon's candescent light
employs their bodies' narrow
flue in shining pale
and cheerful
thro
ug
h

*

Two funnels amble through the night.
Within their body, moonbeams white
converge as they
descend upon
their forest
pathway
and
so
on

(*Christian Morgenstern's Galgenlieder*, Berkeley: University
of California Press, 1963. German into English)

Johann Nestroy

A Man Full of Nothing
(Original title: Der Zerrissene)

HERR VON LIPS:
Your boss throws a party, invites you to come.
You go, for you know where your gravy comes from.
There's Mrs., there's Grandma, there's Junior, and Sis . . .
The wine is not aged, but the Mrs. sure is;
you wish that the beer were as cold as the steak,
and the jokes not as stale as the strawberry cake.
The Sis plays piano, and Junior French horn,
by the time you escape, it is three in the morn.
You say: "Folks, you were charming, your eats were a treat . . ,"
　To pretend in this way is a fabulous feat.

"Your wife has a lover," so says your best friend.
"Confess, shameless hussy, prepare for the end!
Confess, or I'll wallop the tar out of you!"
That's what you would say, feeling mad as you do.
But easy! Find out, before raising the roof,
or you are the fool when she asks for the proof.
She comes in, all dolled up, and says, "Now I must run
to visit Eileen." You say, "Darling, have fun,
just give me a kiss, you look fetching, look sweet . . ."
　To pretend in this way is a fabulous feat.

A man with a corn on each one of his toes
takes a girl to a dance and intends to propose.
She is rich, she is pretty, her figure's divine
but her manner of dancing is elephantine.
She's far more on *his* feet than she is on *hers*
but he smiles at her bravely every time this occurs.
"Your dance is exquisite, it makes life complete!"
　To pretend in this way shows two fabulous feet.

ENCORE
They now have a bomb that more damage can do
than all bombs together in World War Two.
They can poison the air now with horrible stuff,
it's paid for by taxes, and it's never enough.
Populations increase at an ominous rate,
all mankind seems bound for a terrible fate.
And yet, we live on as if nothing were wrong,
We laugh and rejoice in wine, women, and song;
we go to a show and relax in our seat . . .
   To pretend in this way is a fabulous feat.

*

Love Affairs and Wedding Bells

MOON:
They tell me, a man must not live just on bread,
but I do it on crust, and I'm always ahead.
I am quick as a dart, when I run into debt,
but for paying them back, I slow down and forget.
I am what they call a professional moocher,
I've plenty of past, but not much of a future,
yet I eat and I drink, with no sweat on my brow —
   And no one knows how.

The optimist often proclaims with a cheer:
"The best of all possible worlds is right here!"
The pessimist looks at the hullabaloo
and admits he's afraid this might really be true.
Some people are sure that the best man will win,
while others just know you must bear it and grin.
Some believe in a doomsday, some in pie in the sky —
   And no one knows why.

A millionaire banker of three score and ten
takes a girl in her teens when he marries again.
She adores the old man, entertains all his friends.
The husband gets tired but her fun never ends.
After one year of marriage, O blessing and joy!
She gives birth to a baby, a fine little boy.
His friends say that Dad must be proud of the two —
  But no one knows who.

ENCORE
In Metternich's era, to say what you think
meant playing with fire and courting the clink.
The censor, of course, is abolished today,
you say what you want now in any which way —
unless you insist upon keeping your job,
being friends with your neighbors, and pleasing the mob.
True freedom of speech? It will come to all men —
  But no one knows when.

(*Johann Nestroy, Three Comedies*, New York: Ungar,
1966)

Karl Kraus

Der Flieger

Arsenale zu treffen, wäre nicht ohne,
doch werden nur Kinderzimmer ruiniert.
Vielleicht, wer auf einen Säugling visiert,
zerstört endlich doch einmal eine Kanone!

The Aviator

Destroying an arsenal would be fun,
but what does he hit? A baby.
Eventually he would hit a gun
if he aimed at a nursery. Maybe.

*

Kriegswolt

Sie waren bei Laune, es ging ihnen gut,
nur unser Leben hatten sie über.
Tags waren sie schon betrunken von Blut
und gossen des Nachts noch Wein darüber.
Sie lebten und lachten in Saus und Braus
und konnten nicht über Langweile klagen.
Und gingen ihnen die Menschen aus,
so haben die Zeit sie totgeschlagen.

The Warmakers

They spent their lives in laughter and play
while ours were put on the line.
They got themselves drunk with blood in the day
and chased it at night with wine.
They feasted and threw their weight about,
considering boredom a crime;
and when their supply of people ran out,
they turned to killing time.

(*In These Great Times*, Montreal: Engendra Press, 1976)

Ogden Nash

Der Zentral Park von New York

Solltest nach der Sonne Schwinden
du dich hier im Park befinden,
lass die Wege! Eile so
schnell wie möglich in den Zoo,
krieche in den Löwenzwinger -
dort ist die Gefahr geringer.

The Central Park of New York

If you should happen after dark
to find yourself in Central Park,
ignore the paths that beckon you
and hurry, hurry to the zoo,
and creep into the tiger's lair.
Frankly, you'll be safer there.

*

Die Schildkröte

Schildkröten zwischen Panzern stecken,
die praktisch ihr Geschlecht verdecken.
Ich finde es bewundernswert,
dass dieses Tier sich doch vermehrt.

The Turtle

The turtle lives 'twixt plated decks
which practically conceal its sex.
I think it clever of the turtle
in such a fix to be so fertile.

Rat an Ehegatten

Willst du eine gute Ehe,
glücklich, heiter und gesund —
wenn du unrecht hast, gestehe;
wenn du recht hast, halt den Mund.

A Word to Husbands

To keep your marriage brimming
with love in the loving cup -
whenever you're wrong, admit it;
Whenever you're right, shut up.

*

Der Purist

Vor Ihnen steht Professor Haftler,
ein höchst exakter Wissenschaftler.
Vom Kuratorium hoch geschätzt
ward in den Urwald er versetzt.
Dort, lagernd in der Tropen-Au,
vermisst er seine junge Frau.
Es hat, wie ihm sein Boy erklärt,
ein Alligator sie verzehrt.
Da lächelt der Professor still:
"Sie meinen wohl ein Krokodil."

The Purist

I give you now Professor Twist,
a conscientious scientist.
Trustees exclaimed, "He never bungles!"
and sent him off to distant jungles.
Camped on a tropic riverside,
one day he missed his loving bride.
She had, the guide informed him later,
been eaten by an alligator.
Professor Twist could not but smile.
"You mean", he said, "a crocodile."

Geschmackloser Versuch

Es drängte ein Gourmet mich lange:
Versuch ein Stückchen Klapperschlange!
Hab keine Angst — du wirst entdecken,
sie wird wie zartes Hühnchen schmecken."
So war's.
Nun macht mir Huhnfleisch bange —
Es schmeckt so sehr nach Klapperschlange.

Experiment Degustatory

A gourmet challenged me to eat
a tiny bit of rattlesnake meat,
remarking, "Don't look horror-stricken,
You'll find it tastes a lot like chicken."
It did.
Now chicken I cannot eat
because it tastes like rattlesnake meat.

*

Plakatastrophe

Unter diesem Steine
liegt ein armer Wicht.
Er achtete auf die Reklame
statt aufs rote Licht.

Lather as You Go

Beneath this slab
John Brown is stowed.
He watched the ads,
and not the road.

Denthysterie

Mir bangt schon im Vorzimmer —
Beim Zahnarzt, da bohrzimmer.

Obvious Reflection

Dentists' anterooms
give me tanterooms.

*

Die Kuh

Zum Rindviehstamm gehört die Kuh;
ein Ende macht Milch, das andere Muh.

The Cow

The cow is of the bovine ilk;
one end makes moo, the other, milk.

*

Trostspruch für Opfer des Ausspruchs: "Männer, welche Mädchen jagen, meiden die, die Brillen tragen"

Mag sein, dass Mädchen, die bebrillt sind,
schwer Männer finden, die gewillt sind;
doch den begehrteren Geschöpfchen
winkt bald die Windel und das Töpfchen.

Lines to Console Ladies Distressed by the Lines "Men Seldom Make Passes at Girls who wear glasses."

A girl who is bespectacled,
she may not get her nectacled,
but safety pins and bassinets
await the girl who fascinets.

(Ogden Nash, *Der Kuckuck führt ein Lotterleben*,
Vienna: Paul Zsolnay, 1977. English into German)

Gallant Knight

Je ne suis pas . . .

Je ne suis pas de ces gens la
qui font neuf ou dix fois cela
quant ilz sont aupres d'une dame,
mais pour une fois, sur mon ame,
je le fays bien, et puis hola.

L'autre jour une m'en parla
et en m'en parlant m'acolla;
mais je luy dis: par dieu, ma dame,
je ne suis pas, etc.

Tout son conseil me revela
en disant: Mon amy, la la,
entendez a moy, je me pasme.
Et je responds pour estre infame:
Parlez a mon clerc de cela;
je ne suis pas, etc.

I am not . . .

>I am not such a gallant knight
>to function ten, twelve times per night
>when with a pretty femme I lie.
>I do it twice or thrice, oh my,
>and that, I think, should be all right.
>The other day, she held me tight
>and sweetly asked for more delight,
>but I just said: "My lady, why,
>I am not such a gallant knight," . . .
>She didn't like it and took flight
>and left me sitting in my plight.
>When people blame me, I reply:
>"Those who don't want my love, good-bye!"
>Then I defiantly recite:
>"I am not such a gallant knight," . . .

(*A Florentine Chanconnier from the Time of Lorenzo the Magnificent,* University of Chicago Press, 1983. Old French into English)

Animal Jingles

The Emu (Aim-you)

The emu is a nasty bird
of whom some people never heard.
He dwells in puzzles and Australia
and is a sordid sort, I tellya:
He never flies and never sings,
and when he bites your hand, it stings.
Don't emulate the emu, man,
and just avoid him if you can.
    You do not like the emu?
    I don't blemu.

The Arctic Tern

Of all the birds that fly or nest
the Arctic tern's the championest
by flying from the Arctic ice
to the Antarctic yearly twice.
To reach their annual breeding goal
a pair flies almost pole to pole.
When they arrive, the pair unpack,
then make a tern, and double back.

The Kudu

What can a kudu caged in a zoo do?
He's an antelope who cantelope
except by voodoo.
    If you were a kudu, what would you do?

The Camel

The camel, known as desert ship,
has a contemptuous upper lip.
Just watch him haughtily advance,
a picture of pure arrogance.
He thinks he is a genius,
much better than the rest of us,
and that we are creation's blight . . .
   Perhaps he's right.

The Gnats

The gnat is a peculiar thing:
a wisp of nothing with a sting.
Gnats like a picnic and the beach
and fly so close yet out of reach.
They suck the blood and prick the skin
of you, your friends, your next of kin.
You rarely catch them when they park,
and if you do, they leave a mark.
But even a successful slap
will come too late — they have your sap.
   You plan a picnic in a spot
   with gnats abuzz? You'd better gnot.

The Chimpanzee

The chimpanzee, the chimpanzee
is said to be as wise as we.
But I suspect, but I suspect
there is some aspect we neglect
and that is that the chimpanzee
does not build war machinery
but dwelleth peaceful in his tree
and lives his life, lets others be.
   The chimpanzee, the chimpanzee
   may be a wiser ape than we.

The Black Widow

Black widows flourish on a scale
that dwarfs the tiny spider male.
The wedding gives him such a scare,
he wraps her first with silver snare,
which buys him just enough delay
when love is done to run away.
But if he's not enough alert,
she snags and chomps him for dessert.
   I'll say the amorous black widow
   has something wrong with her libido.

The Wombat

The wombat dwelleth in his lair,
akin to the koala bear.
He's not a bat, he's not a wom,
but modest, cute, and frolicsome.
His tail is short, his legs quadruple,
his nose is bare, his pouch marsuple.
He is a truly friendly guy,
his ways are peaceful, meek, and shy.
   The wombat
   shuns combat.

The Oyster

Caged like a monk inside a cloister
sits in its shell the humble oyster.
Men hunt the oyster as a snack
or as an aphrodisiac,
but also to extract a pearl
to deck the bosom of a girl.
   The pearl, though, might prefer the oyster,
   which is less cuddly but more moister.

The Narwhal

The narwhal's horn in an incisor.
(You did not know this? Now you're wiser.)
He doesn't feature other teeth,
not jaw above and not beneath.
   O seniors, what sublime adventures
   to sport a horn instead of dentures!

The Tuatara

On a remote New Zealand isle
a living creature dwells in style.
The tuatara perseveres
for more than hundred million years,
an iguana-type of creature,
which has a very special feature:
It is, to everyone's surprise
equipped by nature with three eyes.
Up, in the forehead, Number Three
sits well content and winks at thee –
   a puzzlement to scientists,
   a problem for optometrists.

(*Zany Zoo* , Berkeley: Kalmar Publishing, 1993)

German Poetry

Mathias Claudius (1740-1815)

The First Tooth

Hurray, hurray, forsooth, forsooth!
It's here, the first white little tooth!
You, Mother, come, and high and low,
all 'round the house, come see the show
and watch it white and brightly glow.

The tooth shall be called Alex. What delight,
oh, darling child! May God keep it for you
and fill your little mouth with more teeth, too.
And may they always have something to bite.

*

Johann Wolfgang Goethe (1749-1832)

The Frogs

A pond was frozen thick with frost,
the little frogs in the deep were lost,
no longer could they croak and spring,
but promised themselves with dreamy eye
that, if they found some space up high,
like nightingales they all would sing.
The spring wind came
the ice was breached,
they paddled and proudly the land they reached,
and settled up and down the shore
and did their croaking as before.

Different Threat

I followed my girl into the wood,
around her neck I fell.
But she was threat'ning me: "Be good
or I will start to yell."

I called defiantly, "I will
kill all who interfere!"
"Still," whispered she, "my darling, still!
So nobody shall hear."

*

Wolfgang Amadeus Mozart (1756-1791)

To his sister before her wedding

In wedlock you will soon find out
what you could only half explain,
and soon it will be known to you
what Eve was once obliged to do
in order to deliver Cain.

But all those wedded duties, Sis,
believe me, you will see as bliss -
they are not hard to do at all.
But everything, then, has two sides:
though wedlock many joys provides,
much sorrow also will befall.

Hence, when your husband's mien is stern,
which, you believe, you did not earn,
and when he vents on you his plight,
just think, his whim will soon be gone
and say: My lord, thy will be done
by day - and mine by night.

Heinrich Heine (1797-1856)

The Lady by the Ocean

The lady by the ocean
sighed long and woebegone.
She felt such deep emotion
about the setting sun.

Young lady, stop your fretting,
it's still the same old tack:
In front the sun is setting,
and rising from the back.

*

Wilhelm Busch (1832 - 1908)

Experience

Once, when I was inexperienced
and more modest than today,
I respectfully paid honor
to what others had to say.
Later, though, I have encountered
grazing with me on the lea
other oxen, and since then
I've valued me.

Fatherhood

Becoming a father - that's a cinch.
Being one - there is the pinch.

Alas!

This always was the situation,
and will, I am afraid, remain:
unless yours is a special station,
virtue is arduous to attain.

To rise requires work, not fooling,
easy enough it is to fall.
The Lord must do a lot of pulling,
the devil needs not sweat at all.

*

Joachim Ringelnatz (1888-1934)

Boomerang

Once there was a boomerang,
just a little bit too long.
Boomerang, on its track,
flew a bit, came not back.
Many hours sat the gang
waiting for the boomerang.

The Wise Ants

Two ants who lived on a dahlia
wanted to walk to Australia.
They marched a mile on the street
until they had hurting feet.
They wisely decided to skip
the final part of the trip.

(From an unpublished anthology of German classical and
modern poetry in translation)

Essays

The Horizontal Society

Last Tuesday night I stood in the dark and watched the moon disappear. There were no clouds, yet the bright disk was being covered slowly as if a black hand had moved acros. I thought how panic-stricken people must have felt before they knew anything about eclipses. I also thought how similar the situation was to what we are experiencing today.

Today, not the moon is disappearing but many familiar values and traditions. And we are panic-stricken because we do not see any reason for what is happening. Fear of the unknown is the greatest fear of all.

We live at a great breaking point of history. Up to now, people have always lived in societies where guidelines for living were given from above – a king, a priest, a teacher, a father. It has been a vertical society, in which the individual found meaning by obeying authority. The meaning of life for a child was to be a good child according to father's standards; for a citizen, to be blindly loyal to the king; for a slave, to be a good servant to the master; for a wife, to obey her husband.

All this is changing. We are rebelling against authority and trying to find our own guidelines. Good is what is meaning fulfilling for *me*. Bad is what is blocking my meaning fulfillment. We are moving toward a horizontal society.

This may sound like an invitation to chaos. It can be. It depends on our definition of meaning. For me, life has meaning if I am aware of some order and that I am part of that order – it *does* make a difference, however small, what I do or neglect to do.

This order has religious and secular names – God, essence, life force, nature, evolution. Its latest name is ecosystem, the awareness that we are part of the universe and will destroy ourselves if we destroy other parts. Paul Tillich calls it the "ground of being."

Vertical societies have a pyramidal order. They make a dogma of it, base their value system on it, and resist change. But our knowledge of the world is not static. New truths are constantly being discovered that change our ideas of that order. For a long time the authorities have been getting away with keeping our belief system static. But people get restless. First one, then a few, then more and more realize that, while ultimate meaning remains constant, our concept of it is changing.

Those who first glimpse new meanings are the philosophers, founders of religions, social reformers. They are threatening to the establishment, are suppressed, ridiculed, often killed. But their ideas live on, and increasingly people realize that the old value system is outdated. Institutions are mistrusted, traditions crumble, there is a vacuum.

The vacuum lasts until a new set of values, institutions, and traditions develop. The process is gradual. The discoveries of new truths come so slowly that they remain unnoticed within the lifetime of one generation. But on rare occasions, fresh discoveries of new truths come so fast that sharp breaks occur. This has happened three times within recorded Western history.

The first break came at the end of antiquity: The Roman society gave way to the new values of Christianity. Zeus was replaced by the Judeo-Christian God. The morals of Homer were succeeded by those of Moses and Jesus. An economy based on slavery gave way to feudalism. The Middle Ages had begun.

The second break came at the end of the Middle Ages when new truths were discovered within a short span. The new discoveries came in three main fields: astronomy, warfare, and communication. The discovery that the earth was neither flat nor the center of the universe had much greater than astronomical consequences. It removed the mysteries of the heavenly bodies from theology, where they could not be questioned, and opened them to inquiry, making way for modern science. Then, warfare: the invention of gun powder in the Western world changed more than our way of fighting. It changed our self-image. No longer was it safe to protect ourselves from attack by individual armament, and the way was opened to the nation-state and nationalism. And communication: The invention of movable type made it possible to spread the knowledge of newly discovered truths and opened the way to faster and faster changes.

Now we are at the third major break. The era we call "Modern Age" has come to an end in our lifetime, and a new era, yet unnamed, has begun. The main changes again come in the areas of astronomy, warfare, and communication. What these changes mean for the future, we can no more foresee than Columbus could have foreseen the city of New York. But we do have an inkling that the exploration of space is more than a feat in astronomy and physics. It may open the way to a new morality. It is one thing to talk about "our shrinking earth," but quite another to actually see the earth, (which to my own parents was a vast expanse populated by strangers) on our television screen as a tiny ball, the home of the entire human race. How will that change our self-image? We do not know. It may lead to the insight that we are truly fellow travellers floating through space on the same fragile life boat. It may indeed have been "a giant step for mankind," as Neil Armstrong put it when he took that first small step on the moon – a giant step toward our awareness of brother- and sisterhood, which so far has been only a pious dream.

The second major invention of our age, nuclear power, is more than another weapon. It's a challenge to make that brother-sisterhood a reality, or we'll all perish. The day we released the atom bomb was the most important day since Creation, it demonstrated how we can *un*create ourselves. It was a blast that can either kill us or wake us up.

The third invention, electronics, is more than communication. Before Gutenberg, the world produced 1,000 books a year. Today, it's more like 1,000 books a second. Television is more than entertainment. It fundamentally affects our institutions – family, education, government – and also our morality. Every child growing up today is raised by three parents: father, mother, and television. And television often is more present than parents. It opens the eyes of our children before they can even read to the schizophrenic realities of our world; they *see* on the TV screen people beaten and bombed while their parents tell them about love and brotherhood. And the commercials present deodorants and brands of beer as having high values for the quality of life.

Thus we are again at one of those sharp breaking points when old values have become obsolete, and we don't know what to put in their place. Not that the old values were bad. Power, production, and propagation were necessary for survival in an age of scarcity. Power was needed in a world where survival meant either you or me; but in a world of nuclear weapons, power leads to destruction of all. What we need today is not more power but more gentleness. Indeed, the meek will inherit the earth or the powerful will destroy it.

Production has meant more goods and food in a starving world. For the first time in history, a majority in at least part of the world is not hungry, and the rest knows that starvation no longer is unavoidable. Production is progress. But *uncontrolled* production is cause of some of the major threats – pollution, waste of non-renewable resources, garbage disposal problems, overcrowding. Having many children was once necessary for survival of the human race. Now survival depends on *limitation* of the birth rate.

One more example of the turn-about in values: our attitude to war. War was the noblest of human enterprises and to die for one's country held great meaning. But in the face of universal destruction, no cause is worth dying for, except a cause that promotes survival and abolishion of war. Why die for a nation when survival of that nation and nationalism will make war and universal destruction *more* likely? War no longer is an extension of diplomacy. The extension of diplomacy is peace.

The values that helped us overcome scarcity included frugality, sobriety, thrift, honest toil, self-denial, perseverance, obedience, loyalty, humility, courtesy, respect for tradition. But survival is threatened no longer by scarcity but by the possibility of total destruction in a world of plenty. The new ethic emphasizes openness in personal relationships, hospitality, cooperation, involvement, experimentation, spontaneity, creativity, participation, self-determination, self-esteem, self-actualization, awareness of one's feelings, honesty in expressing them, and consciousness. A new consciousness is emerging of what life is all about.

Thus, we live through another interim period between two value systems. But this time the consciousness about new truths and values is not limited to a few prophets and philosophers, it is emerging in a sizeable group of people. Lewis Mumford, almost twenty years ago, suggested that humankind's salvation might be achieved if *one* person in ten were fully capable of exercising his or her higher centers of intelligence and morality. This has never been achieved, but many are groping for the awareness that never again must they allow a rigid authority tell them what the meaning of their life should be. This is the job for you and me.

A frightening prospect. We have no experience of finding our own guidelines and meanings. This was always done for us by someone at the top of the pyramid. Even if one authority was overthrown, another took over. The slogan of the vertical society was: "The king is dead – long live the king!" Paganism was replaced by Christianity. Louis XVI was executed, and Napoleon ruled. The Russian czar was assassinated, and the Communist Party took over. Now, for the first time, we live in an order where we have to find our guidelines, in individual search. What is "good" is decided not by some elite. *I* have to decide what is meaningful. We are called upon to live in a society which was only a dream of a few great men like Socrates, Buddha, and Jesus. Now the burden of finding meaning rests on each member. A "horizontal society."

Is a horizontal society within reach? We don't know. But if we fail and let another power-prestige-production-dominated value system take over, we are done for. It is up to you and me to build a new value system in which brother-sisterhood is more than a dream.

Those born after 1945 know that. There *is* a generation gap. We all know that nuclear bombs must not be used, that pollution and surplus population must stop.   The pre-Hiroshima generations know it in their heads, the post-Hiroshimans feel it in their guts. No day in their lives has passed in which they have not known that all life can end in an instant. Many of the young are not much concerned about ideologies on which their elders are still hung up. We all know that death is unavoidable. But the young know that for them death is thoroughly avoidable for a long time, and that universal death would not be the will of God, but the fault of an outdated value system.

That is an unprecedented situation. We are not prepared to find the guidelines of our lives ourselves. Self-reliance was repressed in vertical societies. Imagine the prospects of children to assume responsibility for their lives if they were to grow up under the following circumstances: They are told, as soon as they know the meaning of words, that they were born sinners who cannot change their sinful state by themselves; they are not trusted to make decisions about matters that concern them; they are surrounded by authority figures who tell them, by words and attitudes, that they are stupid, unreliable, untrustworthy, weak, criminal, and mentally unstable, and must be kept under supervision. What kind of adults can we expect such children to grow into? Can we expect them to grow into adults at all? Yet, that is the self-image we have been given in our vertically oriented societies. We have accepted the self-image of a puppet that will collapse unless the strings are pulled by the master; a sinner who can find redemption only by submitting to the master's will; a trained animal that will respond only to rewards and punishments; a computer that will react automatically to data fed into them; a consumer who has no intrinsic worth, only cash value; and the self-image of a child, never trusted, never given responsibility.

Psychological research has shown the self-fulfilling prophecy of one's image. You bring up children telling them they are stupid, and they'll *think* of themselves as stupid, and do stupid things. Then you can say, "See, I told you, you are stupid." And their self-image as stupid persons is reinforced because they now can see that indeed they behave stupidly. Thus, their pattern of life is established. It was to be expected, then, that growing up with the self-image of a puppet, sinner, animal, computer, consumer, and child, we would turn out to be dependent, guilty, instinct-driven, heartless, with no sense of worth, irresponsible. Then we are told, "See, I told you, you need my guidance," and people looked at themselves and their behavior, and agreed.

What, then, should our self-image be to find our own guidelines?

The first requirement is to be aware that we have choices. Scientists tell us we are determined by our genes, drives, and environment. We also have a spritual dimension where we do have choices, where we are not driven but are the drivers.

The second requirement is to consider in our choice-making the consequences for others. In vertical societies responsibilies were given to us, in horizontal societies we have to assume them on our own.

A third requirement is individual uniqueness. In this crowded and computerized world, much of what we do can be done by someone else, or even by a machine. In horizontal societies, we need to stress creative activities and human relationships. Only you can write a poem the way you do. Only you can relate to a friend in a unique way.

A fourth requirement in a horizontal society is to listen to our conscience. It's not a clear voice, it can err; all we can do is follow it to the best of our abilities. As the Harvard psychologist Gordon Allport put it: "You can at the same time be half-sure and whole-hearted."

A fifth requirement is to have self-chosen tasks. In vertical societies tasks were prescribed as duties. In horizontal societies, you have to find your own commitments.

But assuming commitments and responsibilities is meaningful only if a sixth requirement is fulfilled: our awareness that we are a part of a whole, like a cell in a body. Some cells in the eye or the heart may be more important than others, but all cells must function if the whole is to function. If I pick a task, I have to consider not only my needs and the needs of my immediate family and friends, but as wide a human need as I am capable of conceiving. It's the old idea of "brotherhood" which, in an age of nuclear weapons, has moved from a pious hope to a necessity. In modern terms, it's our awareness of being part of the ecosystem.

Can you and I do this? We never have been trusted to develop our potentials. All our institutions – family, school, church, government – were established vertically. Only recently have we begun to rebel against the guidelines of these institutions and to insist on finding our own. Much of today's trouble has been caused by that switch because traditional institutions are slow to change. Examples are Congress, our court systems, our military. But some of our churches, our schools, and our families are beginning to respond to the new requirements: to get to know ourselves better, to see others as individuals not marionettes, to be more honest about our

192

own feelings, to help others to gain self-esteem, to release our own tightness.

Self-knowledge is one requirement; greater self-determination another; and greater trust a third.

What we need most is trust, a feeling that we care about one another. Our government does not trust its citizens to know the facts, it does not trust its voters to decide on the basis of the true issues, and does not trust its minorities and the young. The young and the minorities have to persuade their government that they are trustworthy, and our government is to show it cares.

Thus, we are in the midst of a crucial interim period between a vertical society of outdated values, and a horizontal society with values not yet emerged. It is now up to us to search for these values to the best of our abilities.

If I want my government to be honest, I must start by being honest myself. If I want to avoid pollution, I must stop polluting and stop buying products of pollutors. If I want to avoid overpopulation, I must limit the number of my children. If I want to solve the waste problem I must stop wasting. And if I want to avoid nuclear confrontations, I must practice nonviolence.

These are not fixed goals. They are expanding goals. The further we go, the more we'll see what still needs to be done. Time has passed when a search for meaning was a search for goals outlined by others. The meanings in the Seventies, and thereafter, is more like a search for an ever receding horizon. Do not be discouraged that the horizon is receding. A horizon is nothing but a line that limits our vision, and the requirement of the moment is to expand the vision of ourselves as far as our potential will carry us.

(First Unitarian Church of Berkeley, January, 17, 1971, in *Spirit on Trial*, Berkeley, Self-publication)

Can Ecology Become a Religion?

As we approach the third millennium, an increasing number of people no longer are content with religion's traditional answers to the central question as to the meaning of life and our individual part in it.

Religious persons look for meaning through established religions, but secularists search in other ways, including philosophy, science, and personal insight. The goal of the search, common to all, is to find an order that "binds together."

This is religion's task, by whatever name we may call it.

Intellectually, religion is our attempt to understand the universe and our part in it.

Emotionally, it is our response to the mystery of life in the presence of something bigger than we are, and the sense of security that comes from being sheltered in an orderly universe.

Spiritually, it is our search for the illuminated life beyond our material existence.

Ethically, it is our striving for guidance to live together in harmony.

Existentially, it is our attempt to deal with the realities of life, including suffering, guilt, and death.

Our vast expansion of knowledge, from the tiny atom to infinite space, gives us a new understanding of the workings of nature and our chance to influence it. This frustrates our traditional religious search. Our capacity to influence the cosmic order burdens us with a responsibility for which paternalistic religions have not prepared us.

Intellectually, our increase of knowledge reveals the expanding area of our ignorance.

Emotionally, the complexity of modern society makes it difficult to feel part of a totality, and the bombardment from the mass media, with their emphasis on evil, injustice, and chaos, increases our despair and weakens our sense of security.

Spiritually, we are drained by the reductionism of science and education that presents human beings as nothing but animals that can be trained, or computers that can be manipulated.

Ethically, we feel confused because the guidelines from our secular and religious leaders do not prevent increase in crime, the breakdown of institutions, and the threat of ecological or nuclear disasters.

Existentially, in affluent societies we have exchanged the pain from hunger that was inevitable, for the pain from existential frustration which we feel could be avoided, thereby increasing our guilt.

Unable to find relevant answers in institutionalized religion, we are looking for new guidelines to a meaningful life in a variety of fields, ranging from Oriental religions to psychology, drugs, astrology, encounter groups, and extrasensory experimentation. Some searchers have found a promising new channel in ecology.

Ecology, until recently a minor branch of biology, seems an unlikely path to religion. Being part of the world of science, ecology may appear even antireligious to those who think in science-versus-religion terms. Science, to them, is a search for truth in a world where experiments can be repeated. Religion, on the other hand, is concerned with values and ethics which each of us has to find in the unrepeatable moments of our lives. Science is concerned with the world as it *is*,, religion with the world as it *ought to be*.. Science deals with the what, religion with the why.

These are deep differences which, however, ecology can bridge. Ecology has its roots in science but its goals are religious. It could be the unifying force between scientific knowledge and religious truths, a science that answers religious questions within our expanding knowledge of ourselves and the world around us.

Intellectually, ecology presents the ecosystem, an order of the universe open to research. It discloses our relationship with all other life forms in a chain from the plankton to us and our food supply. It reveals our dependency on the nonliving world: the air, miles above; water, miles below; minerals hidden in mountains; energy locked in atoms.

Emotionally, ecology shows us that mystery can be evoked also by a universe that can be observed, explored, and predicted. The tools of modern science reveal the beauties in atoms and in galaxies hidden from the naked eye. Our awe increases with unfolding knowledge. A universe in which the Earth is a small planet in a minor solar system at the edge of a galaxy of billions of suns is more awe-inspiring than a universe with unexplored Earth as its center. Our existence on earth as the result of evolution is as great a marvel as our creation by God's breathing life into Adam's nostrils. Science has illuminated some corners of our knowledge but also called our attention to mysteries in vast unexplored, perhaps unexplorable, areas.

Spiritually, ecology demonstrates the limitations of the material world and the dangers of its extension beyond a point of no return, which we are approaching. We are beginning to realize that to further increase the quantity of production will lower our quality of life below what we are prepared to accept; perhaps even below survival level. The ecosystem shows us the consequences of a value system that places what is technically possible above what is humanly desirable: that, for instance, we manufacture nuclear weapons and send people to the moon because it can be done, not because it will improve the quality of life for our grandchildren. Ecologists, placing spiritual goals above the material, confirm Thomas Jefferson's scale of values, placing the pursuit of happiness, and not of property, among our inalienable rights.

Ethically, the ecosystem outlines a morality in which the guidelines for living have been changed. The command to "be fruitful and multiply, and fill the Earth and subdue it" was appropriate for small tribes struggling against an untamed nature. Now this call for unending popu-lation growth is a threat to our abundance, comfort, and survival.

In an ecotheology, we see ourselves as trustees rather than masters of Earth's resources. Such a theology will change our economic ideas based on constant expansion, our political systems idolizing power, and our social structure favoring affluence and pleasures. As trustees, we develop different values. "Good" becomes what is good for our species. We will realize that our affluence is achieved at the expense of future generations. Our goal will be redirected from conspicuous consumption to the enjoyment of life's simplicities.

Our priorities will change, not because some higher-ups tell us how to behave but because the ecosystem makes the consequences of "immorality" self-evident. Eventually, the military will see that its own military machine will go up in radioactive clouds. The industrialists will realize that they are polluting the air their children will need to breathe. Business people will see they cannot make profits from dead customers. It will become self-evident that wasting resources, breeding unrestrictedly, and consuming for sheer pleasure are self-defeating.

Today's chaos, increasing crime rates, selfish competition, power struggles, and pleasure seeking are seen by fundamentalists as God's punishment for disregarding the old commandments: we have to obey – or else. But it is increasingly doubtful that traditional values will save our souls, or even our bodies. With conditions of survival drastically changed, we need directions based on respect for the ecosystem and commitment to safeguard it. The traditional rules, enforced by rewards and punishment, no longer seem to work. The rich and powerful get away with exploitation; the meek do not inherit the Earth, and there may be no Earth to inherit. The present chaos is a challenge to every person to find new directives – or else.

Ecology provides a system of guidelines not in the interest of an elite, not even in the interest of the rank and file, but in the interest of life. This is stark, demonstrable reality. In the ecosystem some aspects of the divine have become visible. We see a Great Design to which we can respond and which responds to us. We become aware of a life-sustaining order in which every person is related to every other person, to every form of life, and even to nonliving matter.

To many, a Great Design may not be an acceptable concept of God. But it opens a path to meaning for those who reject the traditional terms yet live in a world where the realities behind these terms are as valid as ever. Even individuals who spurn religious terminology must deal with the question of how to live meaningfully in a world beyond human understanding. They may not speak of their "faith in God" but their sanity will depend upon some belief in an enduring process of which they are an intrinsic part. They may not use words like sin and salvation but cannot avoid groping with their shortcomings and healing processes in a mysterious universe. Ecotheology offers new interpretations of old words. If God means the Great Design, sin is any behavior that disturbs that design; grace, the means by which we can live within the design; salvation, the state of balance with it; and immortality, our participation in actions that will allow future generations to live. To take an example from the literal world of ecology: Sin would be the destruction of a forest by greed or carelessness; grace, the inspiration to rebuild the forest; redemption, the actual rebuilding; salvation, the completion of reforesting; and immortality, making it possible for later generations to enjoy the forest. Human behavior based on this view of life requires a sense of relatedness and responsibility only few at present possess. But humans have shown their capacity to adapt to necessities before. Our ethics may change drastically because these changes are required by observable consequences.

Ecology also helps us find new and healthy perspectives of the old questions of suffering, guilt, and death.

Religion has given suffering meaning by presenting it as heavenly punishment or as a cleansing in preparation for heavenly bliss. This was a comfort when mass starvation and disease could not be prevented. Today, people starve and die because others don't care. Ecotheology is concerned with preventing suffering, rather than mere comforting.

Ecology exposes suffering as the result of our violations of the ecosystem. In this sense, it is still punishment for "sins."

For guilt, too, ecotheology offers an alternate approach to the paternalism of conventional religion. We feel guilty because we disregard the laws of the ecosystem and violate the eternal order. Ecotheology stresses prevention. Rather than cleansed by punishment *after* the violation, we are motivated to meet our ecological obligations in advance. The motivational force still is love – a brother/sister rather than a father/child love, a deep concern for others, including those who will come after us and for whom we are the trustees and ombudspeople.

Death, being unpreventable, was made acceptable by such concepts as afterlife, nirvana, or reincarnation. Ecotheology, by making us see ourselves as servants of a process far greater than our life span, makes us see our death as much a part of life as our birth. What endures is our share in the Great Design. We live and die, not for our own sake, or for the sake of our children, race, or nation, not even for the sake of humankind, but for the sake of the totality of life.

Existentially, ecology helps us face our human predicaments by pre-venting them where possible and, where unavoidable, accepting them as price for being human. Life's goal is not to avoid suffering, guilt, and death but to live meaningfully within our limits, to partake in ultimate order, to flow with it – in terms of the biblical writer, "choose life."

Ecotheology may become a religion that makes sense for our times, but religions are not started by rational processes. They are started by charismatic individuals who set an example of living in new ways that fire the imagination of people who feel their lives have lost meaning under existing values. Only later the ideas of the founders become structured in a rational framework that often falsifies the original insights.

To start a religion from rational premises would be unprecedented. But we live in a tradition-shattering age. The preconditions for a new religious movement are present. Religious growth always begins when people are troubled, and we are in deep trouble today. We feel an emptiness conventional religions cannot fill, and an isolation these religions cannot bridge. Existing values are inadequate to deal with rapidly changing conditions. We are threatened by dangers that are all the more frustrating because we know they are self-made and could be controlled. We are losing confidence in our ability to cope with life in its increasing complexity, and desperately need a sense of security that comes with a sense of belonging. But the institutions that used to provided that sense are crumbling. A "faithquake" is shaking our trust in traditional churches. Our confidence in governments is weakened by their inability to solve the most pressing problems. Work has become impersonal, and the family is breaking up, making any feeling of belonging difficult.

The time is ripe for a charismatic leader to set new goals of a meaningful life. No such leader is in sight. Instead, thousands of individuals are searching for an order to relate to in a life-giving way. They are searching in the ecology movement, in the human-potential movement, the women's liberation movement, political grassroots, communal living, group psychology, and in meditation. The time may have come when, instead of a spiritual genius, a "proletariat of the spirit" is about to found a civil religion.

Ecology is a rational answer to our cry for the connected life. If *homo sapiens* were truly rational, the arguments of ecology would change our behavior pattern. But we are creatures of spirit and emotions. Ecology can become an important force only with the help of a religious fervor which considers the ecosystem as "holy" and inspires believers to sacrifice affluence, pleasures, and status at its altar. A religion of ecology would require us to free ourselves from the self-fulfilling prophecies of religious rulers who stress limitations and belittle potentials. We would have to reexamine our values, customs, and taboos in the light of the emerging vision of universal relatedness. The time may come when it will be as habitual to recycle our waste materials as it is now to brush our teeth; when littering beaches will be as sacrilegious as defacing gravestones, when wasting food as shameful as stealing it; when smoking in company as much of a taboo as masturbating in public; and when it will be disgraceful to fish or hunt for pleasure, drive alone in a large car, or have more than two children. Successful religious movements have been able to perform miracles in changing human habits, values, and institutions, and in a miraculously brief time. A religion of ecology could succeed, even without a charismatic leader, if our religious consciousness is aroused by new conditions of survival and new visions of a meaningful life, and if this consciousness ignites a flash of religiosity that will sweep the earth.

(*Ecology and Religion Newsletter*, Berkeley, November, 1971)

The Chosen People
- Scapegoats and Guinea Pigs

Last Monday the year 5739 started. I wish you a Happy New Year!

In America, the normal reaction to such a wish would be, "Happy New Year to you, too!" Among European Jews, especially from Eastern Europe, the typical answer would be, "May God grant it shouldn't be worse than the last." That's not pessimism. For Eastern European Jews it's realism. Any change, even the change of year, is cause for anxiety. If you live under the shadow of pogroms and are merely discriminated against, and not killed, you are glad when things just don't get worse.

In the twenties they took a census in Vienna. As in previous censuses it asked for your religion. Suspicious, but people accepted it. A new census in the thirties also asked for the religion of your parents and grandparents. An innocent-looking change which later made it easy for the Nazis to pick up people who had been baptised, didn't feel Jewish, and sometimes didn't even know they were Jewish. One of my highschool classmates was active in the emerging and then still-illegal Austrian Nazi Party. By checking the innocent-looking census they found out he had a Jewish grandmother. He committed suicide.

Franz Werfel, the Austrian playwright, wrote a play, *Jacobowski and the Colonel,* about a Polish Jew from the ghetto and an aristocratic gentile Polish colonel, both fleeing from the invading Nazi army. In one scene they both are hiding in a ditch next to a road while Nazi troops march by. After 15 minutes the danger is over and the colonel says to the Jew: "Now I know how you Jews feel." Jacobowski answers: "We Jews have been sitting in a ditch for 2,000 years, and you think you know after 15 minutes how we feel?"

Actually, Jews have been sitting in a ditch for 4,000 years and have survived while other people haven't. Are Jews the chosen people? Chosen for what? In *Fiddler on the Roof* the little taylor Tevye is facing once more a pogrom, and they all flee their village, leaving friends and property behind. Tevye directly addresses God, as he often does, and says: "Dear God, why don't you choose some other people for a change?"

But, of course, he's kidding. For Jews, the belief to be chosen is the reason for survival. It's also the reason for their being hated. In high school, one of my anti-Semitic classmates asked me: "Don't you think it's arrogant of you Jews to call yourselves chosen?" I didn't know how to answer, but after 50 years of sitting in my own Jewish ditch, I think I have an answer. I would have liked to give it to him this summer when we had the 50th anniversary of our high-school graduation, but he had died.

What I am saying this morning is my answer to my old classmate Hermann Gesselbauer who also said, in 1930, when Hitler was on the rise in Germany: "You can say about Hitler what you want, but you must agree the man has clean hands." That was another thing I would have liked to discuss with my friend Hermann, if he hadn't died, the coward.

But back to the chosen people. My theory is that we Jews are chosen as scapegoats and guinea pigs. I have been both, and I can tell you it's not a pleasant experience. Yet, it's good for you. Here I quote another Austrian writer, Stefan Zweig, who could not get over being an exile in South America, in a foreign culture with a language in which he could not write. He committed suicide there but had the insight to say, "Emigration is good for you if you survive it."

This is true for any unescapable suffering. It feels terrible while you are in the midst of it, but looking back you can see the good that came from it. When I look back on my uprooting in 1938, I can see that it made me grow up, I discovered potentials I never knew I had, I made new friends, new doors opened. I found Judith in New York, and consequently had three children and two grandchildren. I am not doing quite as well as Job who first raised the question of undeserved suffering, and ended up, after his tribulations, with seven sons and three daughters, in addition to 14,000 sheep, 6,000 camels, 1,000 oxen, and 1,000 she-asses.

I am not saying that being a scapegoat is good for you, or suffering is good for you, and you should go and volunteer for it. There are more pleasant ways to learn, to grow, develop potentials, and acquire children and she-asses. Pain and suffering comes in many forms. Sometimes you cannot escape it. But you can escape the feeling of guilt and helplessness. If you look to the past and ask why fate did this to you, you will feel a victim. If you accept the unavoidable, look to the present, and ask what you can do now, you will feel a master, at least over the stand you take toward your fate.

Jews know that from long experience. A comedian in a Viennese cabaret caricatured the Jewish situation by saying, "Why shouldn't I be glad to be a Jew? They call me a Jew whether I am ashamed of it or glad. So I might as well be glad."

To be a Jew means to be a scapegoat. It's ironic that the Jews, who were the first to use a goat instead of a human sacrifice, have become scapegoats themselves. They have been blamed for everything, from killing God, to epidemics and unemployment. In pogroms, ghettos, exiles, and concentration camps they didn't ask "why?" but "what can we do now?" They always expected the worst, and usually were right. They were always under a cloud but looked for the silver lining. When hoodlums ransacked their homes, they would say, "It's just lucky they didn't find my jewelry." When, in a pogrom, they lost even their jewelry they would say, "It's just lucky we are still alive." In every catastrophe they found something to be "just lucky" to have been spared something worse. Friedrich Torberg, another Austrian writer, quotes his aunt as saying, "May God protect us from all the things where we were 'just lucky.'"

Maybe things have changed a little. Jews have now their own country, and this makes scapegoating a little harder. They need no longer accept a bad situation, they fight back. But scapegoating dies hard. I know of no other nation that won four wars of survival, and the whole world expects them to return every inch of the conquered land, although they are surrounded by people who openly want to destroy them.

What I would have said to friend Gesselbauer is that one reason Jews are a chosen people is that they have learned to live with suffering in a realistic way. They learned when to fight, and when to accept the unavoidable and see where they could go from there. That brings up my second point: the Jews as guinea pigs.

My career as a guinea pig also started in 1938. Overnight the old values, the foundations of my life, crumbled. The family was scattered. Religion did not save me; it was the reason for my persecution. Material wealth was worthless. It ended up in Hitler's treasury.

When I came to the United States, I found that much of what happened in Austria, also happened in this country – not because of Hitler but in the name of progress. Families were scattered. Children moved from their parents as soon as they finished high school. Old people lived alone. Couples split up. Homes were uprooted because father chased after a better job in other states, or abroad. Children challenged the values of parents, wives those of husbands, students those of teachers.

I see Jewish refugees as guinea pigs in a world of crumbling values. They were forced to live in a moral no-man's land, with no guidelines. What counted was not what they *had* (material things) but what they *were* (human beings with inner resources).

Jewish guinea pigs who survived the holocaust and have come

out strong, are better equipped than the control population of middle-class America, to live under atomic and ecological dangers. When pollution threatens the water supply, Jews are "just lucky" that they are not accused of having poisoned the well. If an atomic holocaust comes, it will not come to them alone. After sitting in the ditch for 4,000 years, they have adapted to ditch-sitting. And they know now we are all sitting in the ditch together.

It's more dangerous to be a guinea pig than a scapegoat. Guinea pigs are sacrificed so people can get healthy and live. Guinea pigs don't know why they die. From their perspective they cannot see the meaning of their sacrifice. Many Jews died. It may be a rationalization on my part, but I wish to believe that if we could view the world from a higher dimension, we would see some meaning in that cruel experiment of virulent anti-Semitism.

It is unkind to call Jews "guinea pigs." A more heroic term would be "pioneers." Jews have been pioneers all along. They found out what it was like to believe in One God in a polytheistic world. What it was like to live in a Christian world and instist that the Messiah had not yet come. They were excluded from all professions except money lending, and then found out what it was like to become bankers in a world where money lending was a sin, thus blamed for the rise of capitalism. They also experienced what it was like to be exploited, and blamed for the rise of Communism. In all these cases, the Jews were guinea pigs as well as scapegoats. Christians blame them for being atheists, atheists for being religious, the Nazis for Communism, and Communists for capitalism.

Einstein, who was born in Germany and was a Swiss citizen, said: "If atomic energy will turn out to be a blessing, the Germans will claim me as a German, and the Swiss will claim me as a Swiss. If there will be an atomic war, the Swiss will say I was German, and the Germans will say I was a Jew."

Where does this leave my answer to friend Gesselbauer? I don't really believe that Jews were preordained to be chosen, any more than the human race was preordained to be what we are. We have evolved, with a lot of mutations and dead ends, and here we are, by no means perfect, but able to ask ourselves what we can do with our lives, imperfect as we are.

I think the choosing started not by God but by the Jews who selected Jahwe as their powerful protector. This belief gave them a security none of their neighboring tribes had. They were envied and persecuted. You can react to persecution in two ways: become unsure of yourself, or show your persecutors that they are wrong. The Jews, strengthened by their belief in a protecting Yahwe, tried to prove their persecutors wrong. They had to try harder than anyone else, become better than others in order to have a chance. This was reason for envy and greater persecution. And the stubborn Jews tried even harder. This vicious cycle made the Jews look better and better, and their persecutors worse and worse.

That's my answer, friend Gesselbauer. To be a chosen people means to live in a world full of injustice, to be scapegoats for this injustice, and guinea pigs in the great experiment of life where injustice is an integral part. To be chosen means to be an example to show that injustice and suffering need not crush you but can strengthen you, that living in the face of pain and suffering has survival value.

There is another lesson. Being a scapegoat and a guinea pig has survival value only if you have a deep commitment. The ancient Jews had their unconditional commitment to Yahwe who moved in a dimension that humans cannot understand, and where things make sense that make none on the human level.

This commitment is the secret of the Jewish optimism in spite of what's happening to them. Life makes sense if you commit yourself to being a part in an order that prevails even when all seems nonsense. Jews are guinea pigs, or pioneers, in a world where injustice, chaos, and pain are part of reality. They show that you have to live *as if* life made sense, even if you don't see it at the moment. That's a message to everyone. Life does not owe you fair breaks, it places demands on you. The Jews see the demand coming from Yahwe, Christians see it coming from Jesus, Buddhists from Buddha, atheists from Life itself. You respond to the demands as *you* see them, as best you can, and you will do your little share to make the world a tiny bit less unjust, chaotic, and painful.

(First Unitarian Church of Berkeley, Feb. 19, 1978)

The Royal Road to the Spiritual Unconscious

Sigmund Freud called dreams the royal road to the unconscious. Viktor Frankl sees the road leading into a much wider land. In his concept, the human unconscious has an instinctual part into which we repress traumas and emotions we do not want to face, but also a spiritual part into which we repress our will to meaning. Repressed traumas may cause neuroses; ignored meanings may cause inner emptiness, frustration, despair.

From our spiritual unconscious speaks the voice of conscience. One of Frankl's early case histories gives an example: A successful composer of popular music dreamed he was trying to phone a woman but the dial was so complex that he never succeeded. The client stated that he had no erotic interest in that woman. Nonetheless, a Freudian interpretation would have explored any repressed desires. The client eventually realized that the number he had tried to reach was not the woman's but the similar number of a recording company for which he had done some serious, extremely gratifying but poorly paid work. In a logotherapeutic dream interpretation he became aware that the dream had placed a value choice before him: between doing well-paid but meaningless composing, or some poorly paid but meaningful work. The symbolism of the dream becomes even clearer when we note that the German word "wählen" means both dialing and choosing.

Another case illustrates a message from the unconscious: A woman dreamed of taking a dirty cat to the laundry along with her dirty wash. When she picked up the wash, the cat was dead. Discussing the dream, she came up with the following associations: she loved cats, and also her daughter who had developed a lifestyle of which the mother disapproved and which caused gossip. The mother was constantly watching and hounding her daughter. The dream expressed a warning not to torment her daughter with exaggerated demands of moral "cleanliness" or she might lose her child.

I have collected samples of my own dreams as well as those of my students and found that dreams are indeed a valuable road to discovering unconsciously selected goals, repressed values, and ignored meanings.

Dreams, just as neuroses, can originate in the body, the psyche, environmental conditions, and also in the spirit. They often are a jumble of these elements. A person suffering from angina pectoris may dream of being chained across the chest. A person with childhood traumas may dream of dragons, and someone sleeping in an overheated room of dying in a forest fire. Dreams are exceedingly fast story tellers and can react to a brief incident with an extended tale. I recently fell asleep while being driven along a highway. I dreamed that I entered a dark room, fumbled along the wall looking for a light switch, bumped into furniture, fell, got up, found the switch and turned on the light. I woke just in time to see that we had driven through an underpass, for a fraction of a second, and that we were coming out from the dark into light.

When working at the University of California, our secretary did her best to make our lives difficult, and we never included her in our coffee breaks. One night I dreamed I lay in bed with her, embracing her tenderly. She responded lovingly. When I woke up I wondered if I could possibly have any repressed sexual desire. If so, they would need years of analytic digging. Then I looked for a logotherapeutic interpretation. Perhaps the dream told me: Be nice to her, and she will be nice to you. The next day I asked her to have coffee with me. We found common interests such as going to plays, or walking in the woods. She became more pleasant, not only to me but to the entire office crew.

I used my newly acquired insight with a woman in a group. In a dream strikingly similar to mine, she had seen herself in bed with her father, kissing him, to which he responded lovingly. Alarmed, she awoke. She had been on bad terms with him since childhood. He had always preferred her older brother, never spent much time with her, never been satisfied with her grades although she was a good student. Did she have any repressed incestual desires? I told the group my dream about the office secretary, and one of the group members asked her, "Why don't you try?" The woman was doubtful but at the next meeting she reported that, after having a similar dream the following night, she called her father, who lived 200 miles away. He immediately suspected that she wanted something from him, which under normal circumstances would have turned her off right away. Under the impact of her two dreams and our group discussion, she told him she just wanted to take him out for dinner. He still was full of suspicion, but she forced herself to be kind. They occasionally had dinner together and talked about her childhood. Her father explained that her brother, having been born with a clubfoot, needed more attention. She was healthy and gifted; the father was proud of her and prodded her so she would get even better grades. He wanted her to go to college. She began to see her childhood in a different light. Two years later she called me. Her father had died and told her in the hospital: "I'm glad I got to know you as one adult to another." The logotherapeutic interpretation of her dream had given them the opportunity .

That dreams, even nightmares, can offer comfort rising from our spiritual unconscious, was shown me many years before I heard about logotherapy. After the war, I learned that my parents and many members of my family had died in concentration camps. I tried to cope with the tragedy as best I could, but I know a lot of repression was going on. One night I dreamed I was walking through a beautiful forest, similar to my childhood memories of the Vienna Woods. Suddenly a huge bird swept down and picked me up. I looked down on meadows and forests, and was not afraid. Then a large area of barren land came into sight, gray and ugly. When we were right over the wasteland, the bird flew lower and I could see a repulsive sight: ditches full of corpses and skeletons as are shown in pictures of concentration camps. While I stared down in horror, the corpses began to disintegrate and formed humus that filled the ditches. Grass started to grow, flowers, and trees. When my bird took me high up again the area looked like part of the rest of the landscape – a forest with birds singing in the trees. When I woke up I felt serene as I had not felt in a long time. The bird lifted me beyond my pain and traumas into the higher dimension of the spirit. No therapist was needed to tell me the meaning.

But often a therapeutic dialogue is required to unscramble the symbolism of dreams. The founder and owner of a successful company was suffering from headaches and depressions, also from marital problems. The counselor tried to explore with him his value priorities, but with no success. Then the client reported a puzzling dream. He saw himself in a dark cellar with his wife and children. When his eyes got used to the darkness, he saw that the room was filled with gaily wrapped packages. His wife asked him to pick one. When he opened it, he was disappointed to find a bust of Richard Wagner. He didn't like operas, and didn't care for Wagner. His wife asked him to select another package, and again he was disappointed. It contained a monopoly game, which he had not played since his children were small. He considered playing games a waste of time. His wife told him he had a third and last chance to unwrap a present. He was disappointed once more. The package contained a plastic Christmas tree and cheap colored decorations. He had always resented spending money on decorations that were used once a year, or even thrown away.

In succeeding therapy sessions the man had an "aha"

experience. He realized the message of the dream: Play! Relax!
Enjoy! Don't be a workaholic! Take time out for music (Wagner),
games (monopoly), celebrations (Christmas tree)! He followed the
advice of his unconscious and his depressions disappeared.

Dreams may be simple and clear, or complex and full of
symbolism. A simple dream: a woman who had lost her husband
after forty years of marriage, was completely lost because there
were so many decisions to be made, and her husband had always
made them. She dreamed that she went to Tibet to see the wisest
guru and ask him for advice. While she climbed the steep mountain
she knew that he would have the answer. The mountain top was
shrouded in mist. When she reached the top she saw a figure sitting
on a throne. She approached the figure and the mist lifted. Sitting on
the throne was she, herself. Upon waking, the message was
immediately clear: it was now up to her to make the decisions. She
was her own best guru.

Dreams can be depressing, but the logotherapist picks up what
affirmative bits they contain. James Yoder, regional director of the
logotherapy chapter in Kansas City, reports about a young man
struggling with self-deprecating attitudes, guilt, and the problems of
a no-sayer to life. He complained about having few friends, job
failures, and fears. In his dream, he wanted to use a power saw but
couldn't because of the rusty power plant from which a tangle of
silver wire extended to his heart. During the therapy session he put
his hand on his chest, complaining that "the power package inside me
is all rusted and corroded. I am afraid to touch it for fear I would be
electrocuted." Yoder, disregarding the rusty part, picked up on the
silver thread and reminded the client that he did have some friends.
"Somehow, the energy is flowing through these silver wires from
you to others, and you rise above your pain." The young man began
to weep, and the dream became a turning point in his therapy. Yoder
commented: "Always the clients are affirmed and given credit for
their positive and courageous stands amidst all their suffering."

Clients with low self-esteem often report nightmares in which
they suffer one failure after another. It only deepens their despair to
dwell on such dreams, trying to find causes of failure hidden in
childhood and life situations over which they have no control. It is
often amazingly simple to switch the client's attention from the
negative to the affirmative. One man repeatedly had dreams in
which he saw himself as a weakling who was pushed around. Once it
was a bull who chased him through a jungle-like thicket in which
thorny branches blocked his path; then it was a giant who kept
pushing him into ditches, and every time he climbed out, the giant
pushed him into another ditch; then there was a mean old witch who

tripped him up with a stick, and kept after him, tripping him again and again. "It's the story of my life," said the man, who saw himself as a helpless victim. The therapist asked him to tell about these dreams again. The man repeated about being chased through the thorny thicket. "Now tell me how you got out of the thicket," the therapist demanded. "I just kept running until I came to the end of the thicket," the man said. When he told about being pushed into the series of ditches, the therapist said: "How did you get out of the first one?" The man said, "I just climbed out." "And how often did the bad witch trip you up?" the therapist asked. "Oh, lots of times," the man said, and then laughed, "I know what you are going to ask me next. I guess I did get up every time she tripped me. There must be something in me that bounces back." The way was opened for a more self-affirming attitude.

I should like to conclude with a dream told not *to*, but dreamed *by* a psychoanalyst. I gave a two-day seminar in Germany to a group of counselors. One of them, Fritz, was a young psychoanalyst who was skeptical and kept asking searching question.s How could a therapy have lasting effects when it took only a few sessions? During the first day Fritz became more and more quiet, and the next morning he told me a dream he had during that night. He was visited by his training analyst who insisted on going with Fritz to the logotherapy seminar to show him the errors of logotherapy. They travelled on bicycles which took hours. When they finally arrived at the seminar they were exhausted and bathed in sweat. When the seminar ended, the analyst asked if he could borrow my car for a fast return trip home. I liked the message of that dream.

(Proceedings of the Seventh World Congress of Logotherapy, Berkeley: Institute of Logotherapy Press, 1989)

The Biological Evolution of the Spirit

I recently discovered books by Hoimar von Ditfurth, a psychiatrist, who was also an evolutionist and biologist. In his writings I found scientific proof of such an "unscientific" concept as the human spirit.

Frankl defines spirit as an exclusively human dimension, not shared with other animals, where we have the freedom to choose our actions and attitudes, determine goals, and discover meanings.

Von Ditfurth sees human beings as the temporary end product of an evolution that began with the Big Bang of the universe some 14 billion years ago. It brought into existence our galaxy, our solar system, our planet, life on earth, and eventually the human species. In the course of this unimaginably long time, animal species evolved with a brainstem that had exclusively vegetative tasks, such as circulation, breathing, hormonal regulation, and other functions of a multi-cell organism. After billions of years, the "brainstem" creatures evolved a midbrain, the seat of inborn reactions over which they have no control, such as drives and instincts. Evolution went on, and the "midbrain" creatures developed a forebrain, first tiny, then increasingly larger, until in humans it takes up the greatest part of our skull. We are the first and (so far) the only species on this planet that has consciousness. "The forebrain grants us freedom of action unknown to previous species," von Ditfurth writes. "It opens up the possibility of self-reflection, consciousness of ourselves, the capacity to see the environment as an objective world that can be manipulated according to plans, and the capacity to foresee the consequences of our actions. We have the freedom to disregard and even oppose the inborn programs of our instincts.These are dimensions of reality which did not exist on earth before. With the forebrain, life on this planet has reached a new step of development."

It is easy to see the parallel between this gradual evolution of the brain and Frankl's three human dimensions: the body (with its vegetative functions), the psyche (with its automatic instincts, drives, and emotions), and the spirit (giving us freedom to disregard, even oppose, the limits of body and psyche). In scientific terms, the brainstem, with its vegetative functions, is a biological precondition for the midbrain with its instincts, and both form the biological basis on which rests the forebrain that gives us consciousness.

The parallel goes further. Von Ditfurth warns against the belief that humans are the ultimate goal of evolution. There is no more reason to think that evolution will stop with the human species than to expect it would have stopped with the ants. Though the development of the human forebrain was a giant jump, it may present just an early stage of further developments. Our descendants, millions of years hence, will consider us the "Neanderthalers" of human evolution. We are the first creatures to have a primitive consciousness, a limited freedom, and a moderate capacity to understand the world as it really is. We have not reached the potential to grasp the world in its fullness. If creatures of an advanced evolution were to explain to us the world as they perceive it, we would no more be able to grasp it than a dog can understand our explanations of the world as we see it. Having existed for a few thousand years only, our capacity to see the world objectively is still rudimentary.

The biological difference between the human forebrain and that of other higher mammals lies in the prefrontal lobes. They affect personality, sequencing events, and planning ahead. Research by brain pathologists, biologists, and behaviorists convinced von Ditfurth that the prefrontal lobes make available several billions of nerve cells which are the "material base for the inexhaustible variations of human actions and attitudes. These nerve cells expand the range beyond anything that was possible on earth before. An almost unlimited field of possibilities is opened, from metaphysical thought to the building of concentration camps, from works of art to criminal acts, from self-transcendence for the sake of others to the capacity to act worse than animals."

Von Ditfurth sees all present functions of the human brain as still belonging to the psyche. But it seems justifiable to see the human forebrain as the biological basis for the spirit – an area of freedom that goes beyond the psyche and the body, yet includes them.

We may be an interim stage between a species dominated by the instinctual midbrain and one whose forebrain allows truly free thought and judgment. Our actions and thoughts are still heavily influenced by emotions. The next, by no means final, stage of evolution may be a species with a more clearly developed freedom from emotions, a more explicit sense of responsibility, and a more distinct voice of conscience. What other human capacities evolution may still develop we cannot guess. Future creatures may reach dimensions that indeed could be called "suprahuman."They, too, will have evolved from a biological base.

Frankl also uses the term "suprahuman" for a dimension beyond the level of the human, with laws we don't fully comprehend but can violate only at our own peril (on a physical level comparable with the law of gravity). Religious persons call them "divine" laws, Frankl sees them as simply "supra" (beyond) human. Von Ditfurth sees them as conditions available to creatures developed to a higher level than we are. We don't know if the purpose of evolution is to develop a "perfect" creature, we don't even know if evolution has any specific goal or purpose. Logophilosophy assumes that life has meaning, that everything, including evolution, follows orderly rules, even if we are not able to know them. This is very close to the belief that we are the "Neanderthalers" of human evolution, and that "suprahuman" creatures will develop, with capacities we see only dimly or not at all.

Another similarity is intriguing. "Logos" (meaning) is seen as the center of the universe since the beginning of creation ("in the beginning was *logos*"). This, again, is in accordance with research in physics, reported by von Ditfurth, that all atoms in the universe, including those in us, were present in the Big Bang, that there is a connection between us and what was present "at the beginning." And that, by being aware of that connection (finding meaning), we feel secure as part in the fabric of life.

Still another biological base for a logotherapeutic assumption is the distinction between values and meanings. Values,"universal meanings," are transmitted through tradition, while meanings, being unique, are a matter of personal discovery. Von Ditfurth sees the difference in biological terms. "Midbrain creatures" are incapable of learning from their own experiences. They survive only through the experiences of their ancestors passed on, as instincts, through their genes. The human species, with its developed forebrain, is able to learn through personal experiences. This is another way of saying that human beings, through their forebrain, can find "the meaning of the moment" in specific situations. But having evolved from "midbrain creatures" we can also rely on the experiences of our forebears – Frankl's "universal meanings" or values. We are influenced by programs stored in our midbrain (traditional values) but in our forebrain we have achieved the freedom to take a stand against being programmed. We can find our own meanings.

Von Ditfurth stresses the order of physics, chemistry, and biology. Order is also the base for meaning. It exists everywhere but, as far as we know, only humans have the brain to be conscious of it.

(*International Forum for Logotherapy*, Berkeley, Spring, 1990)

The Credit-Card Syndrome

The credit-card syndrome dominates our lives. Enjoy now, pay later. Pleasure gratification before meaning fulfillment. We have to have immediately what sometimes needs to be worked for, saved for, sacrificed for. Otherwise we are frustrated, a feeling to be avoided at all cost. So people turn to drugs, gambling, sex, overeating because they ask themselves: Why wait? Why bring sacrifices? What for?

People see no what-for, nothing worth waiting or sacrificing for, nothing and nobody for whose sake it would be worth to give up immediate gratification. Something is missing. An emptiness is to be filled.

Waiting and doing without is meaningful only when directed toward a meaningful goal. A patient said: "I am addicted to alcohol, but haven't touched a drop for a year. My decision to quit came not from therapies. My wife had left me because I drank. I was in poor health, and I wanted to keep my job to support her and our daughter. So I stopped drinking." The man saw a meaning behind his abstinence for the sake of his family. But many people stay on the level of their body and psyche. The spirit is disregarded. Their needs are satisfied – now. Their drives are abreacted – now. The meanings that lie in the future remain unfulfilled.

An example of the credit-card syndrome: A high-school student passes his driver's test and has to have a car – now. He borrows money, has dates, borrows more money to buy electronic equipment that provides "fun" for him and his dates. In one of the better scenarios he takes on a meaningless job to pay back his debts, doesn't go to college, and has an empty life. In a worse scenario he holds up a bank and lands in prison.

Examples fill addiction centers, unemployment offices, prisons, newspaper columns, and counseling centers. If these people are lucky, they'll meet counselors, who will direct them toward meanings rather than pleasures and the money needed to pay for them.

The credit-card syndrome is not limited to things money can buy. It exists where a long-range meaningful goal is jeopardized for the sake of imminent gratification: High-school drop-outs whose classes are not enough "fun"; bored housewives who go on shopping sprees and end in divorce courts; teenage girls who give in to their physical urges and become pregnant; drug addicts who steal to raise money for their addiction; and politicians who make shady deals (the pleasure principle disguised as lust for power) and are disgraced.

The credit-card syndrome begins in childhood, long before children are eligible for the plastic tempter. Their rooms are filled with gimmicky toys, soon disregarded. At Christmas and birthdays, children go through their expensively wrapped packages like hungry wolves. These gifts cost money but have no value.

When children go to school, they expect learning to be fun or they "won't play." There is nothing wrong with making education enjoyable but this is not its main goal. One task of school is to teach children what they should learn in their homes: that many meaningful values need working and waiting for. It is impossible to become a surgeon, attorney, or architect without many years of hard study. A second task of education is to teach children (what they also should learn at home) that we need to change from a consumption-centered life to one where people take pride in what is creative, varied, and meaningful.

When young persons enter mainstream America, the credit-card syndrome hits them with full force. They have to have their own home, swimming pool, two cars, and all the gadgets advertisers dangle before their eyes. NOW. The main problem of the affluent is no longer to feed the children but the plastic creditor. Both parents work, the children come from school to an empty home. Juvenile and divorce courts, rehabilitation and addiction centers, mental hospitals and jails are filled with people who pay for immediate gratification. This payment cannot be made by credit cards.

Then comes old age, retirement. At this stage, many people could use their credit cards for pleasures they have earned to enjoy – luxuries, hobbies, trips. Money may no longer be the problem. The problem is time. They have time on their hands, and have never learned how to spend it meaningfully. The credit-card syndrome takes on a different aspect. They have lived a life where pleasure was measured by money and the things money can buy. Their value system, their self-esteem, are built on money. They possess three treasures needed by the world – time, experience, and wisdom – but they refuse to use them unless they are paid. Meaning could fill their last years through service to others. But if they are not paid for it, it has no value for them. And so, retirement, too, ends in frustration.

The credit-card syndrome impacts the mental health not only of individuals but of society. The problems of education, drug abuse, marriage, divorce, economics, ecology, and politics are all rooted in our emphasis on Pleasure Now, Affluence Now. The idea of Sacrifice Now is not considered a proper way to gain meaning later. The principle of the credit card goes far beyond the magic little plastic.

Loggers cut entire forests for quick profit. Rain forests are cut, without regard of ozone depletion and erosion that turns large areas into deserts and causes famine for us and future generations. To live in affluence we need energy now – foreign oil, never mind the consequences; atomic power, never mind the radioactive waste. We bury it – its poison won't leak out for hundreds of years. And then? We risk the health and lives of our descendants for our comfort bought at their expense. Profits, jobs, the comforts of affluence are important but some sacrifice is required for the survival of our great-great-grand children. We are not even willing to do without big cars and unnecessary trips, car sharing, or a minor gasoline tax to help reduce our gasoline consumption.

We are on a consumption binge. Advertising and tax policies have discouraged saving. A penny saved is no longer a penny earned. Rather, a dollar borrowed is a dollar to be spent. The credit card is not just a convenience; it's an addiction. We keep on borrowing. Personal debts doubled in the United States in the past nine years from 300 to 600 billion dollars. Not coincidentally, personal bankruptcies doubled as well.

Our wealth depends on productivity. Productivity depends on investment. And investment depends on savings. Pleasure-oriented America has the lowest personal savings rate in the industrial world – a third of that in Germany, a quarter of that in Japan. These two countries have learned the lesson of saving today in order to build a meaningful tomorrow after their resources were destroyed in World War II. Going to college and prepare for a career is a prize to be worked for by hard learning.

Saving is the opposite of using credit cards. Its principle is to provide an umbrella for a rainy day. Well, the rainy day is here *now*. Our shortage of capital spells economic disaster. We must break free from our obsession with the immediate. We must get away from borrowing, consuming, and producing trash. We must think not just of quick and easy profits, the next quarterly report, or the next election, but of the next generation and the next century. We borrowed from the whole world, so for ten years we had an economic boom. Now our federal debt runs to more than 3,000 billion dollars. The interests we have to pay run to more than 170 billion dollars a year. Who will pay for our pleasures? Our children, and they won't be able to use credit cards.

We live like the farmer who eats up his seed crop, instead of planting it. We have to shake the credit-card addiction and forego instant pleasure for the sake of a meaningful future.

(*Proceedings of the Eighth World Congress of Logotherapy*, Berkeley: Institute of Logotherapy Press, 1993)

In Search of Reality

Human beings are in search of reality. We want to know what the world is really like, the world of things, relationships, ideas, emotions, causes, and potentials – all of it. We want to know the what, how, and why. This unquenchable curiosity is universally and exclusively human. It's our religious search for the ultimate. Religion, thus defined, has no room for atheists.

A second aspect of religion, equally universal, is the human need to feel sheltered, not forsaken, cared for. Here, too, there are no atheists.

The human species has tried to satisfy these two innate longings through science, philosophy, psychology, and theology. We have come closer to glimpsing reality than any other creature, but are still far from knowing the ultimate. We are the first beings on the evolutionary ladder to suspect that there is more than what we can perceive, but not evolved enough to know the totality. All creatures live in a reality they conceive as complete, with no inkling that there may be infinitely more. Humans alone are conscious that there are things unknown, perhaps unknowable. We have begun to penetrate the forces of the cosmos and the atom, but the reali ty of eternity and infinity, life and death, ultimate truth and justice, meaning and purpose, remain mysteries. We know of the existence of such suprahuman laws as physics, chemistry, genetics, gravity, electricity. But we don't know if corresponding metaphysical moral laws exist as part of a reality still hidden from us.

Our consciousness of the unknown directs us toward the search for ultimate reality, the religious search. Prophetic individuals, perhaps mutants of the next evolutionary step, have gained glimpses of a more inclusive reality than most of us can perceive, but they were not able to communicate their insights. Their disciples tried to preserve their precious divinations in "holy" books, rites, myths, and symbols but these remain only wrappings of the truth. As Bishop James Pike observed, the great religious insights were put in bottles for safekeeping by the priests of various theologies; but as time went on, the precious contents evaporated, and only the empty bottles are worshipped.

That's the tragedy of our religious search. While bottles are necessary to hold the truths that are to quench our thirst, they must not become the subject of our quest. There are many bottles, but the content is universal. There is only One Reality, One God.

The word "God" has always been used to explain the unknown. Early societies needed many gods, to explain the fury of the ocean, the movements of the stars, the emotions in our hearts. Yahwe was, as far as we know, the first godhead who explained the total reality within human understanding, but left many mysteries inaccessible to us. Besides,Yahwe remained a tribal Jewish god. Founders of other religions glimpsed what they claimed universal godheads. But there still is no true belief in One God for the entire universe. Jews have their Yahwe, Christians their Trinity, Moslems their Allah, and Eastern religions have different concepts still. Adherents of the various God concepts fight religious wars. In secular wars, too, each nation appeals to "its" god. We are still far removed from true monotheism, the belief in One Reality.

The multiple approach to the one common reality would not be harmful if we were tolerant enough to grant others the benefit of the doubt that their approaches may be as valid as ours. But every theology has its fanatics, convinced that theirs is the only way, trying to "save" other-believers by "fire and sword." They are convinced they see the whole reality and the only way to reach it.

Wise people have defined God monotheistically as unmoved mover, creative force, ultimate concern, ground of being, or spirit of life, but these cerebral concepts do not touch the heart. In our religious search we grope for dimensions beyond the human, but do they exist? The Austrian writer Franz Werfel may have had a precious insight when he said, "Our thirst is the best proof for the existence of water." Perhaps our unquenchable thirst for dimensions far beyond the human is proof that they exist, though barely glimpsed at our low stage in human evolution.

We are now at a crucial moment in our search for reality. We see the need for a post-patriarchal, post-colonial relationship of non-exploitive partnerships. We see the danger of following ideologies rather than guidelines that ask, "What is good for our children?" We are starting to think in global, perhaps universal, terms.We have discovered our ecological interdependence. We may be ready for true monotheism, a monoreality.

It is time for a unifying religious revolution. The Swiss theologian Hans Küng maintains that nations and races will not find peace until the various religions (theologies) make peace with one another. We are far from that goal. But the fanatical clinging to traditional beliefs may be the last desperate clutching of an obsolete security blanket. The clutching, however, has become dangerous because the clutching hands hold mass-destructive weapons.

Acceptance of a truly universal God-reality, even if beyond our present understanding, is a precondition for human survival.

Here we come up against a dilemma. A universal God-reality seems incompatible with the personal godhead we crave. The second aspect of our religious need, a God who cares for each of us individually, remains unfulfilled. A reality does not care.

Or does it? We cannot conceive of a creative universal force that responds to us personally. Perhaps this blindness is the result of our low evolutionary level that gives us a human-centered view of reality. We see ourselves created in the image of a father (or mother) figure who cares, rewards, and punishes like a human parent would – a godhead reduced to the human level. At the same time we crave a superhuman God, all-powerful, good, and just for the entire universe. Every theology has gone to great lengths to reconcile the irreconcilable.

This contradiction has made theologies come up with twisted explanations that turn people into atheists. How can an all-powerful and loving God allow catastrophes like earthquakes, defective babies, wars, and holocausts? Why do bad things happen to good people? Answers emerge when we see the universe ruled by an orderly life force that requires earthquakes to settle continental tensions, flawed babies as mutations necessary to drive evolution forward, and human evil, including wars and holocausts, as consequence of our having evolved as creatures no longer forced to follow instinct but having acquired a dimension where free choice is possible. The sense of shelteredness then comes from a belief, not in a just "Father" or a caring "Mother," but in a universal life force that is "good," not because it provides us with pleasures but because it is orderly and reliable. To expect a godhead to be concerned about the personal well-being of each creature living at the far edge of one of billions of galaxies is conceit at the highest, resulting in disappointment, doubt, and guilt.

And yet, and yet. We do have that unquencheable thirst for a God with whom we can personally communicate, and who will respond. We *can* communicate – one way. But a Ruler of the Universe who answers personal requests, is not likely to be the true universal God-force. Our prayers are dialogues with our highest possible self, dialogues with Reality of which we are a part. Realistic prayers are not requests to a power outside of us, but appeals to the highest power within, for strength, growth, insights, meaningful attitudes, reaching potentials, for hearing the small voice of our conscience, and for giving thanks.

But reality offers us more than an impersonal safety net. We ourselves, everyone, are part of that net, a tiny strand in the fabric of life, interconnected with everything and everyone else, sheltered and providing shelter. Isn't it possible that the caring we long for may not come (at least not exclusively) from outside but from within and from each other? All major theologies have recognized this force: love.

True, our capacity for love (beyond the instinctual) is still weakly developed. There may be many rungs ahead on the evolutionary ladder of creation. We have been given a modest brain (to distinguish truth from falsehood). More highly developed creatures may be provided with an organ enabling them to hear the still-small voice of conscience more clearly (to discern right from wrong), a distinct sense of the aesthetic (to separate beauty from ugliness), a deeper awareness of responsibility (to specify the just from the unjust), and a greater certainty in values (to identify the genuine from the convenient).

Some mutants of a higher evolution may already have walked the earth, unrecognized, often considered dangerous, even killed when their revelations did not fit traditional theology. It may well be that evolution moves toward creatures more conscious of their inner resources and their interconnectedness within the fabric of life, qualities developed only weakly in *homo sapiens*. The awareness that each person is linked with every other, with neighbors and even enemies, has only been glimpsed by some of the mutants and may become better developed in *homo moralis*, a future step in evolution.

Relying on our own resources does not preclude the existence of a universal life force that delegates the caring to its evolving creatures. Life provides a shelter of orderliness and assurance that we are not forsaken. What lies beyond our control and understanding we have to accept on faith. Struggling against the unavoidable will only exhaust us needlessly. There, we only can bow our heads. In other instances we are challenged to reach for the reachable. The serenity prayer applies: change the things over which we have control, accept those over which we don't, and strive for the wisdom to know the difference. There still is a vast area of the unknown that fills us with awe and mystery, a precious goal in our religious search.

Recognition of a universal life force does not make the various theologies superfluous. They approach Truth from different directions. Theologies tend to divide, compete. This need not be so. Religion, as the Latin root indicates, unites. The search for reality is a unifying force.

This unifying force is the precious content of Bishop Pike's "bottles." We have to see the bottles as what they are:

symbols, myths, parables, approaches, not reality itself. Even though reality remains shrouded in mystery, new attitudes can be found: Evil need not be seen as a flaw in creation, but a necessary part of an imperfect world on its way to perfection. We are not punished for any original sin but, as the theologian Matthew Fox suggests, buoyed by the "original blessing" of an orderly universe allowing us freedom, consciousness, and potentials. Sin would be a falling short of potentials. Salvation, approaching our potentials. Faith, the belief not to be forsaken but sheltered in a reliable universe. Immortality (on a physical level), the pretty much accepted fact that all atoms existing today, in us and in the immense cosmos, were present at the birth of the universe and will be present at its inconceivable ending. Whether a similar eternal presence exists on a spiritual level, we are not evolved enough to know. We, the human race on our tiny planet, are neither helpless victims nor complete masters of our fate. We have no right to demand special favors from life. We have been given the ability to respond to life's offerings, the response-ability to love, to care for each other, to forgive, to achieve reconciliation. The command, "Thou shalt have no other God before Me" deserves the widest possible interpretation. We can doubt the existence of a God of nations, ideologies, and theologies, we can even come to believe that such a God is dead, but no one can deny the existence of reality.

(*Human Spirit on Trial* , Berkeley: Self-publication, 1992)

Epilogue

Memorial Service for Max Knight

Welcome, friends of Max whose life we are here to celebrate.

Max was a man of strong convictions, and we are trying to honor them the best we can There will be deviations from the usual memorial services. He was a believer in tradition but rejected cliches and customs which merely were done because they were expected.

He did not care for organ music at memorial services because he felt it overemphasized th solemnity which should come naturally at such occasions. He was a master of the understatement, and let the readers and listeners come to their own conclusions, and not – as he expressed it – hit them over the head.

We chose the piano, and selected not the obligatory masses, and requiems, and hymns, but music that had meaning in his life. You already heard a polonaise by Chopin which was traditionally played at the opening of the Viennese balls which he loved as a young man. At the end of the service we will hear the "Voices of Spring Waltz" by Johann Strauss because spring was his favorite season and conjured up in his mind youth and romance, and the flowery meadows of the Alps which he loved and visited, even when the altitude was risky for his heart. The dedication in his book he was most proud of, read, "To the girl on the Alpine meadow." He had not *one* specific girl in mind, nor *one* specific meadow, but all girls on all Alpine meadows.

We also decided to do this memorial without the help of clergy, because they represent a god in which he did not believe.

Max was an editor to his core and, as he himself said, lived his life not according to the Bible but according to Webster. And he never was able to go beyond Webster's first definition of God as "a being of more than human attributes and powers." In his editorial classes he taught his students that you define a word the first time you use it, and then continue using it in the same sense. The first time Max used the word God was in anti-Semitic Vienna. God was responsible for the good as well as the bad, or he did not exist at all.

He edited religion as he did everything else in his life. He believed in order, and planning, and logic, and was quite disdainful of anything that was unplanned and disorderly. It was just as important to him to have the colons and hyphens at the proper places in a sentence, as it was to have his socks lined up in his drawer, or the crystals in his collection, orderly placed and labeled. Nothing irritated him more than a *non sequitur*.

Of course, he liked facts and figures, so I should mention that he was born June 8, 1909 in Pilsen, then Austria, moved to Vienna as a child, fled from Hitler in 1938, first to London, then Shanghai, and finally to the United States, was able to rescue his parents, married Charlotte Lowes in 1942, had two sons, Anthony, born 1947, and Martin, born 1951, and one granddaughter, Samantha, born 1983. He was productive in his writing, and his bibliography fills 12 pages, including books, short stories, articles, translations, poetry, reviews, and plays. For 26 years he edited more than 200 books for the University of California Press, and after his retirement taught editing classes at the University Extension. For the past 62 years we wrote and published together, using a common pen name, Peter Fabrizius. We shall now read selections from his writings, letting Max tell in his own words what was important to him.

[Members of his family read from Max's writings , ending with the following passage from his autobiography:]

"While I edited and taught and Joe gained increasing recognition for his crusade in psychology, we were as close as a generation earlier. One day we talked about what we would like to be remembered by. He mentioned his writings in logo-therapy, and I the *Return to the Alps*, the translation of Kelsen's *Pure Theory of Law,*, and my version of Christian Morgenstern's *Galgenlieder*.. We have different interests but Peter Fabrizius lives on.

On one of our periodic strolls in the El Cerrito cemetery, standing on a hill overlooking the San Francisco Bay, we saw a new section of the cemetery opening up.

"How about it?" Joe said.

It seemed a logical conclusion; not the surprise ending of the old short stories but a natural finale – nothing morbid, just a well-edited ultimate period at the end of a story.

We went to the cemetery office and signed up – two plots, one for Joe and Judith and one for Charlotte and me, side by side. A few days later the four of us clambered up that hill and Joe's son Richard, a fine photographer, took a picture of the site, with the four of us, the first of four projected. He is commissioned to take the second when there are only three to be photographed, then a third, and eventually the last. Sic transit gloria Fabrizii.

(First Unitarian Church of Berkeley, October 2, 1993)